The I Was A Teenage Juvenile Delinquent Rock 'n' Roll Horror Beach Party Movie Book!

The I Was A Teenage Juvenile Delinquent Rock 'n' Roll Horror Beach Party Movie Book!

A Complete Guide to the Teen Exploitation Film, 1954–1969

Alan Betrock

Plexus, London

Published by Plexus Publishing Limited
30 Craven Street,
London WC2N 5NT

Betrock, Alan
I was a teenage juvenile delinquent rock 'n' roll horror beach party movie book.
1. American cinema films, 1954–1969
I. Title
791.43'0973

ISBN 0-85965-1959

Published by arrangement with St. Martin's Press, New York

Book designed by Flicky Ford
Cover designed by George Corsillo
Manufactured in Great Britain

Contents

Dedication and Acknowledgments

For Marilyn Laverty, Without Whom
Life Itself Would Be Impossible.

Many people helped me along the way in compiling, writing, and finishing this book. I would like to take this opportunity to thank them publicly: Mamie Van Doren, Sam Arkoff, Roger Corman, Charles Beesley, Miriam Linna, Ed Strait, Billy Miller, Michael Weldon, Todd Abramson, Andy Schwartz, Chris Capece, Richard Foos, David Gahr, Gary Goldsmith, J. H. Beal, Ruby Merjan, Toby Byron, and all the books, magazines, fanzines, and monographs I liberally borrowed from over the years.

Also, a great debt is owed to the New York Public Library and their overworked staff, and, of course, the most important thanks goes to all the actors, actresses, directors, screenwriters, musicians, businessmen, and poster artists who made these films under the most trying of circumstances. I hope this book helps to offer them all the recognition they justly deserve.

And finally, deep gratitude goes to all the fine people at St. Martin's Press, especially the indefatigable Lisa DiMona, and the benevolent warlord, Bob Miller.

Without all the above people and many more, this book would not exist.

INTRODUCTION

What exactly is a teen exploitation movie? That's a difficult question to answer in words. It's like asking what is a rock 'n' roll record, or what is soul music. Everybody has a different answer and different criteria. To me, the term connotes both content and advertising. What does the movie represent, how is it presented, and who is it aimed at? They usually are centered on the lives of teenagers, fantasies of teenagers, or trends, fads, or problems of teenagers. They are presented with sensationalistic advertising campaigns that usually promise more than the movies deliver, and their goal is to lure you into the theater. Obviously, the goal of all movie advertising is to get you to see the film, but exploitation advertising is lurid, violent, sexy, wild, and overblown. It brings things down to the simplest and basest emotions and preys on those feelings most easily manipulated. Teenagers, as a group, are less sophisticated and experienced than adults, and because of this are easily lured toward something that speaks to their interests, fears, or escapism. They have a significant amount to spend each week, and going to the movies is a traditional way to spend that money, either on a date or with friends. To the exploitation filmmaker, they are easy fish out there waiting to be hooked.

This book covers the years from 1954 to 1969, the golden age of teenage exploitation. Every few years there was a new trend or cycle which the producers would jump on, exaggerate, and get millions of teens to the theaters to see. There were rock 'n' roll films, juvenile delinquent films, motorcycle and hot-rod films, teen pregnancy and marriage films, problems-in-school films, bad-girl films, teen horror films, beach movies, drug movies, rebellion movies, and hippie films. There were dramas, comedies, and fantasies—all produced with the teenager in mind, and their dollars in hand.

Why do we want to look back at teen films? For one, it's a matter of moviegoing history, a repeating trend that started primarily in the fifties and continues today. And as we all know, those who forget history are condemned to repeat it. But more importantly they mirror the fascination with youth culture and trends that is not only part of history, but part of our lives. There is the campy fun of looking at these films and laughing at the characterizations, lingo, and farfetched stories, but they also bring us back to that time in our lives when we too felt these things, acted this way, and thought these thoughts. These films not only captured the teen culture, but influenced it as well, helping to create trends, fads, and personalities. Besides television, the movies were the most influential medium in the country to help teens across the land know what the rest of their peers were doing and thinking, wearing and saying, and how they were getting through life. Many modern-day stars and directors came out of these films and it is novel and interesting to see their early work. And when you get into it even more, there's a whole group of B-movie teen performers who made their whole careers in these films, going from one to the other until they were too old, without ever becoming above-ground notables. To me it's just as much fun to see Jack Nicholson in *The Cry Baby Killer* as it is to see Richard Bakalyan in *The Delinquents.* Both have their own histories and stories to tell, and both were integral to the popularity and development of teen films.

For the most part this book tries to meld together the fun and the important history. We see where the films came from, how they developed, and who the movers and shakers were. The filmographies try to place the films in perspective, seeing how they were received at the time of their release, and how they stand up today. Together with my thoughts, I've tried to mix in reviews from such varied sources as *Variety, The New York Times,* the reviews of theater owners whose main concern was box-office grosses, and the reviews from trade magazines such as *Boxoffice, Motion Picture Herald,* and *Film Daily.* I think by using these disparate sources you can not only glean what they felt about each picture, but what the historical perspective of the times was.

In the filmographies, I've not only listed producer, writer, and director, along with the main cast, but running time, musical director, and date of release. In these days of home video recording the running time can be important (and it also helps you determine whether your television versions of these films have been edited); and the musical directors played an important role in teen films, probably moreso than in many other genres of film. Additionally, although most filmographies only list the year of release, I've tried to track down the exact date of release for each film, because with teen trends coming and going so fast, I found it interesting to see whether a film was released in, say, January 1958 or December 1958. That could be a lead not only to historical facts and trends, but it also helps show which film was first, last, or in the middle of a particular trend, fad, or theme. (These dates indicate when the films first opened, but they may not have gotten to your town until three or six months later. Most teen exploitation films opened city-by-city or region-by-region, taking a playdate whenever and wherever they could get one. So if you're trying to remember when it was you had your first date and went to see *High School Confidential!,* use this information only as a guide.)

Many of these films are very hard to find nowadays. There was a time, not too long ago, when many of them were still on television, even if it was at two A.M. But now most of them have been lost or pulled from circulation in favor of more recent, and usually color, films. They still do pop up, especially in markets not in the top ten or twenty nationally, and also occasionally show up in revival houses or various festivals. Recently, some of the films have begun to be released on home video, and two of the reasons for this guide are both to help spur interest and reissues, and to help you decide which films to view or purchase. I hope you find this book both informative and fun. Try to catch these films. Get into their spirit. And of course, happy viewing.

—Alan Betrock
April 1986

The I Was A Teenage Juvenile Delinquent Rock 'n' Roll Horror Beach Party Movie Book!

Roots of Exploitation: 1900–1925

Exploitation movies didn't begin in the 1950s with American International Pictures. They didn't even begin in the 1940s or 1930s. In actual fact, exploitation movies are almost as old as the moving picture itself. From the early days of the Edison kinetoscope (1894), and the variations that followed, through the development of the nickelodeons (1905), and the ensuing rapid rise of short films, and then longer features, exploitation movies have played a major role in the popularity and development of the motion picture business. And although modern motion picture techniques and progressions have made these early films seem totally archaic in comparison, many of the rules, styles, trends, and marketing ploys used back in the early 1900s are still being used today, albeit in an updated guise.

Most early moving pictures were little more than short vignettes; the novelty of "moving pictures" alone was enough to draw in the curious crowds. Then, as films became longer, they basically copied stage plays, both in style and substance. Certainly there were artistic trendsetters, but the large percentage of films were static and derivative. Soon, producers tried to outdo one another with sensational stories and pictures, and the first wave of exploitation films concentrated on human vices and failings—sex, drink, gambling, and so on. These early films were geared toward the lower-class working immigrants whose nickel or dime provided them with some period of escapism. As soon as one film or subject would prove to be popular, a dozen lookalikes quickly crowded the marketplace. Early titles (1900–1915) included *Gambling Exposed, The Downward Path, Ten Nights in a Barroom, The Fate of the Artist's Model, The Curse of Drink,* and many others.

Controversy soon arose as to whether these films were good or bad for the public. One side believed that evils must be shown and talked about so others wouldn't fall prey to their temptations. The opposition felt that motion picture producers were merely exploiting the basest elements of society for pure greed. As a result, and to protect themselves from such criticisms, most producers prefaced their films with a serious statement, which offered the opinion that such-and-such vice or problem really existed, and that this film was produced to educate the public, and finally ending with the hope that this motion picture would aid in stamping out the problem at hand. With this preface firmly in place, and often receiving prime exposure in advertisements for the film, the picture could then go on to show all kinds of scenes of vice and degradation, because ultimately it was all for the public good. This technique was used for many years, and is occasionally still used today, not only in films, but in books and magazines as well. When the "scandal magazine" boom hit America in the mid-fifties, such publications rationalized their preoccupation with sex, drugs, vice, alcoholism, etc., by stating their disgust for such occurrences, and when the Supreme Court gave their landmark decision on pornography, stating that, to be declared obscene, the material must be totally without socially redeeming value, the explanatory preface was used in books, magazines, and films telling the viewer exactly what the redeeming social value of their work was. Then it was much easier to get by the censors, and into public hands. "It's a dirty job, but somebody's got to do it." (When the juvenile-delinquency boom hit films in the mid-1950s, many pictures had explanatory prefaces or epilogues. Some of these included *The Blackboard Jungle, The Cool and the Crazy, The Delinquents,* and numerous others.)

"FOR GOD'S SAKE DO SOMETHING!"

White Slavery
Horrors of the Traffic

Will You Help Free Me ?

The Greatest Crime in the
World's History

PRICE 50c.

A paperback book published in 1910 showing public interest in "white slavery."

In 1913, the Rockefeller Commission released a report on prostitution, which received wide public attention and discussion. Within months, busy motion picture producers were churning out films on the problem of white slavery, (presumably "black slavery" was not much of a public concern). The most famous film of this kind was 1913's *Traffic in Souls,* which cost under $10,000 to produce, but grossed over a quarter of a million dollars. This became a trademark of exploitation filmmakers—market like crazy, take the money, and run. Then followed the copycats: *The Inside of the White Slave Traffic, Lure of New York, Smashing of Vice Trust, Serpent of the Slums, Is Any Girl Safe?, Human Cargoes, Protect Your Daughters,* and many more.

Soon, a repeating trend emerged: a lurid exposé would receive wide public attention via newspapers, magazines, or a government report (the wave of vice-trust movies, also known as "red-light" films, followed District Attorney Whitman's report "Investigation of the Vice Trusts"); then some quick-buck entrepreneur would rush out some low-budget film to capitalize on the event. Eventually, when the more conservative, bigger studios saw that there was money to be made, they would produce a "classy" version of the story. By the third year, less inventive producers would try to wring out what was left in the public's interest by making low-budget imitations with similar titles. After that, the public's interest was sated, and the genre disappeared for a few years, always to return later, when events proved auspicious. This cyclical nature of exploitation filmmaking continued for decades, and still continues today. American International Pictures, for example, based their whole enterprise on creating cycles—juvenile-delinquent pictures, rock 'n' roll pictures, horror pictures, beach pictures, biker pictures, protest pictures, and so on—and also knew when to get out before losing their shirts on films that the public was no longer interested in.

Another early cycle for the exploitation filmmakers was geared to drug abuse. In 1913 came *The Accursed Drug* and *Slave of Morphine,* followed by *The Devil's Needle* (1916), with Norma Talmadge. But the biggest shot in the arm for drug films (no pun intended) came in 1923, when matinée idol Wallace Reid went public with his morphine addiction and entered a hospital to take "the cure." This event received wide attention in the daily press, but took an unexpected turn for the sensational when Mr. Reid died during withdrawal. His wife dedicated herself to exposing this terrible vice by producing a film based on drug addiction and withdrawal called *Human Wreckage.* It was a huge success. She followed with a film the next year called *Broken Laws,* concerning juvenile delinquency, and other studios jumped on the delinquency bandwagon. Other popular delinquency films included *As The World Rolls On* (1921), *Romance of a Million Dollars* (1926), *Youth Astray* (1928), *Our Dancing Daughters* (1928), and its sequel *Our Modern Maidens* (1929), these last two both starring Joan Crawford.

The wave of marijuana exploitation films flooded not only the U.S. but numerous foreign countries during the 1930s.

Other cycles and genres of exploitation films in the teens and twenties included pictures on magical cure-alls; child labor; social diseases; birth control; abortion; girls astray; and another wave of white-slave films. There was even an antimarijuana western, *Notch Number One* (1924). Another trick of the exploitation filmmaker was to rerelease the same film over the years with a new title and advertising campaign. Perhaps the greatest example of this pattern was with the film now currently known and shown as *Reefer Madness.* During the thirties and forties it played all over America as *The Burning Question, Tell Your Children, Dope Addict, Doped Youth, Assassin of Youth,* and *Love Madness.*

By 1921 the motion picture business had grown into an industry. Weekly attendance was fifty million admissions. There were fourteen thousand theaters. The numerous film companies released about seven hundred pictures annually. So it was left to the producers to try to outdo each other with sensationalism. Some of the pre-code exploitation titles included: *A Shocking Night, The Naked Truth, Street of Forgotten Men, Luring Lips, Sheltered Daughters, Foolish Wives, The Truant Husband, Sacred and Profane Love, Road to Ruin, She Could Not Help It, Port of Missing Girls, Her Purchase Price, Where Are My Children?, Confession, Curse Of Drink, Flames of the Flesh, Forbidden Love, Lure of Youth, Passion's Playground, Probation Wife, Reckless Youth, Wild Girl,* and many more. Usually the titles and advertising campaigns were far wilder than the films themselves, but this uncensored flood of exploitation began to cause trouble. As movie stars began to lead rich and wild public lives, and the industry was attacked on several other fronts, many citizens and officials began to call for censorship. Eventually, to protect their businesses, the bosses of most major studios rallied behind a plan to police themselves—they formed the Motion Picture Producers and Distributors of America (MPPDA)—better known as the Hays Office.

The Hays Office

As America entered the 1920s, the most prevalent social topic was the "Jazz Age"—as pictured on the screen, a period of wild dress and dance, loose sex and speakeasies, and a general atmosphere of carefree abandon. In response, a vicious battle between Jazz Age supporters and public moralists began in earnest. And for a while it seemed like the protectors of decency were winning. The president of the Christian Endeavor Society declared that the modern "indecent dance was an offense against womanly purity, the very fountainhead of our family and civil life." Other religious journals called Jazz Age styles "impure, polluting, corrupting, debasing, destroying spirituality, and increasing carnality." The president of the University of Florida stated: "The low-cut gowns, the rolled hose and short skirts are born of the devil and his angels, and are carrying the present and future generations to chaos and destruction." Immediately, elected officials saw this as a topic for vote-getting. One bill was introduced "providing a fine and imprisonment for those who wore on the streets skirts higher than three inches above the ankle." In Virginia a bill was proposed forbidding women from wearing skirtwaists [sic] or even gowns which displayed "more than three inches of her throat." In Ohio, the proposed limit for decolletage was two inches, and the bill strove to prevent the sale of any "garment which unduly displays or accentuates the lines of the female figure" and would have barred any "female over fourteen years of age from wearing a skirt which does not reach to that part of the foot known as the instep."

In the U.S. Senate the target was motion pictures. One senator stated: "Hollywood is a colony of these people where debauchery, riotous living, drunkeness, ribaldry, dissipation, and free love seem to be conspicuous. Many of these 'stars' it is reported were formerly

The Jazz Age: In the 1920s the public was already being warned to be wary of "bad girls."

bartenders, butcher boys, sopers, swampers, variety actors and actresses, who may have earned $10 or $20 a week. Some of them are now paid, it is said, salaries of $5,000 a month or more, and they do not know what to do with their wealth, extracted from poor people in large part by 25¢ or 50¢ admission fees, except to spend it in riotous living, dissipation, and 'high rolling.' These are some of the characters from whom the young people of today are deriving a large part of their education, views of life, and character forming habits. From these sources our young people gain much of their views of life, inspiration, and education. Rather a poor source, is it not? It looks as if censorship is needed, does it not?"

By 1921, thirty-six states had censorship bills pending, and in 1922, a congressman from New Jersey introduced a bill to create a Federal Motion Picture Commission, with a license provision covering all films entering interstate and foreign commerce. But perhaps the biggest blow to the motion picture industry came in 1921 when famed comedian Fatty Arbuckle was linked to an "orgy death party" that resulted in the death of starlet Virginia Rappe. News and rumors of wild parties, drink and drugs, paid women, and exactly what Arbuckle did to Rappe, flew in the tabloids and corner stores across America. Arbuckle had to go through three trials, under a massive blaze of publicity, before he was finally acquitted. But not before charges of manslaughter, assault, bribery, perjury, suppression of evidence, intimidation, and coaching of witnesses were brought forth. Arbuckle's million-dollar career was ruined, and outside the trial he was greeted with jeers from the crowd who called him "murderer," "big, fat slob," "beast," "degenerate" and worse. His films were withdrawn from circulation, and several already "in the can" were not released.

Resentment, jealousy, and even bitterness began to sweep across the country, as tales of huge salaries and wild living by those in the movie colony became commonplace. One member of the industry, sensing this growing change in public opinion, stated: "For several years the stories of huge wages were regarded as showman exaggerations, merely the reckless boasting of inspired press agents. People thought it preposterous that a girl, unknown a year or two earlier, should be earning $2,000 a week, or that a plumber's assistant should have become a comedian worth a quarter of a million a year. But gradually theater patrons came to realize that these stories were true, and realization was accompanied by mixed emotions that in many instances turned to bitterness and hostility. Admiration and adoration of movie celebrities had developed without any sound basis, and now many people who had formed the habit of idolizing their favorites as superior beings were shocked to discover that their divinities were money grubbers of the most ordinary variety. Merchants and professional men, struggling to earn five or ten thousand dollars a year, began to curse the 'pretty boys' of the screen who received as much in a month or a week, and their wives grew caustic in commenting on the 'dough-faced girls who hadn't brains enough to act, but were lucky enough to get a fortune for being clothes-horses.' "

In 1921, with the industry facing pressure from both government and the public, film-colony leaders decided to form the Motion Picture Producers and Distributors of America. In late 1921 they approached the highly regarded Postmaster General Will H. Hays to head the organization. On January 14, 1922, at age forty-two, he accepted the job, along with a $100,000 yearly salary. Hays saw his main goals as keeping the industry free from government censorship and interference; strict self-regulation that would maintain standards; and a campaign to raise both the quality of films made, and the public's tastes. The forming of the MPPDA, and Hays's lofty goals, quieted down the public clamor somewhat, but most took a wait-and-see attitude before dropping their calls for "cleaning up" the motion picture industry.

Hays's activities did make some progress over the next several years, but there were still abuses, and with the advent of sound, the new realism available to filmmakers proved to be a shock to the public. Now, once again, public indignation began to rise. So in 1930 the MPPDA came up with a specific "code" of conduct, detailing content, language, image, advertising, and almost every aspect of the industry. By the mid-1930s the code was firmly in place and being enforced; the quality of films was improving rapidly; and the industry stars were on

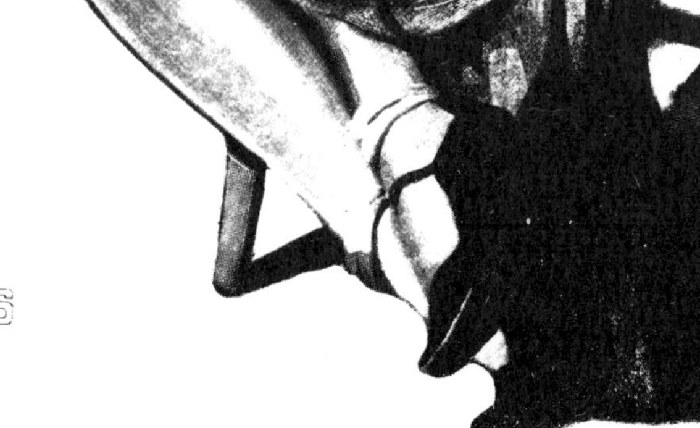

A 1933 magazine publicizing scandal in Hollywood.

their best behavior. After all, this was the depression, and no one wanted their golden goose consumed. The industry was fast becoming dominated by a few big companies who controlled the major share of production and distribution, and only a few daring outsiders succeeded in breaking the code either artistically or financially. But there was a new public fascination sweeping the country, and Hollywood would soon jump in with both feet—the world of crime and gangsters.

The Thirties and Forties

The 1930s burst onto the screen in a blaze of gunfire. With the Hays office firmly keeping a lid on sex, violence came to the fore, passable as long as the bad guys got it in the last reel. Crime movies were the rage, and stars were born. Edward G. Robinson, James Cagney, Humphrey Bogart, and others all went to the top of the Hollywood heap by starring in crime movies, and they were typed as gangsters for many years. It was only after they were able to assert some measure of power over the studios that they were slowly able to branch out and star in other kinds of roles, many atypical of their earlier characterizations. Similarly, the Dead End Kids became popular as tough, poor juvenile delinquents, until, over time, they became happy-go-lucky good guys. These 1930s crime movies were important to the later development of 1950s teen movies because they were quick-paced, relatively inexpensive to make, and the lines between right and wrong were clearly delineated. And slowly, most particularly with the Dead End Kids, they began to add social themes and subplots to the stories. Were these criminals just born bad, or were they a product of their environment? If the latter were so, what could society do to break the repeating pattern?

Even though the Production Code was firmly in place, exploitational films like* Confessions of a Vice Baron *still managed to be released.

During World War II, the movies concentrated on helping the war effort by portraying the military in a strong and winning light. Obviously, this was not a time for crime movies. Every branch of the military was shown on screen, occasionally with problems, but those were always overcome. There were spies, traitors, Nazis, and "Japs" to be dealt with. This was war for real and Hollywood's effort played a major role in raising spirits, rallying patriotism, and pulling the country together. But with so many fathers away from home, newspapers and magazines began to be filled with stories of juvenile delinquency, and it seemed to be mushrooming into a major national problem. Some went so far as to offer the opinion that America was at danger from within, and that our youth were becoming prime targets for our enemies to exploit, lost as they were in loneliness and confusion.

In 1943, sensing a commercial topic on their hands, RKO invested $400,000 to produce *Are These Our Children?*, a film that examined juvenile delinquency. Some questioned whether we should show such problems on the screen, images which might show America in a weak light at a time when strength was needed so desperately. Director Val Lewton replied: "Is it more important to produce worthwhile films to combat a tangible danger on the home front, or to neglect this because of an intangible fear that some of the pictures might possibly be used as propaganda in Europe?" Amid a great deal of national publicity, the picture was made, along with some other quicky copycats: Monogram's *Where Are My Children?* and PRC's *I Accuse My Parents.* Also in 1944 came two talked-about Broadway plays concerning wayward youth, *Pick Up Girl* and *Hickory Stick.*

In the late forties came three important films dealing with juvenile crime: *Gun Crazy* with John Dall and Peggy Cummins as two teenagers on a wild crime spree; *Knock on Any Door,* which introduced John Derek as a delinquent product of a bad environment, and which introduced

During World War II juvenile delinquency became a major topic of public interest. An example was this 1942 exploitation magazine's cover story on a "teenage vice wave."

the popular slogan "Live fast, die young, and leave a pretty corpse"; and *City across the River,* a toned-down version of Irving Shulman's bestselling novel on teenage gangs, *The Amboy Dukes.* All three of these films received a lot of publicity, captured the public's fancy, and introduced many themes and images that were to follow.

Moreover, the late forties and early fifties brought a new cinematic style to the screen—film noir. These dark and brooding pictures added a psychological edge to criminality and they were rushed out by the dozens. A new crowd of antihero stars were being born in Hollywood, a group whose screen personas were tough, violent, sexy, and antiestablishment. Even their looks ran against the grain of the Hollywood "pretty boy" image. This was real life—gritty, dirty, and living on the fringes of society. Repelled by the actions they saw onscreen, the public also seemed fascinated with this darker side of life, and these

This low-budget film was rushed out in 1944 to compete with such films as Are These Our Children, *and* Where Are Your Children? *The poster was quite beautiful; the film quite miserable.*

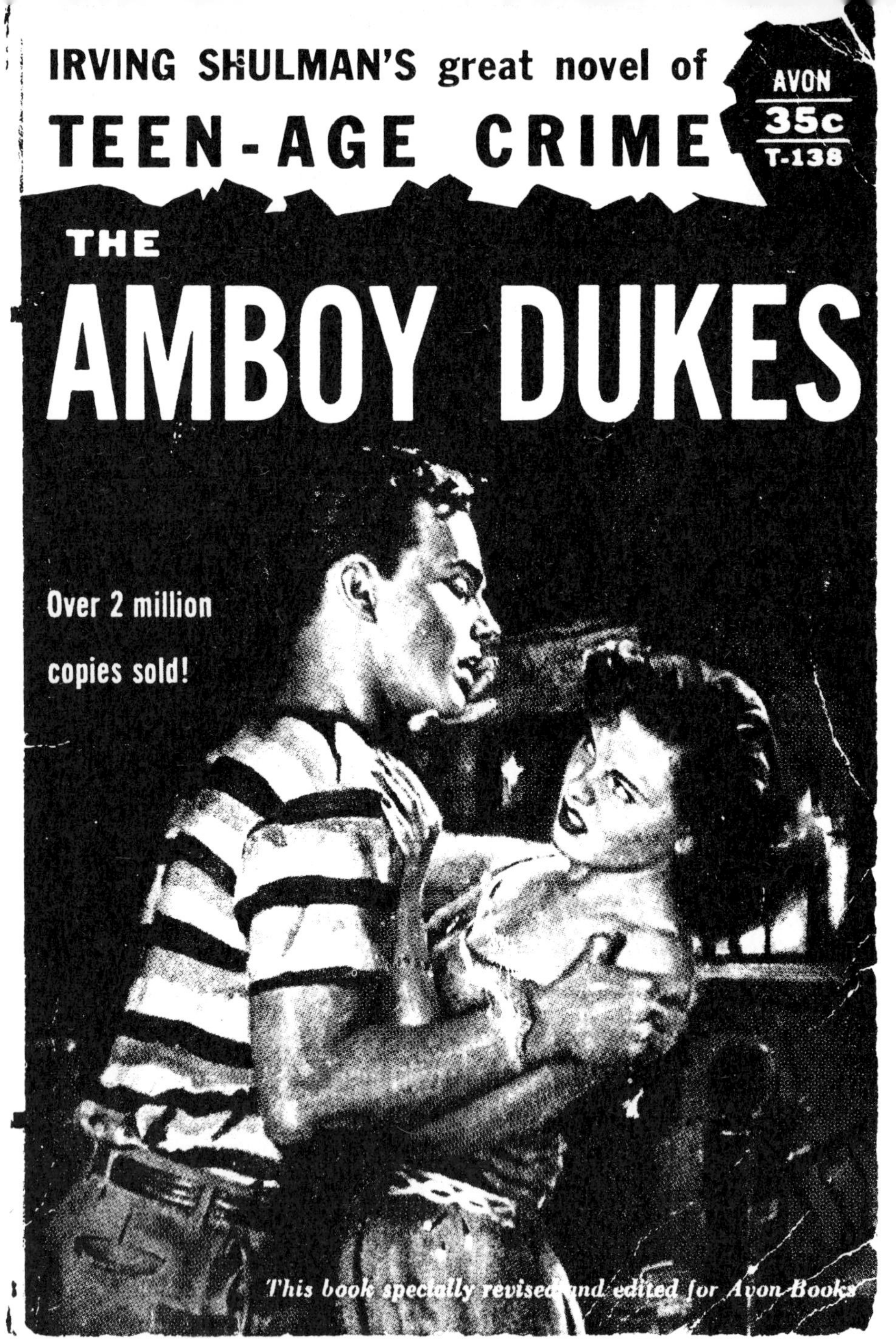

Irving Shulman's gritty best-selling novel was made into a tamed-down motion picture, City Across the River, *in 1949.*

There were many exploitation films in the thirties and forties with teenage themes, but most, like Cocaine, *made their advertising pitch to adults.*

films, to the surprise of many, were quite successful. In some ways they were cathartic, but they were also indicative of a postwar malaise that seemed to permeate much of the country's psyche. A revolution had occurred in America during the war years, and things were never quite the same again. Millions who left as boys returned as men, and despite economic prosperity, there seemed to be a discomfort with new roles and events. There was underlying confusion not only with one's place in the world, but right here on Main Street, U.S.A., as well.

And finally, Hollywood decided to tackle tough social issues on the screen. Almost every social ill and problem became ripe for vivid and often adult characterizations. There were movies on alcoholism, divorce, rape, infidelity, racism, mental illness, kidnapping, drug addic-

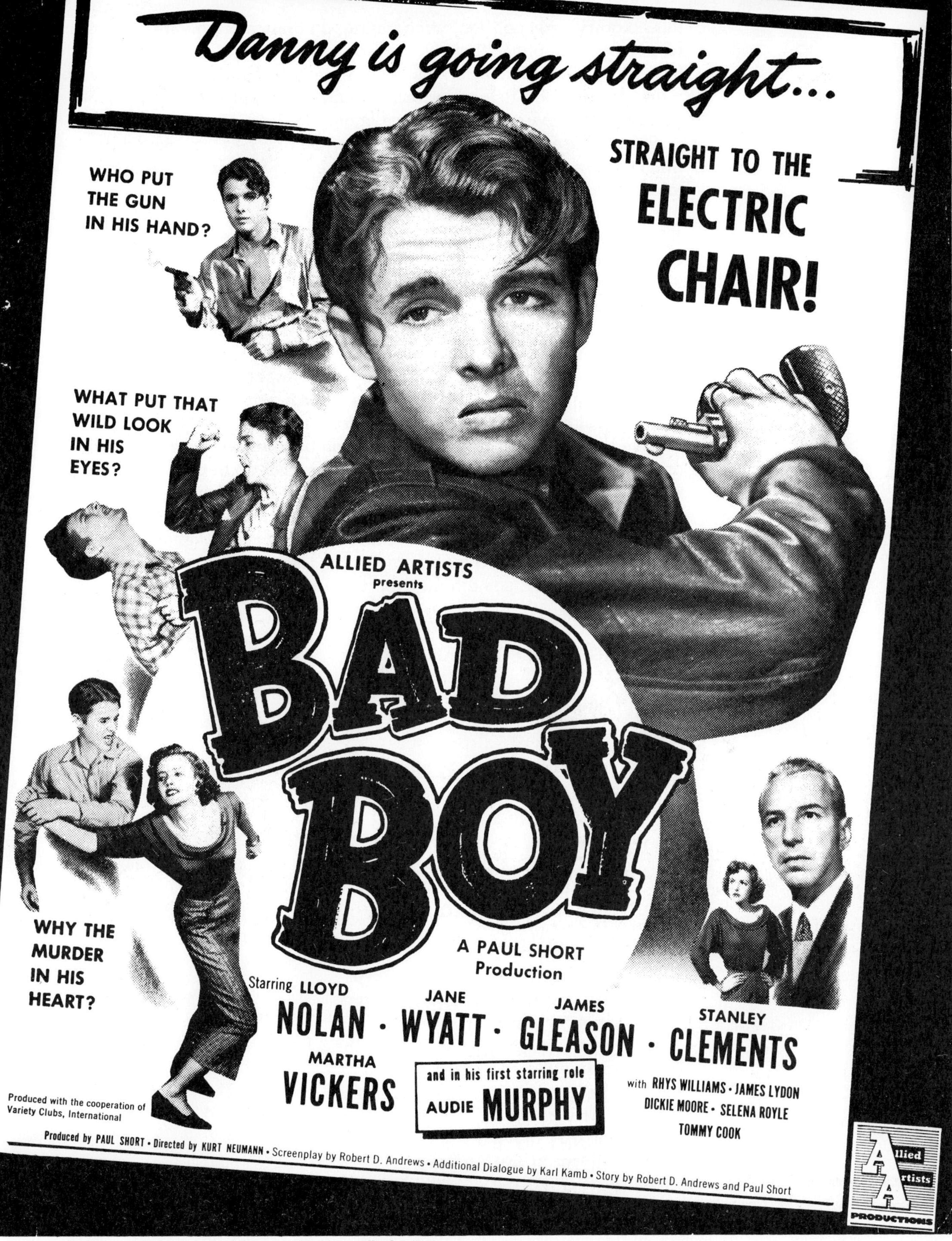

Bad Boy, a 1949 juvenile delinquent film from Allied Artists.

tion, bigotry, sex, political wrongdoing, and much more. Many of these were fine films, but Hollywood seemed to be testing the code, to see how far they could go—and just what the public would accept. (Finally, a few pictures had to be released without code approval, until in 1956 the code was liberalized, but more about that later.)

It was these three trends—crime movies, film noir, and social theme films—that would help to contribute to the teen film explosion of the mid-fifties. There were to be other developments and important contributing factors, to be sure, but these three cinematic trends helped to pave the way and open the door for what was to follow. Some felt that fifties teen films developed in a vacuum, but it would be more accurate to say that they had been developing over many years. The forties and early fifties were filled with (usually) cheap exploitation films—there were literally dozens and dozens—that promised much for the cinematic voyeur. They usually didn't break much new ground past their lurid advertising campaigns, but they were important pace-setters for what was to follow in terms of themes, characterizations, and marketing. They played throughout the country, in big cities and small towns. To give you an idea of what was going on beneath the façade of glamorous Hollywood, here are some of the films that dealt primarily with teenagers, their problems, and related exploitational themes. I think a look at the titles will tell you that teen exploitation was alive and well prior to the mid-fifties explosion, although one big difference was that these films were geared mainly to adults, rather than to teens themselves. But clearly, something was rumbling, and about to explode:

BIG TOWN SCANDAL
CAGED
GIRLS ON PROBATION
HOT ROD
MAN CRAZY
THE MARIHUANA STORY
PICKUP
PRISON GIRLS
TEEN AGE
ON THE LOOSE
PROBLEM GIRLS
SO YOUNG, SO BAD
SKID ROW
SECRETS OF A CO-ED
THE WEAK AND THE WICKED
THE YOUNG AND THE DAMNED
GOOD TIME GIRL
GIRLS IN CHAINS
GIRLS IN THE NIGHT
FLAME OF YOUTH
NOT WANTED
JOHNNY HOLIDAY
THE DEVIL ON WHEELS
BAD BOY
CURSE OF A TEENAGE NAZI

And so on. Now approaching the mid-fifties, things began to move quickly—not only sociologically but in the movie business as well. First we will look at a pioneer of exploitation films in the forties and early fifties, Kroger Babb, and then we will see how this all led up to the huge explosion of teen exploitation films of the fifties and sixties.

Some late forties and early fifties advertisements for teen exploitation films.

A trade magazine advertisement for So Young, So Bad, a 1950 teenage 'bad-girl' delinquent film.

Master of Exploitation—Kroger Babb

There were studios in business solely for the production of the B picture, studios that made short, fast-paced films by the dozens, made a small profit, and then moved on to more films. But rarely has an organization been built on just a few films—pictures that were advertised like crazy, and continued playing in small town across the country for five or even ten years after they were first produced. Only a true wizard of exploitation could carry that off, and one such man was Kroger Babb.

Kroger Babb was born in Lees Creek, Ohio, in 1906, and at the age of fourteen became a reporter and sports editor for the Wilmington, Ohio, *Daily News Journal.* He took four years off to go to college, and after graduation he returned to the paper as advertising manager. In 1934 he became advertising director for Warner-Chakeres Theaters, where he presumably learned about publicity and promotion, and in 1945 he formed his own company, Hallmark Productions, with J. S. Jossey. The first film they produced, under the banner of Hygienic Films, was *Mom and Dad,* which they described as "the world's only educational sex-hygiene film." *Mom and Dad* was an incredible success, thanks mainly to Babb's outrageous advertising campaigns and machinery. From growing up in a small town himself, Babb realized that there were thousands of small towns across the country that had no movie theaters (or theaters with only limited, conservative fare), so he decided to bring the theaters to them. For a week or two before the film came to town, the citizens were deluged with handouts, huge posters, and even sound trucks. If there was no available theater, Babb would rent a meeting hall, a warehouse, or, if all else failed, he would even set up a portable tent. The film, projector, and advertising materials were carried in a van or truck, and would simply move from town to town, not unlike a carnival or a medicine show. Babb would often heighten the sense of the forbidden by scheduling two shows, one for men and one for women. Occasionally the film was preceded by a lecture of "educational value," and more money was made by selling books or pamphlets relating the film to the audiences. And so it went, day after day, week after week, month after month, and year after year. By 1950, Babb claimed that *Mom and Dad* had been seen by over forty million people, in over fifty countries, and had grossed more than fifteen million dollars.

Babb acquired full control of Hallmark, and began producing exploitable pictures in earnest. Perhaps his biggest success came with *The Prince of Peace,* a color film which told the story of Jesus Christ, and, by Babb's estimate, the biggest-grossing film of 1949 and 1950. By 1950, he had several other shows on the road, including a sports show which was basically clips of action sports such as wrestling, bowling, golf, baseball, football, and so on. His hook here was promising "$2,500 in sports merchandise prizes at every engagement." Since the film only grossed a few hundred dollars a showing, it's probably safe to believe that the prize values were somewhat inflated. For the adult audiences, "to be shown at midnight only," came *She Shoulda Said No,* which asked the question: "How bad can a good girl get?" ("Thinking mothers and fathers will be the first to acclaim it!")

You may never have heard of these movies, but thanks to Kroger Babb, they played in every town in America, and grossed millions of dollars.

On August 31, 1948, fledgling actress Lila Leeds was arrested along with Robert Mitchum for possession of marijuana. By 1950, Babb was already distributing *Devil's Weed,* "the inside dope about dope, starring the screen's new blond bomb, Lila Leeds, and her exposé of the marijuana racket." This was usually co-billed with the short featurette, *G.I. Love,* which was a rather hot title for a tame picture about G.I.s sightseeing in Europe, padded with some names of the day doing their thing overseas. In 1949 also came *The Lawton Story of the Prince of Peace* a drama set around the annual passion play in the Witchita Mountains. Also in 1950: *One Too Many,* the story of alcoholism and Alcoholics Anonymous. The film starred Ruth Warrick, who had risen to Hollywood fame with her first role in 1941's *Citizen Kane.* By 1950 she was doing films for Babb, and for the Protestant Film Commission, where she starred in *Second Chance,* a tale of a woman who dreams she has gone bad, only to wake up and begin life anew with the church as her foundation. Babb continued with *Delinquent Angels,* the true story of a tough female jurist who turns bad kids straight, and *Side-*

road, a remake of *Mom and Dad*. He forged on with *Father Bingo* ("the most delightful comedy of all time"), and *The Best Is Yet to Come* ("all there is to know about cancer"). Throughout it all, Babb ballyhooed his pictures in the newspapers, movie trades, and of course in every small town. He promised (and usually delivered) extra profits for the exhibitor, and of course profits for himself. He called his offices in Wilmington, Ohio, "the world headquarters of the greatest showman's organization to be found anywhere in the world today." Babb would often travel to trade shows and exhibitions speaking on "The Secrets of Showmanship," promising "a hypodermic for boxoffice grosses that any Dr. Exhibitor can inject into his own community and create an epidemic of S.R.O."

DON'T MISS MR. SHOW BUSINESS!

SEE and HEAR

KROGER BABB

THE MAN WHO PRODUCED THOSE HALLMARK 'DOOR-BREAKING' . . . MONEY-MAKING HITS . . .

"MOM AND DAD" "PRINCE OF PEACE" "ONE TOO MANY" "SECRETS OF BEAUTY" "SHE SHOULDA SAID NO"

A SUCCESSFUL INDUSTRY

SPEAKING ON

"SECRETS OF SHOWMANSHIP"

A COMPREHENSIVE exploration of the fields of Advertising and Publicity . . . and how to use them for Greater Profits!

AN ALL-NEW Illustrated Talk . . A Hypodermic for Boxoffice Grosses that any Dr. Exhibitor can inject into his own community and create an Epidemic of "S.R.O." . . . (a disease associated with Profititis).

AT THE

National Allied Drive-In Theatre Owners and Kansas-Missouri Allied Spring Convention

Kroger Babb not only hyped his films— he hyped himself. Here was a chance to meet "Mr. Showmanship."

Joe Solomon, who became a millionaire running his own exploitation film company, Fanfare Films, in the late sixties and seventies—mostly with biker films—got his start in the business hawking some of Babb's films. He had the New York, New Jersey, and Pennsylvania markets. A 1971 article in *Esquire* described how Solomon plied some of the tricks of the trade. "Solomon was an advance man. He'd go into Allentown, say, and book the picture and set up a campaign. The picture itself wasn't much; something about a girl who fell in with the wrong crowd and got pregnant. It was in black and white, but at the end they'd spliced on a live childbirth in full color. [This was *Mom and Dad.*] 'I think they bought it from some educational film company,' Solomon recalled. 'They just spliced it onto the end of our story, and nobody could tell the difference.' "

Solomon, as advance man, hit on the idea of having sexually segregated showings. Women in the afternoon, men in the evening, "so as not to offend the delicate." He also advertised that a uniformed nurse would be on duty at all times. Before each screening, a man in a business suit would climb onto the stage and make a speech about the book they were selling on birth control, sex hygiene, venereal disease, and the hazards of promiscuity. Then a woman in a nurse's uniform would

A 1955 ad for some of Babb's productions — at this point some were ten years old and still getting playdates.

Walk the Walk. ***One of Babb's final promotions — the "anti-drug" feature***

peddle the books up and down the aisles.

"Just the campaign alone, we'd have the whole town steamed up," Solomon said.

"And then at the afternoon show, I'd turn off the ventilation in the theater, or throw some kind of crap into the ventilation, some gas to make them nauseous, and I'd call the local paper to come and get a picture of the people fainting. The women would be pouring out of the theater holding their heads and moaning. By now we had every guy in town ready to see that picture. They broke down the doors for the evening show. The funny thing was, when the childbirth came on, the men fainted for real. This was the middle fifties. It was a great gag. It was good for two weeks in any town in the country."

By 1955, Babb was still at it, flogging his pictures away, and selling his ideas on showmanship. It's true that some other companies tried to duplicate Babb's success with pictures similar to his, but they just couldn't compete with his incredible organization, drive, belief, and total commitment to advertising, promotion, and exhibition. By the mid-fifties Babb had added several pictures to his roster: *Karamoja* ("the world's lost tribes, weird shocking rites, authentic, uncensored, shocking!") *Monika* ("nineteen and naughty, the story of a bad girl, starring the sensational Swedish actress, Harriet Andersson"), *Mixed-Up Women* (starring Ruth Warrick; "Is there one in your house?"), and finally "Kroger Babb's most fearless production," *The Birds and the Bees* ("It might be all about S-E-X").

Finally, in 1958, Babb sold his company, but still managed to keep the machine going. In 1970, he was promoting *Walk That Walk,* the "true" story of a Catholic priest hooked on booze and heroin—and finally cured. Babb's pressbook for the film overflowed with "proven" success strategies and odd ways to hype the film.

Eventually, Babb faded from the scene, but in the 1950s, with the impending rise of independent film companies, and the need to compete with television, future producers and companies would look back at Kroger Babb's style, update it slightly, and forge onward into the world of exploitation and dollars. Whatever was to happen in the fifties and sixties, Babb had led the way and showed them all how it was to be done. All that was needed was for the new mavericks to follow in his footsteps, and he left tracks that anyone could follow. And they did.

An early teen-exploitation double-bill:* Teen Age *and* Youth Aflame, *seen here in a sensationalistic theater display in Dallas, 1949.

1954–1958
I Was a Teenage Moneymaker

Perhaps Kroger Babb was making money hawking his exploitation films around the country, but the rest of the movie industry was running scared. Their biggest problem, as they saw it, was the rise of television, an appliance that one theater owner called "that little monster in the living room that gives away programs for free." The rise in television ownership and viewing had indeed been monumental. In 1950, there were only four million televisions in use, and by 1960 that figure had grown to fifty million. At one particularly manic point in 1956, televisions were being sold at the rate of twenty thousand a day. Movie attendance and theater ownership began to drop proportionately. During the postwar boom, weekly theater attendance had topped out at 90 million, for each of the years 1946, '47, and '48. By 1955 that total had fallen to 45 million, and by 1959 the number had dropped to 42 million. And despite a rise in ticket prices, the total gross was down from $1.5 billion at its peak in 1948, to $1.1 billion by the end of the fifties. On top of that, the cost of producing films for the major studios had increased substantially, so their profit margin was shrinking from both the manufacturing and consumption ends. And the number of theaters was dropping as well, from a peak of twenty thousand in the late forties, to a total of seventeen thousand by the end of the fifties. The one saving grace, perhaps, was the rise of drive-ins, from little more than a thousand in 1949, to almost five thousand by the end of the fifties. Theater owners liked drive-ins because they found that they could book cheaper films, and the audience still came, and they also realized that concession sales were about four times as great as in a normal theater—and concession sales was where the theater owners made most of their money.

On top of these grim numbers, the major studios had been forced, by a 1948 divestment decree, to rid themselves of the theater chains they owned. This was a startling blow to the studios, because before divestment they had been guaranteed a certain number of screens and a resulting guaranteed income. It took five years for full divestiture to take place, but by 1953 all theaters were independent operators or chains that could book their own films, and attempt to dicker for prices and better percentages. Without a guaranteed distribution for their output, and with weekly attendance dropping, the production of the eight major studios dropped precipitously. In 1951 they had produced a total of 320 films; by 1960 that number had fallen to 184. Other new independents stepped in to fill the gap somewhat—Allied Artists and American International were the most notable—but still the total of all features released in the United States had fallen from 654 in 1951 to 387 in 1960—a forty-percent decline.

The industry tried to fight back with all kinds of gimmicks. Wide-screen, CinemaScope, VistaVision, Smell-O-Vision, and so on. In 1953, 3-D was heralded as the salvation of the industry, but the concept was dead within a year. Some of these technological gimmicks did bring people back to the theaters, but they were certainly not the cure-alls that the industry was searching for. With all these problems rampant, this would not have seemed like the time to go into the movie business, but two entrepreneurs saw it otherwise. They were Samuel Z. Arkoff and James Nicholson, and in 1954 they decided to go into business as the American Releasing Corporation.

Arkoff was a lawyer who had experience working for many small and medium-sized entertainment clients. Nicholson had a background in theater management, and was, in 1953, working as sales manager for Realart Pictures. Both wanted to make movies, and through a circuitous series of events they met, discovered their mutual interests, and began producing films together. Initially they started with low-budget westerns and action pictures—*The Fast and the Furious, Five Guns West,* and *Apache Woman.* These were true B pictures in the sense that not only were they inferior to A pictures, but they only played the bottom of bills to better productions. The A films could get a percentage of the gross revenue, but the B film was only rented out on a flat-fee basis, and this amount was small—so small that shortly after their first few pictures were released, Arkoff and Nicholson realized that they couldn't make their money back by playing only dates at the bottom of the bill. So they began making horror pictures, as mediocre as they were, and sent them out on double bills with elaborate and sensationalistic advertising campaigns (some of the posters and campaigns were better than the films themselves). With double-bill packages, they could go to theater owners and provide an entire show for less than the theater owner would have to pay for one Hollywood feature. Besides, Nicholson and Arkoff would then be operating on a percentage basis. With their wild advertising campaigns, and the fact that horror and sci-fi pictures were the rage in the early and mid-fifties, patrons, mainly kids, flocked to the theaters, and American Releasing Corporation began to make money. In 1956 they changed their name to American International Pictures, and they were on their way.

Nicholson and Arkoff geared their pictures to a young audience because they reckoned that seventy percent of moviegoing patrons were between twelve and twenty. Not much of a scientific study went into this formulation—it was just a hunch—and like so many of AIP's hunches, it was right. A few years later a "scientific study" came out with the proclamation that fifty-two percent of those who went to theaters once a week or more were between the ages of ten and nineteen. And by the time the study was done, almost all of them had paid to see numerous AIP films.

Simultaneous with the rise of AIP, teenagers began to get noticed. The biggest force, of course, was the rise of rock 'n' roll, with Elvis Presley as the kingpin who knocked down the doors. Alongside rock 'n' roll came a media infatuation with juvenile delinquency—there were numerous magazine articles, dozens of popular paperback novels, radio and TV shows, and even Senate committees that talked about the whys and wherefores of the problem. And daily, newspapers across the country were filled with the crimes, vandalism, hot-rodding, drug-taking, and general exploits of teenage delinquents. Something was indeed stirring, and by mid-1956, AIP was right there with their first all-

GOLDEN STATE PRODUCTIONS
SUNSET PRODUCTIONS
BALBOA PRODUCTIONS
ROGER CORMAN PRODUCTIONS
CARMEL PRODUCTIONS

FOR 1957-58 RELEASE . . .

ROCK ALL NIGHT
DRAGSTRIP GIRL
I AM A TEENAGE WEREWOLF
INVASION OF THE SAUCER MEN
GIRLS REFORM SCHOOL
MOTORCYCLE GIRL
THE AMAZING NTH MAN
WOLVES OF DARKNESS
JET SQUADRON
HELL RAIDERS
ISLAND OF PREHISTORIC WOMEN
GIRL FROM 1,000,000 A.D.
THE CAT GIRL

An early trade magazine advertisement for forthcoming American-International films.

The first AIP all-teenage double-bill, mid-1956.

teenage-bill combination of *Girls in Prison* and *Hot Rod Girl,* followed four months later by *Shake, Rattle and Rock,* and *Runaway Daughters.* Over the next three years AIP would release numerous types of pictures, but their bread and butter was the teenage double bill—by the end of 1959, they would release twelve such packages, and all of them made money.

AIP was not alone in pursuing such lofty goals. By the time the teenage exploitation film had bloomed fully, every major studio and most independent companies and producers would try their hand with such topics. But AIP's two main competitors in the annals of teenage flicks were Sam Katzman and Albert Zugsmith. Katzman had been in the business for years, making jungle serials, horror pictures, westerns, adventure films, and the like. But Katzman's true talent came with being Mr. Topicality. He rolled out a series of films on topical themes so quickly that there wasn't a chance for the fad to fade before the film hit the screen. In the fifties there were films on calypso music, the cha-cha, rock 'n' roll, beatniks, and so on. In the sixties he had the twist, hot rods, and hippies. It was all the same to Katzman—churn 'em out and wait for the money to roll back in.

The third master of this triumvirate, Albert Zugsmith, was a writer, producer, and director who was also tied to topicality, but who always spiced his films with more sex and violence per screen foot than was usually tolerable. And in the late fifties and early sixties, he had Mamie Van Doren under exclusive contract, and despite the Platinum Powerhouse's possible acting deficiencies, she certainly spiced up the films and pulled crowds into the theaters.

Despite competition from all sides, despite new times and trends, and despite new young blood entering the fray, AIP, Katzman, and Zugsmith were always there holding court over teen exploitation films. From their onset in 1955 until the demise of the golden era in 1969, these three led the way, and whatever criticisms might have been leveled against their films or marketing techniques, there was at least one thing you could say for them: they were dependable.

There was one more important element in this mixture that contributed to the rise of teen films—the popularity of James Dean. His only released film during his lifetime was *East of Eden,* but it was with *Rebel Without a Cause,* released one month after his death, that the unforeseen Dean explosion began. Although adults didn't like or even

One of the many magazines devoted to the burgeoning James Dean cult, 1956.

Four 1950s paperback novels, showing the media infatuation with teenagers and juvenile delinquency.

understand his screen persona, to the kids he became an idol. When *East of Eden* was released in April 1955, *The New York Times* called Dean "a mass of histrionic gingerbread. He scuffs his feet, he whirls, he pouts, he sputters, he leans against walls, he rolls his eyes, he swallows his words, he ambles slack-kneed—all like Marlon Brando used to do. Never have we seen a performer so clearly follow another's style. Mr. Kazan should be spanked for permitting him to do such a sophomoric thing. Whatever there might be of reasonable torment in this youngster is buried beneath the clumsy display." For *Rebel Without a Cause,* a film they generally praised, the *Times* was once again critical of Dean: "We do wish the young actors, including Mr. Dean, had not been so intent on imitating Marlon Brando in varying degrees. The tendency, possibly typical of the behavior of certain youths, may therefore be a subtle commentary, but it grows monotonous." But Dean's popularity skyrocketed. In 1956, there were four "one-shot" magazines published about him, alongside numerous newspaper and magazine articles, Dean merchandise, and Dean fan clubs. Not only was *Rebel* to become archetypical for many of its characterizations and plot lines, but every low-budget producer hoped that they had another James Dean on their hands when they rushed out their teen exploitation films—and many actors did their best to follow in his footsteps.

With the business side on one hand dictating cheap double bills geared to teenagers and the popularity of drive-ins predominating, and on the other hand the social phenomena of rock 'n' roll, juvenile delinquency, and the Dean craze gaining momentum, the stage was set for an explosion of teenage exploitation films. And explode they did.

Violence-Sex Twin Bill Big St. Louis Grosser

"Curse of a Teenage Nazi" and another exploitation picture, "Unwed Mothers," were booked into the Ansel Bros. Enterprises Ritz Theatre out on Delmar boulevard in St. Louis where Don Meyers is manager.

Meyers pulled out all the stops in promoting the violence-sex twin bill, proclaiming from a shocker front, handbills, etc. "Trapped, They Defied Their Killer Captors . . . ROMANCE . . . SHOCKING . . . VIOLENCE . . . REALISM . . . See Women Enslaved by Nazi Werewolves . . . It Screams the Terrifying Truth . . . Girls Choose Death to Nazis . . . Now It Can Be Told . . . It Will Tear Your Mind With Fury."

With this kind of advertising, the twin bill went on to outgross such films as The Big Fisherman, Solomon and Sheba, The Unforgiven, the Last Voyage and Porgy and Bess at the Ritz, Meyers reports. He comments he would be pleased to forward a copy of his campaign to anyone writing him at the Ritz Theatre, 6267 Delmar Blvd., St. Louis.

This trade magazine story shows what lengths theater owners would go to in their sensational approach to advertising.

In 1955, it was pretty much all *The Blackboard Jungle* and *Rebel Without a Cause,* two different sides of the same coin—confused youth and juvenile delinquency. Both films were taken seriously by the adult media, with many thought pieces published both pro and con, and both films were patronized by adults and teenagers. The result was box-office grosses of over five million dollars for each film, making them both artistic and commercial successes. But more important, for the first time in a long while, teenagers were beginning to be seen as a unique force unto themselves—and with the burgeoning popularity of rock 'n' roll, and the rollout of such influential national teenage magazines as *Dig,* this huge age group began to get serious attention. All of a sudden, not only were teenagers perceived as an important social force, but advertisers and promoters began to see them as a massive economic power as well. In late 1955, two films were rushed out to

Evan Hunter's best-selling novel, The Blackboard Jungle, *became a surprise hit motion picture in 1955.*

capitalize on these trends, Universal's *Running Wild,* starring Mamie Van Doren, and Sam Katzman's *Teenage Crime Wave.* But for a while this remained a very minor trend because filmmakers were falling over each other to make pictures about rock 'n' roll.

The first one to reach the theaters was Sam Katzman's *Rock around the Clock,* quickly followed by Katzman's *Don't Knock the Rock,* both featuring sparse plot lines and lots of rock 'n' roll groups. AIP jumped in with *Shake, Rattle and Rock,* which was teamed with *Runaway Daughters,* one of the first low-budget films to deal with "delinquent parents," about three high school girls who run off to Los Angeles, only to find that life is much tougher than they had imagined. These early rock 'n' roll films did so well that Hollywood responded with *The Girl Can't Help It,* a wonderfully funny film that also managed to capture some classic rock 'n' roll performances. AIP rushed out their first all-teen-exploitation double bill, *Girls in Prison* and *Hot Rod Girl,* and with their success, others began to follow suit. These AIP double bills were cheaply made, with each feature costing in the range of $50,000 to $100,000 each. Then they were marketed like crazy—the ad campaigns emphasized the wild, the sensational, and the teenage—adults were often just peripheral figures. AIP would often ask their distributors their reaction to a potential new title. If they got a good response, they would go ahead and make the film. If not, they would come up with something else. Often the final title remained nebulous until the picture was completely shot, and then AIP would add on a title that seemed most current and most exploitable. With the major studios making fewer features (and few of them expressly for teenagers) and the continuing growth of the drive-in market, AIP began to see a good return on these releases. Initially it wasn't enough to make the majors take an interest, but for a small, tightly run organization, the profits were significant. AIP's early films were often clumsy, wooden, and featured no known stars, but kids flocked to them just to see themselves onscreen. With rock 'n' roll showing signs of becoming a continuing phenomenon rather than a passing fad, and juvenile delinquency receiving continuing media attention, exploitation producers who had been waiting on the sidelines jumped in with both feet, and by 1957 the explosion was fully underway.

While 1956 had seen perhaps a total of ten features geared primarily to teenagers, 1957's total was almost forty. Said *Variety* in their year-end wrap-up: "Sci-Fi, horror, shockers, rock 'n' roll, and JD [juvenile delinquency] became patterns for the short budgeted new crop of features. Somewhere in between the last two categories came the reefer and dope-addict themes. True enough. Now there were not only teenage films by the dozen, but there were numerous subgroups to be found: the bad kids–wild youth genre; the good kids–mild youth genre; the personality films (e.g., Elvis Presley features); the horror and sci-fi teenage flicks; the dope-addict teenage flicks; the well-meaning poor-environment kids-in-trouble flicks; and so on. The adult media jumped on these films with a vengeance, criticizing them in print, on television, and on the radio. The fact that hardly any of these critics had actually seen any of the films was usually not mentioned. Sure there were some wild scenarios and exploitative marketing campaigns, but the bad guys usually got it in the end, and good and bad were clearly delineated. The fact that these films may have mirrored real life, rather than the fantasy world that Hollywood had been churning out, also received little attention. But the bottom line was that the films were making money, so they kept rolling on out.

Most were put on double-bill packages, and they made enough money for their producers to pocket a nice piece of change and still have enough left over to go back and make some more. Some, like *I Was a Teenage Werewolf,* made enormous sums by 1957 standards—*Werewolf* cost roughly $100,000 and grossed more than $2 million in its first year. And overall, quality began to improve as well. For the most part these productions couldn't afford name stars, so they tried to build and create stars, sort of a mini version of the now-crumbling old studio-system contract players technique. A few, like Sal Mineo, were able to graduate and become real stars, but most spent their brief careers as prisoners of teen flicks. Toughie Richard Bakalyan was in *The Delinquents, Dino, Juvenile Jungle, The Cool and the Crazy,"* and *Hot Car Girl;* Brett Halsey appeared in *High School Hellcats, Hot Rod Rumble, The Cry Baby Killer,* and *Speed Crazy;* Yvonne Lime was in *Untamed Youth, I Was a Teenage Werewolf, Dragstrip Riot, Speed Crazy,* and *High School Hellcats.* Other early teen stars were Fay Spain, Scott Marlowe, John Ashley, Susan Cabot, Frank Gorshin, John Saxon, and Yvette Vickers. Together, the major and minor players formed a tight little group who partied together on the outskirts of major Hollywood stardom. They hung out, went to acting classes, improvised, drove around, and formed a hip little Hollywood outpost. And with experience, most of their acting improved as well. Some were quite good, others less so, chosen merely for their looks—some going on to major film roles with little experience or formal training. But together they forged a semirealistic vision of American teenaged life. Many who appeared in these films were able to move into lasting careers—Jack Nicholson, Dean Stockwell, Sal Mineo, Tom Laughlin, Edd Byrnes, Connie Stevens, Michael Landon, Sally Kellerman, Robert Vaughn, and Robert Blake—but for the most part it took years of scuffling and hard work. Their rise to fame was usually not a direct result of their work in teen movies—that was just a stepping stone.

These films also provided work for a new breed of Hollywood writers and directors. In the beginning, most of the teen movies were turned out by people who had worked in the thirties, forties, and early fifties—producers, writers, directors, cameramen, musicians, and so on—most of whom just saw it as another job and another film. But slowly a new group of young and hip people began to get their breaks. In many cases their films were more realistic, more in tune, more adventurous,

Hurt at Rock 'n' Roll Show, Teenager Asks $40,000

PHILADELPHIA—A $40,000 damage suit—first of its kind ever brought in a federal court—was filed against the Stanley Warner Management Corp. by the parents of a 14-year-old boy who allegedly was beaten and stomped by an audience of frenzied teenagers at a rock 'n' roll movie.

Katherine E. and Joseph G. D'Angelo are asking $25,000 damages for their son, Joseph A. and $15,000 in their own right.

The Warner chain operates the Orpheum Theatre here, where, the complaint alleges, young D'Angelo suffered a fractured nose during the showing of a double bill, "Rock, Rock, Rock" and "Hot Cars" last December 16.

The complaint states the boy was watching the show "quietly and peacefully" when he was tumbled out of his seat by the maddened audience, beaten, kicked and imperiled of "life nd limb."

The theatre was charged with "carelessness and negligence" in exhibiting a picture that aroused its viewers "to acts of violence, frenzy, savagery, undue excitement and criminal and immoral conduct." The management also was accused of failing to provide adequate police protection, and with negligence in admitting persons "whom they knew or had reason to know would become aroused."

One of the many reports of 1950s teen violence, this time at a movie theater.

"High School" Premiere Held at Atlantic City

Atlantic City gave producer Albert Zugsmith and four of the principal players of "High School Confidential" a lively welcome for the opening of the picture there. Mr. Zugsmith is a native of the resort city. In the party were Jan Sterling, Charles Chaplin, Jr., Jackie Coogan and Diane Jergens. On their arrival they were escorted by a motorcade, followed by a Junior Chamber of Commerce luncheon in the ballroom of the Shelburne Hotel. New York Avenue at the Boardwalk was ceremoniously renamed Jan Sterling Avenue. Mr. Zugsmith addressed the student body of the Atlantic City High School in the morning and visited the Cerebral Palsy Clinic in the afternoon. A dinner preceded the opening at the Apollo theatre, owned by Warren Wielland. Emery Austin, MGM exploitation manager, was a member of the party.

and more with it. There was Roger Corman, Charles Griffith, John Frankenheimer, Robert Altman, Irvin Kershner, Mark Rydell, and numerous others who got their first credits on teen exploitation movies. Without years of rules behind them, they experimented and made their own rules. The sparse sets and hip dialogue of Corman and Griffith; the on-location no-sets shooting of Robert Altman; the inventive lighting and quick cuts of John Frankenheimer—all added new dimensions to the teen film genre.

In 1958 there were still thirty or thirty-five teen flicks churned out, but a large percentage of these were by new producers, often first-time outfits who made cheap imitations of successful teen films without regard for quality or content. While AIP had been struggling to build a lasting enterprise and improve their films, these new quick-buck artists had only one thing in mind—the bottom line—and they would often take the money and run. The pure rock 'n' roll film had faded by this time, and the only personality films still making money were those of Elvis Presley, and these were having less and less teenage content. As the spate of poor pictures began to flood the market, even AIP began to howl. In March 1958, the company called a meeting of all their officials to discuss ways of fighting the "cheap imitations." For a company whose stock was built on low-budget topical quickies, this must have set the industry laughing, but for AIP, it was no laughing matter—they took their exploitation seriously. "The exploitation market will die if program pictures don't maintain some semblance of quality," said Sam Arkoff at their convention. "We spend about $200,000 on an average film," he continued, "while others are now only spending $50,000. These films are poorly written, brutal for sensationalism alone, produced in a shoddy fashion, and dishonestly advertised. . . ." The fact that these criticisms were basically the same leveled against AIP for some time

THE NEW GENERATION – AND PROMOTION

DO YOU KNOW THEM? — If you don't, you will soon. The girl on the left who looks like a young edition of Sophie Tucker is Mrs. Jackie Coogan. The man next to her with the high forehead is Jackie Coogan. The little girl with the freckles is Diane Jergens. Looking over her shoulder is Albert Zugsmith, producer of "High School Confidential" for MGM, and the big fellow in the white coat is Charles Chaplin, Jr. The photo was made as they landed at Atlantic City for the opening of the picture at the Apollo theatre.

Four mass market magazines showing the different images of teenagers and movie stars. "The Teen-Age Jungle" is from 1956, the other three are from 1957.

didn't seem to dissuade Arkoff. This was now big business—eight thousand theaters depended upon AIP-type films, and his company could produce an entire show (two features) for about $400,000 while one Hollywood feature could cost that much or more. He saw his market being killed by poor films that would turn off both the paying customer and the theater owners and bookers as well. It was not only independent outfits that were releasing these films; almost every major studio had bought or produced a teen exploitation film, some of them quite miserable, and the market was overwhelmed.

Perhaps as a result, and as a way to stay one-up on the competition, AIP came up with the theory of cycles—not exactly a new concept, but one that was now put to work regarding solely teenage pictures. A cycle could run for about three years at most. In the first year, a topic of public interest sweeps the country and the first few films sneak out to test the waters. If these are successful, the second year the market is established and there's big bucks to be made. By the third year, the public is tiring of the subject and story lines and only the latecomers and fast-buck entrepreneurs come in and try to pick up the few remaining dollars. AIP's entire career was built on the cycle theory—juvenile delinquency pictures, sci-fi pictures, the Poe horror cycle, beach pictures, and teen protest pictures—which took them comfortably from 1956 to 1969, with only a few gaps or false starts in between. Between 1956 and 1959, AIP had made twelve double bills geared totally to teenagers—twenty-four pictures in all—and they had covered all the bases: rock 'n' roll pictures (*Shake, Rattle and Rock, Rock All Night,* and *Rock Around the World*); juvenile delinquent pictures (*Runaway Daughters, High School Hellcats,* and *The Cool and the Crazy*); hot rod and motorcycle pictures (*Hot Rod Girl, Dragstrip Girl, Motorcycle Gang, Hot Rod Gang,* and *Dragstrip Riot*); teen horror pics (*I Was a Teenage Werewolf, I Was a Teenage Frankenstein, Invasion of the Saucer Men, Teenage Caveman,* and *Blood of Dracula*); and miscellaneous teen themes (*Reform School Girl, Sorority Girl, Daddy-O* and *Diary of a High School Bride*). They had covered all possible scenarios, sometimes even one or two times too many, and by the end of 1958 had realized the cycle was coming to an end. There were some good teen flicks in 1957 and 1958: *The Delinquents, Teenage Doll, Untamed Youth, The Cool and the Crazy, High School Confidential,* and several others, but public interest was near the saturation point. The competition consisted mainly of second-rate imitations, and besides, times were changing. These films once taken seriously as examples of teen malaise and significant social problems, exploitative as they may have been, were becoming the butt of many jokes. Jerry Lewis parodied juvenile delinquents in his film, *The Delicate Delinquent;* Ernie Kovacs did a skit on TV called "I Was a Teenage Justice of the Supreme Court"; and one popular Los Angeles industry joke revolved around two small-time producers who meet for lunch: one says to the other, "What shall we do this afternoon? See the Dodgers or make a horror picture?" So it was time for a change, and, for better or worse, a change did come.

Filmography '54–'58

The Blackboard Jungle

Producer: Pandro Berman
Writer: Richard Brooks
Director: Richard Brooks
Music: Charles Wolcott
MGM: 101 minutes
Released 3/25/55

Cast: Glenn Ford, Anne Francis, Margaret Hayes, Louis Calhern, Richard Kiley, Sidney Poitier, Vic Morrow, John Hoyt

Adapted from the best-selling novel by Evan Hunter, *The Blackboard Jungle* was one of the first and most important films to deal with mid-fifties juvenile delinquency. It was a serious film, and treated as such, and paved the way for many of the plot lines and characterizations for the more exploitative films that followed. *The New York Times* called it a "full throated, all out testimonial to the lurid headlines that appear from time to time, reporting acts of terrorism and violence by uncontrolled urban youths." They cited Vic Morrow (in his first film role) as a "sinister replica of a Marlon Brando roughneck" and dubbed the film "nightmarish and bloodcurdling." But the *Times,* along with much of the rest of the public, still had serious doubts about the film's impact, asking whether

Vic Morrow gets ready to smash his teachers' prized records in **The Blackboard Jungle.**

this was "responsible reporting . . . and a desirable stimulant to be put before the young." They finally concluded that "this is unfirm ground from which to reach for 'public awareness' of a problem of great contemporary concern." Later that year, Bosley Crowther in the *Times* placed *The Blackboard Jungle* in his second-best ten films of the year, praising its "vitality."

The film is also credited with kicking off the rock 'n' roll craze by featuring Bill Haley's "Rock around the Clock," and helping to send it to the top of the charts. Director Brooks later went on to make such classics as *Cat on a Hot Tin Roof, Elmer Gantry, Sweet Bird of Youth,* and *In Cold Blood.*

The Careless Years *marked Dean Stockwell's return to film after a six-year layoff, following a previously successful career as a child star.*

The Careless Years

Producer: Edward Lewis
Writer: Edward Lewis
Director: Arthur Hiller
Music: Leith Stevens
United Artists: 70 minutes
Released 9/3/57

Cast: Dean Stockwell, Natalie Trundy, John Larch, Barbara Billingsley, John Stephenson, Maureen Cassidy, Alan Dinehart III, Virginia Christine

A rather tame film about the problems of young love. Look for Beaver Cleaver's mom, Barbara Billingsley, in a featured role. This film is also notable for starring Dean Stockwell, in his first adult part after a six-year layoff, following his previously successful career as a child star. The *Times* called it "drab and routine," but Stockwell is always interesting. "I didn't want to love him . . . but I didn't want to lose him either!" This was Arthur Hiller's first feature film. He later directed *The Wheeler Dealers, The Tiger Makes Out, Love Story, Plaza Suite,* and a handful of mediocre middle-class comedies.

Carnival Rock, *a Roger Corman quickie, featured some obscure rockabilly bands, as well as a cameo appearance by The Platters.*

Carnival Rock

Producer: Roger Corman
Writer: Leo Lieberman
Director: Roger Corman
Music: Walter Green, Buck Ram
Howco International; 75 minutes
Released 1958

Cast: Susan Cabot, Brian Hutton, David J. Stewart, Dick Miller, Iris Adrian, Jonathan Haze, Ed Nelson, Chris Alcaide

A low-budget quicky released on a double bill with *Teenage Thunder, Carnival Rock* is a story of teen night-clubs, mixed-up love, gamblers, rock 'n' roll singers, arson, and redemptive marriage. "It's got a heat beat—hear ten exciting songs by Bob Luman, The Platters, David Houston, The Shadows and The Blockbusters." Said *Variety:* "Overtones of Pagliacci and out and out rock 'n' roll have been mixed together by P-D Roger Corman for okay results—film has a couple of very good performances in Susan Cabot and Dick Miller." There's also some good rockabilly performances.

The Cool and the Crazy

Producer: E. C. Rhoden, Jr.
Writer: Richard C. Sarafian
Director: William Witney
Music: Raoul Kraushaar
American International; 78 minutes
Released 5/1/58

Cast: Scott Marlowe, Gigi Perreau, Dick Bakalyan, Dick Jones, Shelby Storck, Marvin J. Rosen, Caroline von Mayrhauser, Robert Hadden

Filmed on the streets of Kansas City, and utilizing some of the same cast and crew as *The Delinquents, The Cool and the Crazy* is a solid and interesting JD flick. It was hyped as the story of a "stricken dope addict who even performs murder for his supply of dope," and featuring "seven savage punks on a weekend binge of violence" in this "twin rock 'n' riot show" (it was co-billed with AIP's *Dragstrip Riot).* The *Hollywood Reporter,* criticizing AIP's fare, said: *"The Cool and the Crazy* is a badly written, sloppily edited, poorly directed, low-budget film. . . ."

The Cool and the Crazy *was one of the best JD flicks — this time with a dope subplot.*

Actually, by teen JD standards, it is realistic, well-acted, and fast-paced, although the effects of marijuana are inflated considerably. Scott Marlowe stands out with a fine performance, even if he does ape James Dean a bit, and Dick Bakalyan throws in a few nice bits. Best line from a gang member to a prospective newcomer: "Hey, we like you—you're stupid!" And we just love Bakalyan's "Wow." Definitely recommended.

Crime in the Streets

Producer: Vincent Fennelly
Writer: Reginald Rose
Director: Don Siegel

Music: Franz Waxman
Allied Artists; 91 minutes
Released 6/10/56

Cast: James Whitmore, John Cassavetes, Sal Mineo, Mark Rydell, Malcolm Atterbury, Denise Alexander, Virginia Gregg, Will Kuluva

Originally a television drama, *Crime in the Streets* is a fairly standard action film dealing with crazed gangs, violence, and social workers, with a bit of the New York "method" style thrown in. *The New York Times* called it a "meager drama of juvenile delinquents—they talk more jivey lingo and dance to a rock 'n' roll beat, and wield switch-blade knives . . . a cheap little slum-pent film . . . looks exactly like some of those B-grade agonies of yore." At the time, one theater owner said: "It was a cruel picture of what can happen when youngsters, who grow up without any religious teaching, launch a crime wave." Director Don Siegel, known for his hard-hitting films, also worked on pictures for Elvis Presley and Fabian, and later directed such taut classics as *Madigan* and *Dirty Harry.*

A typical high school class in teen exploitation films. That's teen star Scott Marlowe in the middle with jacket and white pants.

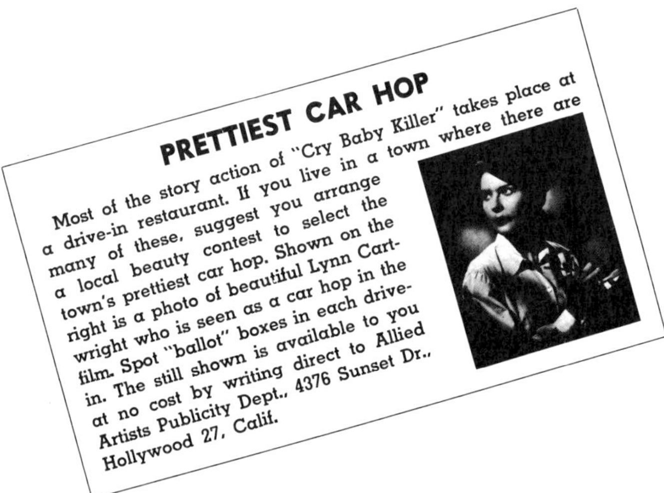

PRETTIEST CAR HOP

Most of the story action of "Cry Baby Killer" takes place at a drive-in restaurant. If you live in a town where there are many of these, suggest you arrange a local beauty contest to select the town's prettiest car hop. Shown on the right is a photo of beautiful Lynn Cartwright who is seen as a car hop in the film. Spot "ballot" boxes in each drive-in. The still shown is available to you at no cost by writing direct to Allied Artists Publicity Dept., 4376 Sunset Dr., Hollywood 27, Calif.

Producers were always thinking up crazy schemes to promote their films. Here's a typical plan.

Cry Baby Killer *marked Jack Nicholson's first screen performance. That's him abducting the frightened female.*

Cry Baby Killer

Producers: David Kramarsky, David March
Writers: Leo Gordon, Melvin Levy
Director: Jus Addiss
Music: Gerald Fried
Allied Artists; 61 minutes
Released 8/17/58

Cast: Harry Lauter, Jack Nicholson, Carolyn Mitchell, Brett Halsey, Lynn Cartwright, Ralph Reed, John Shay, Barbara Knudson

A short, minor film, notable mainly for Jack Nicholson's first screen appearance, where he plays a young criminal who is holed up and surrounded by the police. The film moves quickly from fights to shootings to the siege, which then concentrates on crowd psychology and ultimate capture. Executive producer Roger Corman saves money by utilizing mainly two sets, while Nicholson alternates between viciousness and, ultimately, tearful surrender. Co-billed with *Hot Car Girl,* the film was hyped as the story of "a teenage rebel and a mad-dog slayer—a sizzling teenage shocker." Newcomer Carolyn Mitchell was, as the trades put it, "a twenty-year-old redhead beauty discovered in Phoenix by producer David Kramarsky." Best line: "Teenagers—we never had 'em when I was a kid!"

Curfew Breakers

Producer: Charles E. King
Director: Alex Wells
Screen Guild; 1957

Cast: Regis Toomey, Paul Kelly, Cathy Downs, Marilyn Madison, Sheila Urban

An obscure little film that only received limited national distribution, *Curfew Breakers* is the story of drug addicts and murder, with a nice Elvis Presley imitation thrown in for good measure. The ads hyped: "Pent up punks on a penthouse binge!" The film starred Regis Toomey, whose screen career began in 1929, and who ultimately appeared in over 150 films. His other roles in fifties teen classics included *Joy Ride* and *Sing, Boy, Sing.*

Dangerous Youth

Producer: Anna Neagle
Writer: Jack Trevor Story
Director: Herbert Wilcox
Music: Stanley Black
Warner Bros.; 98 minutes
Released 6/7/58

Cast: Frankie Vaughan, Carole Lesley, George Baker, Jackie Lane, Katherine Kath, Thora Hird, Eddie Byrne, Kenneth Cope

A British film, starring aging teen idol Vaughan, who gets mixed up in a story of delinquent gangs, the army, AWOL, redemption, and ultimate return to the army—not too radical. The same team had previously come up with *Teenage Bad Girl* the previous year. *Motion Picture Herald* said: "The film would probably best be sold on the rock 'n' roll angle. As a melodrama it is contrived and full of clichés. Despite British locale and slang, young U.S. audiences should have no difficulty in getting the message—it tends to prove conclusively that juvenile delinquents the world over can be equally obnoxious under stress." Also released as: *These Dangerous Years.*

The Delinquents

Producer: Robert Altman
Writer: Robert Altman
Director: Robert Altman
United Artists; 75 minutes
Released 3/57

Cast: Tom Laughlin, Peter Miller, Richard Bakalyan, Rosemary Howard, Helene Hawley, Leonard Belove, Lotus Corelli, James Lantz

A gritty, realistic, and sometimes arty film, occasionally quite violent and often shot in cinema-verité style, *The Delinquents* was Robert Altman's first film, and an obvious sign of his talent. It was actually shot in 1955, all on location in Kansas City, using many locals as extras, and real cops, real drive-ins, etc., for most of the scenes. The film was made for $63,000, later sold to Warner Bros. for $150,000, and then hyped as "the screen's most shocking exposé of the baby faces who have just taken their first stumbling step down sin street U.S.A. The kids who live today . . . as if there's no tomorrow . . ." The story concerns gangs, robbery, violence, misunderstood teens, and a bit of a social statement. Tom Laughlin scores well as the "good" teen, while Richard Bakalyan kicks off his

Dangerous Youth *was a 1958 British import, starring aging teen Frankie Vaughn.*

JD career, to be continued with roles in *Dino, Juvenile Jungle, The Cool and the Crazy,* and *Hot Car Girl.* Laughlin later became a star with his series of *Billy Jack* movies. This film is solid and often daring, and definitely recommended.

The Delinquents, ***shot on location in Kansas City, was director Robert Altman's first film.***

TEEN-AGE GIRL AND BOY STREET BALLYHOO

Employ a good-looking teen-age girl and a good-looking teen-age boy to carry signs such as those illustrated through the busy intersections of your town. They could start from your theatre each day, make their rounds and return to your theatre where they should walk in opposite directions much as pickets do. It is important to note that both these teen-agers should be dressed very conservatively and in good taste. Try to arrange with local newspaper photographer to follow them for any crowd display or other special interest.

Another funny publicity scam from the producers.

Dino

Producer: Bernice Block
Writer: Reginald Rose
Director: Thomas Carr
Music: Gerald Fried
Allied Artists; 94 minutes
Released 7/21/57

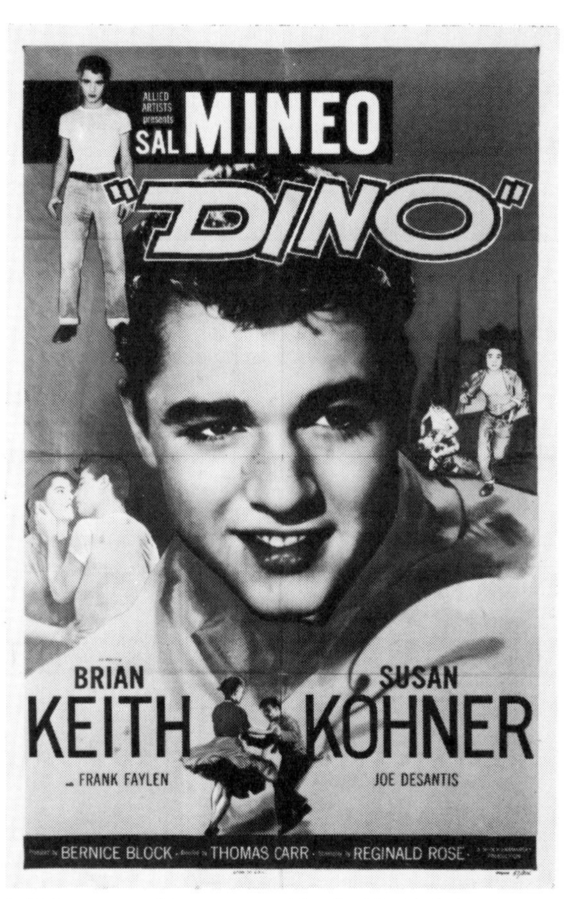

Sal Mineo starred in many teen films besides **Rebel without a Cause,** ***among them*** **Dino, The Young Don't Cry,** ***and*** **Rock Pretty Baby.**

Cast: Sal Mineo, Brian Keith, Susan Kohner, Frank Faylen, Richard Bakalyan, Joe De Santis, Penny Stanton, Ken Miller

Another Sal Mineo vehicle where he's a mistreated little boy on the inside and a tough guy on the outside. The film deals with reform school, violent parents, social workers, and redemption. By this time Mineo had this role down pat, having played similar parts in *Rebel without a Cause, Crime in the Streets,* and *The Young Don't Cry.* Look for Sal's brother Michael in a supporting role.

Dragstrip Girl

Producer: Alex Gordon
Writer: Lou Rusoff
Director: Edward L. Cahn
Music: Ronald Stein
American International; 69 minutes
Released 4/24/57

Cast: Fay Spain, Steve Terrell, John Ashley, Frank Gorshin, Russ Bender, Tommy Ivo

A fast little picture that concentrates on hot rods and drag racing, as well as a bit of robbery and murder, but ultimate right choices made. This went out on double bill with *Rock All Night*, and Fay Spain is quite good, while Frank Gorshin camps it up as he did in other teen films like *Runaway Daughters, Hot Rod Girl* and *Invasion of the Saucer Men.* One exhibitor said: "I think they must have made this picture in one day, but even at that, it's better than some that take a month. The two make a good double bill." Another said: "The acting in this may smell a little like last year's senior class play in spots, but the story isn't bad, and the business was darned good. It's an inoffensive story built around the hot rods the kids love."

Dragstrip Riot

Producer: O. Dale Ireland
Writer: George Hodgins
Director: David Bradley
Music: Nicholas Carras
American International; 68 minutes
Released 5/1/58

Cast: Yvonne Lime, Gary Clarke, Fay Wray, Connie Stevens, Bob Turnbull, Gabe DeLutri, Ted Wedderspoon, Marcus Dyrector

Released on a double bill with *The Cool and the Crazy,* this is a story of motorcycle gangs, hot rodders, death, romance, and redemption. Yvonne Lime became a veritable superstar of teen JD movies, usually playing the "good girl," while Connie Stevens gets to sing a few rock 'n' roll numbers. See: "Hot rods versus motorcycles"; the "train drag"; and "beach party rumble." Not bad.

Eighteen and Anxious

Producer: Edmond Chevie
Writers: Dale and Katherine Eunson
Director: Joe Parker
Music: Leith Stevens (and all-star jazz musicians)
Republic Pictures; 93 minutes
Released 11/15/57

Cast: William Campbell, Martha Scott, Jackie Loughery, Jim Backus, Ron Hagerty, Jackie Coogan, and Mary Webster (as the girl who is "eighteen and anxious")

An adventurous ad campaign for a rather tame picture regarding teen motherhood: "Not a child—maybe not yet a woman—already a mother. But mother, we did get married—honest! Parents may be shocked, but youth will understand!" Perhaps the key to the failure of this picture was a misguided attempt to appeal to adults: "Notice—no one over 35 will be admitted to see *Eighteen and Anxious*—unless you want to get [young ideas]." No self-respecting teenager would go to a flick like this if their parents were also interested. Useful trivia: Mike Wallace recorded the promotional radio spots. Look for

In* Dragstrip Girl, *the kids spent most of their time studying cars and curves. Both attracted audiences.

***Frank Gorshin* (right) *and pal ham it up in* Dragstrip Girl.**

***Yvonne Lime leads the kids in a dance in one of the lighter moments in* Dragstrip Riot.**

Connie Stevens in her first, albeit small, role. She later followed with teen epics *Young and Dangerous, Dragstrip Riot,* and *The Party Crashers* before achieving fame in TV's *Hawaiian Eye* and a slew of fluffy sixties teen movies.

The Flaming Teen-age

Producers: Ervin S. Yeaworth, Charles Edwards
Writers: Ervin S. Yeaworth, Charles Edwards
Directors: Ervin S. Yeaworth, Charles Edwards
Truman Enterprises
Released 1957

Cast: Noel Reyburn, Ethel Barrett, Jerry Frank, Shirley Holmes

A very obscure film which only received minimal release. It's a semi-verité story of alcohol and drug abuse, with scenes of wild make-out sessions, intense police interrogation, robbery, jail, and withdrawal. Definitely a strange one, with some of the oldest "teenagers" around.

Kids have a private party in* The Flaming Teen-age *an obscure 1957 teen film.

James Franciscus got his first starring screen role in* Four Boys and a Gun*, a fast-moving teen-crime film.

A trade magazine advertisement for* Eighteen and Anxious*, a teen film geared to both adults and kids.

Four Boys and a Gun

Producer: William Berke
Writers: Philip Yordan, Leo Townsend
Director: William Berke
Music: Albert Glasser
United Artists; 73 minutes
Released 1/57

Cast: Frank Sutton, Tarry Green, James Franciscus, William Hinant, Otto Hulett, Robert Dryden, J. Pat O'Malley, Diana Herbert

Standard action-crime drama, released on a twin bill with *The Wild Party.* The ads blared: "These kids are going straight . . . to the electric chair," and "the shock stories behind the rock 'n' roll generation in one sensational package!" This was James Franciscus's first screen role.

Girls in Prison

Producer: Alex Gordon
Writer: Lou Rusoff
Director: Edward L. Cahn

Girls on the Loose ***was a tough and sexy teen film geared to leering adults.***

American International; 87 minutes
Released 7/56

Cast: Richard Denning, Joan Taylor, Adele Jergens, Lance Fuller, Helen Gilbert, Jane Darwell, Diana Darrin, Mae Marsh

An early AIP exploitation picture, originally teamed with *Hot Rod Girl,* asked the burning question, "What happens to women without men?" This film is rather old-fashioned, and in fact features many old-time Hollywood stars, and concerns the usual trials of inmates, money, and the prison chaplin. Edward L. Cahn began directing in 1931 and in 1956 began directing teen movies. Over the next few years he turned out *Runaway Daughters, Shake, Rattle and Rock, Dragstrip Girl, Motorcycle Gang,* and *Riot in Juvenile Prison.*

"Okay, are you going to give me your allowance, or what?" (From* Girls on the Loose.*)

Girls on the Loose

Producers: Harry Rybnick, Richard Kay
Writers: Alan Friedman, Dorothy Raison, Allen Rivkin
Director: Paul Henreid
Music: Joseph Gershenson
Universal–International; 78 minutes
Released 4/21/58

Cast: Mara Corday, Lita Milan, Barbara Bostock, Mark Richman, Joyce Barker, Abby Dalton

Produced and directed by the same team who brought you *Live Fast, Die Young* (with which it was originally co-billed), *Girls on the Loose* is a fast-paced picture concerning female gangs, robbery, murder, runaways, and possible salvation. Packed with some dynamic ladies, whose physical attributes may have outweighed their acting ability, the ads promised girls who were "trigger tough and ready for anything. Crime-crazy girl gangs looting, lying, and living only for thrills." This picture was geared more toward leering adults than escapist-minded teenagers.

Going Steady

Producer: Sam Katzman
Writer: Budd Grossman
Director: Fred F. Sears
Music: Mischa Bakaleinikoff
Columbia; 79 minutes
Released 2/58

Cast: Molly Bee, Alan Reed, Jr., Irene Hervey, Bill Goodwin, Ken Miller, Susan Easter, Linda Watkins, Byron Foulger

A light piece of teen fluff from the master of quickies, Sam Katzman, this picture features pleasant faces and a little excusable mischief—perhaps a forerunner of the beach films. Said one exhibitor: "An entertaining little picture. Fits today's tempo. A little more time plus 'scope and Columbia would have had a gasser."

The Green-Eyed Blonde

Producer: Martin Melcher
Writer: Sally Stubblefield
Director: Bernard Girard
Music: Leith Stevens
Warner Bros.; 76 minutes
Released 12/14/57

Cast: Susan Oliver, Linda Plowman, Beverly Long, Norma Jean Nilsson, Tommie Moore, Carla Merey, Sallie Brophy, Jean Inness

Another "behind-the-walls" drama, featuring a bevy of good-looking newcomers, that takes place at an institution for wayward teenage girls. The plot revolves around illegitimate babies, car theft, murder, and death. The ads promised: "It's shameful but it's real! The naked truth told by a girl who lived in a home for unwed mothers. She dates her guys through a barbed wire fence!" This was nineteen-year-old Susan Oliver's first screen appearance. She later was seen in *The Gene Krupa Story, Butterfield 8, Looking for Love,* and *The Love-Ins,* among others. Trivia: The title song, "Green-Eyed Blonde," was sung by Cornelius Gunter, of Coasters fame. Marty Melcher was Doris Day's husband.

High School Confidential!

Producer: Albert Zugsmith
Writer: Lewis Meltzer, Robert Blees
Director: Jack Arnold
MGM; 85 minutes
Released 6/13/58

Cast: Russ Tamblyn, Mamie Van Doren, Jan Sterling, Jackie Coogan, John Drew Barrymore, Diane Jergens, Ray Anthony, Charles Chaplin, Jr

The racy little film,* The Green-Eyed Blonde *was produced by Martin Melcher, Doris Day's husband.

This can only be described as a marvelous camp classic. The plot careens wildly, and often unbelievably, the lingo is totally gonesville, and Mamie Van Doren, as a seductive aunt(!), just about punctures the screen. Other highlights include Jerry Lee Lewis on a flatbed truck singing the title tune, a tremendous beat poetry reading, and an excellent performance by John Drew Barrymore as a compulsive hipster. This picture garnered a lot of publicity for its themes and portrayals which were best summed up by the two major trade journals of the day. Said *Boxoffice:* "A hard-hitting, controversial film . . . it's sure-fire box office. The story touches on both marijuana smoking and drug addiction among high school students, but not offensively so, and includes a hotrod race and jive session by Jerry Lee Lewis, additional selling angles for the younger and most movie conscious element." But the *Motion Picture Herald* felt differently: "In an epilogue to *High School Confidential!* it is solemnly stated that a serious purpose motivated the making of the film—that, the audience is informed, was the exposure of the activities of narcotics peddlers in the nation's high schools. In view of what has been happening on the screen for almost and hour and a half before this revelation, it is hard to take this pronouncement seriously. . . . Here are some typical episodes in the film. (1) A fresh punk insolently mocks the principal and asks an attractive teacher for a date in front of the whole class; (2) at home he

'High School Confidential' Narcotics Theme Crusading One, Says Producer

NEW YORK—Anticipating some public controversy over "High School Confidential," his picture on the use of marihuana by juveniles which MGM is releasing, Albert Zugsmith, producer, sought to set the record straight in a tradepress interview Tuesday (27). He foresaw some disinclination on the part of adults to believe that the conditions outlined in the picture exist, and an inclination to believe the picture was produced for sensational reasons.

Zugsmith cited the cooperation of the narcotics committee of the Los Angeles County Medical Ass'n and named areas in the U. S. where marihuana is peddled and used in the schools. He called the situation "a cancer that can spread like wildfire" if not exposed. He said that juveniles smoking marihuana cigarettes almost invariably go on to heroin, and must be made to understand that.

The picture is of the crusading type like his "Slaughter on Tenth Avenue," and he will continue to make crusading pictures, he said. Unlike "Blackboard Jungle," it has a clear-cut moral lesson and it shows only a few juveniles as delinquents as contrasted with a whole class, he said. Furthermore, Zugsmith said, the children themselves solve their own problems in the picture.

The idea for the picture originated with the true incident of the son of a Texas Ranger killed by narcotics pushers who joined the gang and got evidence against them. The other incidents in it are true, gained through chats with juvenile marihuana users in schools and homes, Zugsmith said.

He reported that the code administration of the Motion Picture Ass'n of America was worried before it read the script but approved it and the completed picture with only one deletion. The British version has a prolog spoken by an authority on the subject to dispel any belief that juvenile use of marihuana is common in the U. S. and to make the point that it is a threat rather than a widespread menace.

***Mamie Van Doren tempts Russ Tamblyn in* High School Confidential, *reissued later as* The Young Hellions.**

***Russ Tamblyn and Jackie Coogan fight to the death over the dope traffic in* High School Confidential.**

spends a great deal of his time warding off the seductive advances of his aunt while his uncle is away; (3) several of the other students are part of a dope ring and have 'hooked' a number of their classmates.

"For other entertainment the teenagers hold a dangerous 'drag' race in hot rods. Sexual promiscuity is taken for granted, and a trip to jail is all in an evening's fun. . . . Is the film exploitable? Strictly to sensation seekers. There is loads of 'jive' talk but overall the film produces an effect of excess, and finally, disbelief. It thus becomes appropriate that several events first presented as facts are later exposed as hoaxes."

This is an exploitation classic, and should not be missed. Rereleased in 1961 as *The Young Hellions.*

High School Hellcats

Producers: James Nicholson, Samuel Arkoff
Writers: Mark and Jan Lowell
Director: Edward Bernds
Music: Ronald Stein
American International; 68 minutes
Released 6/58

Cast: Yvonne Lime, Brett Halsey, Jana Lund, Suzanne Sydney, Heather Ames, Nancy Kilgas, Rhoda Williams, Don Shelton

Originally released on a double bill with *Hot Rod Gang, High School Hellcats* is much the better of the two. It tells the story of a wild girl-gang ("The Hellcats") and a good girl who is forced to belong. Ultimately there's some robbery, murder, a sadistic gang member, and of course some romance and final salvation. Jana Lund is good as the head hellcat, and the story moves along briskly with some occasionally interesting photography. The ads said: "What must a good girl say to 'belong'—the *facts* about the taboo sororities that give them what they want!" This featured the battle of teen stars—Halsey appeared in *Hot Rod Rumble, The Cry Baby Killer,* and *Speed Crazy,* while Lime emoted in *Untamed Youth, I Was a Teenage Werewolf, Dragstrip Riot,* and *Speed Crazy.*

The Hot Angel

Producer: Stanley Kallis
Writer: Stanley Kallis
Director: Joe Parker
Music: Robert Drasnin, Richard Markowitz
Paramount; 73 minutes
Released 12/58

Cast: Jackie Loughery, Edward Kemmer, Mason Alan Dinehart, Emory Parnell, Lyle Talbot, Zon Teller, Heather Ames, Steffi Sidney

An advertising campaign that was much better than this meager picture. The plot concerns lost uranium,

High School Hellcats, ***a good teenage film about "bad-girl" sororities, robbery, murder, and sadism.***

delinquent gangs, and finally love. Paramount said: "Hot rod hot-shots and their tailgate babes! Teenage gangs rip highways and skies with thrills and terror." Oh, if it were only so.

Hot Car Girl

Producer: Roger Corman
Writer: Leo Gordon
Director: Bernard L. Kowalski
Music: Cal Tjader
Allied Artists; 71 minutes
Released 8/17/58

Cast: Richard Bakalyan, June Kenney, John Brinkley, Robert Knapp, Jana Lund, Sheila McKay, Bruno Ve Sota, Grace Albertson

Another typical story for teen exploitation flicks—car theft, murder, crime spree, gun battle, and death, but this film moves along nicely, and is peppered with appearances from Corman's teen stable. *Motion Picture Herald* was quite taken with the film, and said: "A new personality has hit the screen in a hard hitting realistic story of defiant young people on the loose. His name is Richard Bakalyan—tough, flat nosed, with an air of authority that should have fans asking for more of his films. Executive producer Roger Corman has a winner in this one, which is being teamed with another of his productions, *The Cry Baby Killer,* as a combination package program. Directed with considerable finesse by Bernard L. Kowalski and produced by Gene Corman, with an exciting musical background by Cal Tjader, Leo Gordon's excellent screenplay, which is flavored by a complete cast of competent new faces, comes to life in bold realism."

This film was still getting playdates in 1965, as a reissue with *The Singing Idol* (formerly *Expresso Bongo*). One exhibitor said: "Personally, I think the whole program smelled to high heaven!"

***Richard Bakalyan* (center) *tries to sweet-talk June Kenney over some fizz Cola, in* Hot Car Girl.**

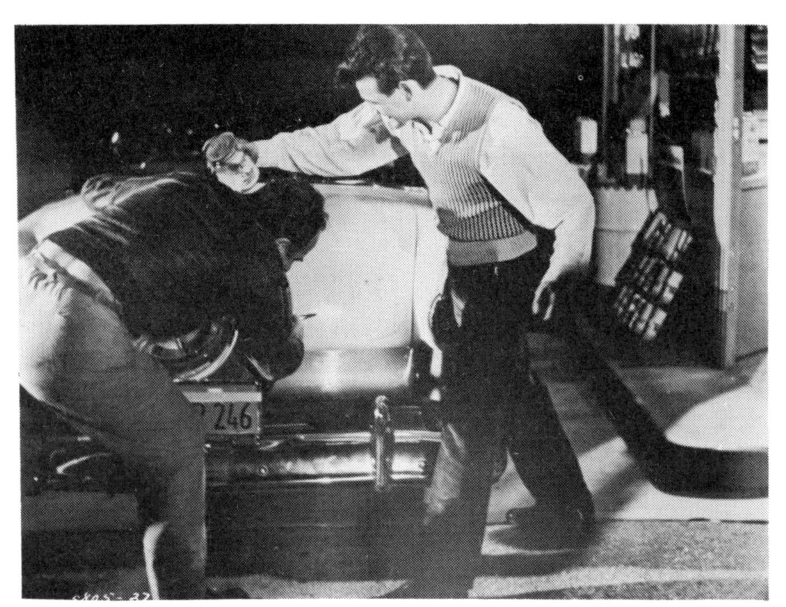

"That'll teach you to be so slow to fill my tank." (Scene from Hot Car Girl.)

Hot Rod Gang

Producer: Lou Rusoff
Writer: Lou Rusoff
Director: Lew Landers
Music: Ronald Stein
American International; 72 minutes
Released 6/58

Cast: John Ashley, Jody Fair, Gene Vincent, Steve Drexel, Henry McCann, Maureen Arthur, Russ Bender, Gloria Grant

A pretty silly teen flick dealing with grandpa's fortune, hot rods, rock singers, robbery, romance, and the essential happy ending. The plot centers too much on the rather dull Ashley and his various disguises, and the boring subplot with adults and grandparents. The ad line of "crazy kids living to a wild rock 'n' roll beat" is never quite realized. The saving grace of the film is the several musical performances (and a big acting part) by Gene Vincent—these are top-notch. There's lots of hip lingo, and a small, unbilled appearance by Eddie Cochran. Behind-the-scenes personnel may have helped: associate producer was Lou Kimzey, publisher of America's hippest teen magazine, *Dig* (he also performed the same function on *High School Hellcats,* with which *Hot Rod Gang* was originally co-billed); and associate musical supervisor was Jerry Capehart, ace songwriter and producer who teamed with Eddie Cochran on the latter's great recordings. Lew Landers directed almost 150 films beginning in 1935, mostly low-budget quickies for RKO, Republic, Columbia, and Monogram. *Hot Rod Gang* was his next-to-last film. Best line: from a policeman hearing Jody Fair belt out a tune: "Sounds like an Indian massacre going on in there . . ."

Hot Rod Gang *featured Gene Vincent singing four songs and doing some bit acting.*

Hot-Rod Girl

Producer: Norman Herman
Writer: John McGreevey
Director: Leslie Martinson
American International; 75 minutes
Released 7/56

Cast: Lori Nelson, John Smith, Chuck Connors, Roxanne Arlen, Mark Andrews, Frank Gorshin, Dabbs Greer, Carolyn Kearny

An early AIP quickie, originally teamed with *Girls in Prison,* revolving around hot-rodding, death, chicken runs, good policemen, and reconciliation. The ads promised: "Youth on the loose. *See* the death defying 'chicken race'—teenage Russian roulette. *See* teen-age terrorists on a speed crazy rampage—violent—reckless," but the film never really quite delivered. Said *Variety:* "A well-knit programmer with juve interest . . ."

Hot-Rod Girl ***was one of AIP's earliest teen exploitation movies.***

Hot Rod Rumble

Producer: Normal T. Herman
Writer: Meyer Dolinsky
Director: Leslie H. Martinson
Music: Alexander Courage
Allied Artists; 79 minutes
Released 6/9/57

Cast: Leigh Snowden, Richard Hartunian, Wright King, Joey Forman, Brett Halsey, John Brinkley, Chuck Webster, Larry Dolgin.

Originally sent out with *Calypso Jo, Hot Rod Rumble* featured hot-rod clubs, drag racing, death, and salvation. The cast was peppered with minor teen stars and a host of new, young faces. (The producers bragged that ninety percent of the cast was under age twenty-three). Leggy Leigh Snowden (later married to Dick Contino) was "discovered" as a walk-on in a Jack Benny TV show and picked for stardom, but it never came. The ads said: "Revved up youth in a souped-up jungle of thrills! You'll need shock absorbers—dragstrips and slick chicks!" Alexander Courage later did music for the "Star Trek" series, and *Hot Rod Rumble* features some good instrumental music by famed jazz musicians including Barney Kessel, Shelly Manne, Maynard Ferguson, Frank Rosolino, Pete Candoli, Bob Cooper, Bud Shank, and Dave Pell. One theater owner said: "The best one we have played yet of this type. Wherever teenage pictures are doing business, this should continue to do the same."

Leigh Snowden and Richard Harunian contemplate the problems of teen life.

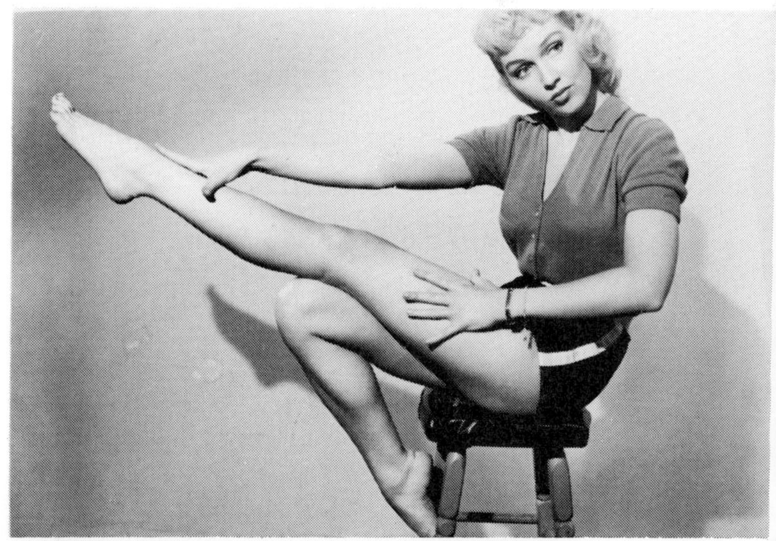

Leggy Leigh Snowden provides some cheesecake for **Hot Rod Rumble.**

I Was a Teenage Frankenstein

Producer: Herman Cohen
Writer: Kenneth Langtry
Director: Herbert L. Strock

Music: Paul Dunlap
American International; 74 minutes
Released 11/23/57

Cast: Whit Bissell, Phyllis Coates, Robert Burton, Gary Conway, George Lynn, John Cliff, Marshall Bradford, Claudia Bryar.

A quickie followup to *Teenage Werewolf, I Was a Teenage Frankenstein* is a dull story of a mad doctor and his quest to create the perfect human from dead body parts. There's very little teenage influence in the pic, beyond the title, and the fact that the monster is a teenage boy (Conway). There are some semi-gross body-part shots, extremely tame by today's standards, and a boring subplot love story. This went out on a bill with *Blood of Dracula,* and went out with a campy ad campaign which boasted: "The most gruesome horror show ever, not for the squeamish, free first aid and smelling salts. Don't come before dinner. Warning for people who faint easily!" More likely a warning was needed for those who fall asleep easily.

This follow-up to* I Was a Teenage Werewolf *was quite inferior to its predecessor.

I Was a Teenage Werewolf

Producer: Herman Cohen
Writer: Ralph Thornton
Director: Gene Fowler, Jr.
Music: Paul Dunlap
American International; 76 minutes
Released 6/19/57

Cast: Michael Landon, Yvonne Lime, Whit Bissell, Tony Marshall, Malcolm Atterbury, Guy Williams, Louise Lewis, and Ken Miller

This film was one of 1957's biggest success stories, and spawned a wave of imitations. The film cost in the neighborhood of $100,000 and within a year had grossed $2 million. This one has a good teenage milieu, and Landon is solid as the "moody" teenager with problems. Special effects are okay, and the film moves along briskly. This was originally co-billed with *Invasion of the Saucer Men,* and later rereleased as "starring Michael Landon, star of 'Bonanza.' "

Invasion of the Saucer Men

Producer: James H. Nicholson, Robert Gurney, Jr.
Writer: Robert Gurney, Jr., Al Martin
Director: Edward L. Cahn
Music: Ronald Stein
American International; 69 minutes
Released 6/19/57

Cast: Steve Terrell, Gloria Castillo, Lyn Osborn, Frank Gorshin, Raymond Hatton, Russ Bender, Ed Nelson, Douglas Henderson

Originally released on a twin bill with *Teenage Werewolf, Invasion of the Saucer Men* was a strange little tale of teenagers, hot rods, and make-out sessions. Only trouble is, some aliens move in and their method of attack is to inject alcohol into the kids' systems. Oh boy, now what authority figure is going to believe that? This is pretty good, and moves along briskly, with a couple of fun performances. It was also released as *The Hell Creatures,* and poorly remade in 1965 as *The Eye Creatures.*

Joy Ride

Producer: Ben Schwalb
Writer: Christopher Knopf
Director: Edward Bernds
Allied Artists; 60 minutes
Released 11/23/58

Cast: Rad Fulton, Ann Doran, Regis Toomey, Nicholas King, Robert Levin, Jim Bridges

"What'll we do tonight for kicks? The hot cars—the cool parties—the easy dames." Hot-rodders hassle middle-aged sports car fan and throw in a bit of robbery, violence, followed by adult revenge and a tough's tears. Said one exhibitor: "A good teenage picture for a double bill. They liked it here." Another offered: "Teenage story of a bad apple in a barrel evolving from a kid's desire to drive a new T-Bird. Average business."

Juvenile Jungle

Producer: Sidney Picker
Writer: Arthur T. Horman
Director: William Witney
Music: Gerald Roberts
Republic; 69 minutes
Released 4/24/58

Cast: Richard Bakalyan, Corey Allen, Anne Whitfield, Rebecca Welles, Joe Di Reda, Joe Conley, Walter Coy, Taggart Casey

Thrown out on a double bill with *Young and Wild* (and filmed in "Naturama"!), *Juvenile Jungle* is the story of teenage gangsters and a kidnapping. The ending is not pretty. "A girl delinquent—a jet propelled gang—out for fast kicks!" The poster was a lot better than the film.

Life Begins at 17

Producer: Sam Katzman
Writer: Richard Baer
Director: Arthur Dreifuss
Columbia; 75 minutes
Released 7/58

Cast: Mark Damon, Dorothy Johnson, Edward Byrnes, Ann Doran, Hugh Sanders, Luana Anders, Cathy O'Neill, George Eldredge

"The lowdown on teenage love. Out for thrills, in for trouble, these shook-up teenagers are feeling that first surge or that old urge." This is a not-too-wild pic about a teenage love triangle. Twist is, it's about sisters. "He's going to marry me! He can't, I'm going to have his baby! Both of them are lying!" With Edd ("Kookie") Byrnes.

Live Fast, Die Young

Producer: Harry Rybnick, Richard Kay
Writer: Allen Rivkin, Ib Melchior
Director: Paul Henreid
Music: Joseph Gershenson
Universal-International; 82 minutes
Released 5/58

Cast: Mary Murphy, Norma Eberhardt, Sheridan Comerate, Michael Connors, Carol Varga, Jay Jostyn, Peggy Maley

A seedy story that went out on a bill with *Girls on the Loose.* The story features teenage rebellion, runaways,

In* Joy Ride*, an adult takes revenge on juvenile delinquents.

This Sam Katzman Production, about a teenage triangle, featured Edd "Kookie" Byrnes in a supporting role.

bar hostesses, robbery, prison, psychiatrists, and correction. As the ads put it: "Teenage runaway! Rock 'n' roll is her lullaby! The nearest bar her only home . . . the road she travels tonight is a one-way highway to hell! Hear music in the mood of today's 'beat' generation!" Starring Mary Murphy of *The Wild One* fame, along with Mike "Mannix" Connors. Look for Troy Donahue and Dorothy Provine in supporting roles.

Motorcycle Gang

Producer: Alex Gordon
Writer: Lou Rusoff
Director: Edward L. Cahn

Music: Albert Glasser
American International; 78 minutes
Released 10/22/57

Cast: Anne Neyland, Steve Terrell, John Ashley, Carl Switzer, Raymond Hatton, Russell Bender, Paul Blaisdell, Jean Moorhead

A semi-sequel to *Dragstrip Girl,* this time on motorcycles instead of hot rods. "A wild girl cyclist forces a showdown in a thrilling motorcycle race! Wild and wicked—living with no tomorrow!" Have's a story of romance, motorcycles, drag racing, gang violence, jail, and correction. It went out with *Sorority Girl,* and featured loads of jive talk, a bit of sex, and some good performances. *Motion Picture Herald* said: *Motorcycle Gang* should draw a better than average response from the teenage crowd, albeit there is little interest for anyone outside this age category. While Lou Rusoff's screenplay is sound in characterizations and the dialogue is packed with juvenile jargon that gives it a feeling of authenticity, it is short on plot and what there is concentrates too heavily on motorcycle action. The new-faces cast, Steve Terrell, John Ashley, and Anne Neyland, show individually and collectively that they can do better than the merely competent work herein displayed." *Film Daily* was less sympathetic: ". . . will undoubtedly satisfy those youngsters who find reckless speed exciting and disregard for the law completely understandable."

TODAY'S "SHOOK-UP" KIDS
SHAKING LOOSE!

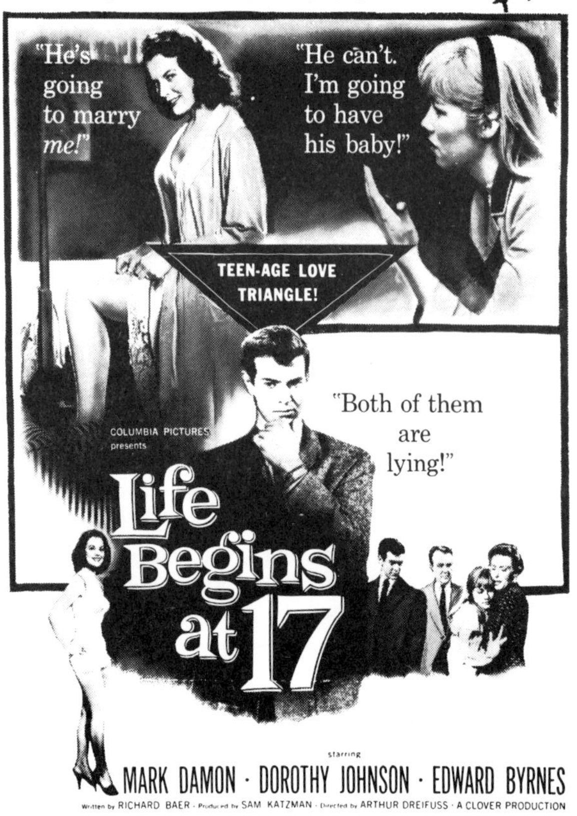

Dorothy Provine strikes a delinquent pose for Live Fast, Die Young.

The Narcotic Story

Producer: Robert W. Larsen
Director: Robert W. Larsen
A Police Science Film/Harry Stern Releasing; 75 minutes
Released 2/58

This was a semidocumentary originally made for police viewing and subsequently released to the public, first in Los Angeles, where it created quite a controversy over whether it should be shown to "nonprofessionals." A lurid ad campaign was mounted—"The whole story—from the first 'connection' to the 'hooked' addict." The cast? "Dope addicts, narcotic investigators, the alleys of our towns, dope pushers, and the temptation put in the paths of both teenagers and adults, police officers." The film only received limited exposure. In 1962 it was rereleased as *The Dread Persuasion.*

This police film caused a furor when it was released to the general public in 1958.

No Time to Be Young

Producer: Wallace MacDonald
Writer: John McPartland, Raphael Hayes
Director: David L. Rich

Would you buy a used motorcycle from these guys? Said* Film Daily: *"*Motorcycle Gang *will undoubtedly satisfy those youngsters who find reckless speed exciting and disregard for the law completely understandable."

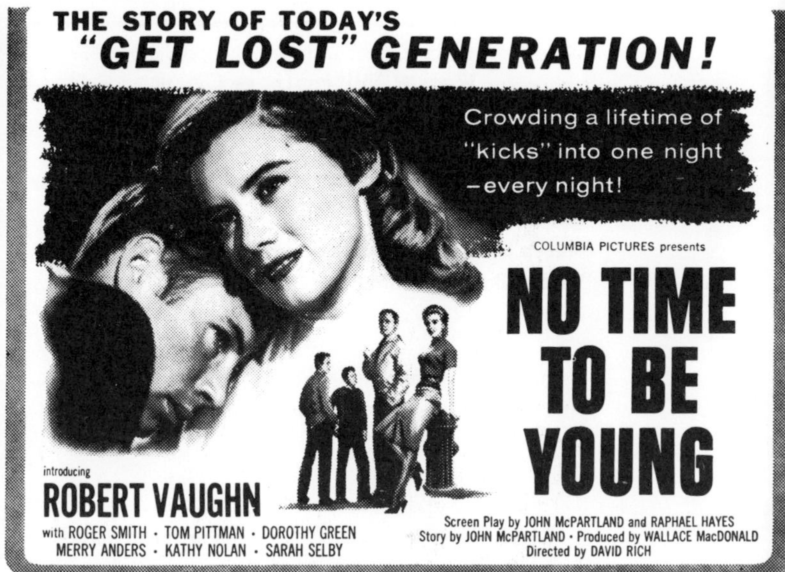

Robert* Man From U.N.C.L.E. *Vaughn starred in this 1957 teen flick.

Columbia; 82 minutes
Released 8/15/57

Cast: Robert Vaughn, Roger Smith, Tom Pittman, Dorothy Green, Merry Anders, Kathy Nolan, Sarah Selby

This is a fast-paced story of teenage robbery, murder, chases, and death, originally co-billed with *The Young Don't Cry.* "Too old to be teenagers, too young to be adults. Crowding a lifetime of kicks into one night—every night. The story of today's 'get lost' generation." Not too much teen lingo here, more like a traditional crime drama. The film was the first big role for Robert Vaughn—also look for him in *Unwed Mother,* and *Teenage Caveman.* Tom Pittman later starred in 1959's *High School Big Shot.* This was David Rich's first film, he later directed over fifty TV movies.

The Party Crashers

Producer: William Alland
Writer: Bernard Girard, Dan Lundberg
Director: Bernard Girard
Paramount; 78 minutes
Released 9/58

Cast: Mark Damon, Bobby Driscoll, Connie Stevens, Frances Farmer, Doris Dowling, Walter Brooke, Gary Gray

A "bad youth" teen flick revolving around bad parents, party crashing, death, and reform. "Who are the delinquents? Kids or their 'respectable' parents?" Fledgling teen star Mark Damon also appeared in *Young and Dangerous, Life Begins at 17,* and *The Young Racers. The Party Crashers* is also notable for the return to the screen of Frances Farmer after a sixteen-year absence. This was her lone movie comeback.

Rebel Without a Cause

Producer: David Weisbart
Writer: Stewart Stern
Director: Nicholas Ray
Music: Leonard Rosenman
Warner Bros.; 111 minutes
Released 10/29/55

Cast: James Dean, Natalie Wood, Sal Mineo, Jim Backus, Ann Doran, Corey Allen, William Hopper, Rochelle Hudson

Released after *East of Eden* (4/9/55), and before *Giant* (11/24/56), *Rebel Without a Cause* was the most influential Dean film as far as teenagers and teen exploitation films were concerned. This was a serious film, although it too started out as a low-budget project. The film was a huge success with kids, though many parents and media just did not get it. From *The New York Times:* ". . . A violent, brutal, and disturbing picture of modern teenagers . . . excruciating flashes of accuracy and truth in this film . . . however we do wish the young actors, including Mr. Dean, had not been so intent on imitating Marlon Brando in varying degrees. The tendency, possibly typical of the behavior of certain youths, may therefore be a subtle commentary, but it grows monotonous . . ." One theatre exhibitor wrote in to *Boxoffice:* "It has everything my patrons ask for—drama, action, and suspense in liberal doses. Has a good lesson for delinquent parents. Drew good houses and many good comments, though one lady walked out and said, 'crazy picture.' My thought was 'delinquent parents,' because I think if there were less delinquent parents, there would definitely be less delinquent children." Red jackets and dungarees were never the same again.

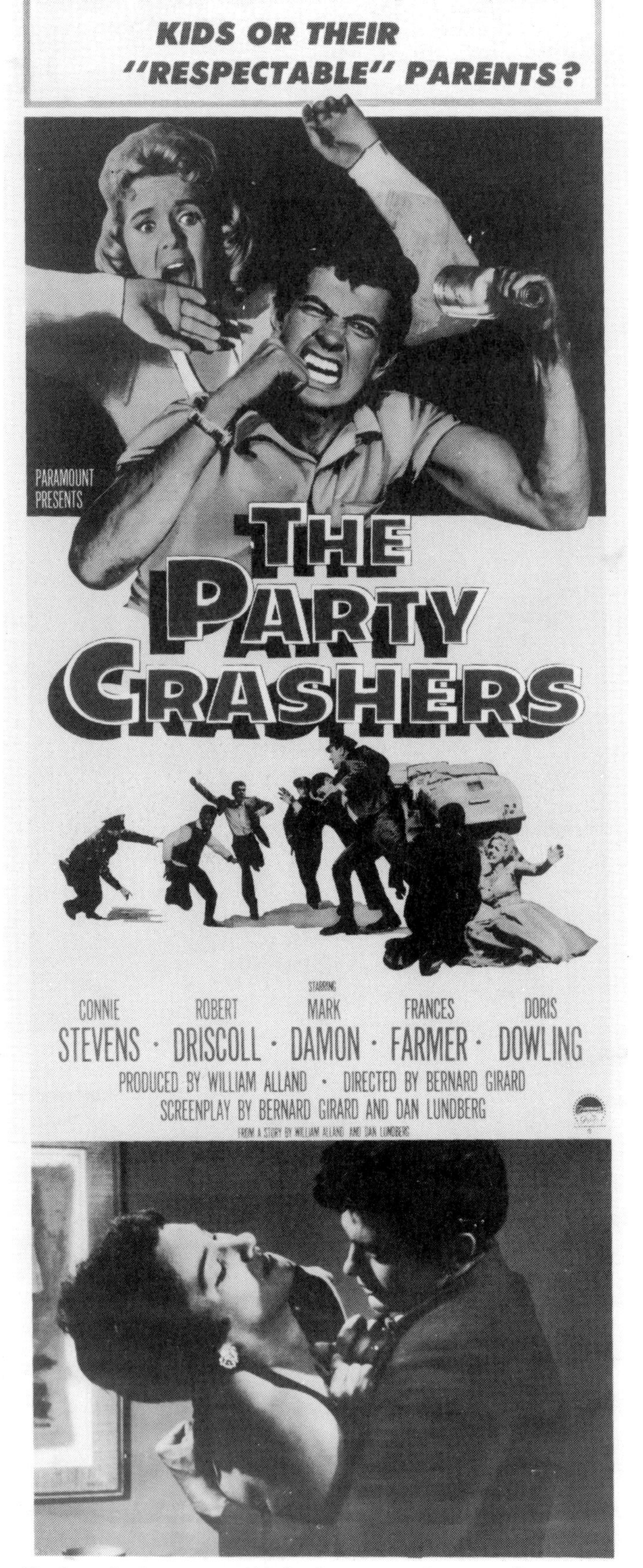

The Party Crashers ***was notable for the return to the screen of Frances Farmer after a sixteen-year absence. This was her lone movie comeback.***

WARNER BROS. PUT ALL THE FORCE OF THE SCREEN INTO A CHALLENGING DRAMA OF TODAY'S TEENAGERS!

JAMES DEAN

The overnight sensation of 'East of Eden' becomes the star of the year in

"REBEL WITHOUT A CAUSE"

...and they both come from 'good' families!

WARNERCOLOR · CINEMASCOPE · STEREOPHONIC SOUND

Warner Brothers had no idea that Rebel Without a Cause would be such a smash hit, and catapult James Dean to cult stardom.

***Some down and dirty cat-fighting in 1957's* Reform School Girl.**

From* Rockabilly Baby. *Does this look like rockabilly to you?

Reform School Girl

Producer: Robert J. Gurney
Writer: Edward Bernds
Director: Edward Bernds
Music: Ronald Stein
American International; 71 minutes
Released 8/21/57

Cast: Gloria Castillo, Ross Ford, Edward Byrnes, Ralph Reed, Jack Kruschen, Yvette Vickers, Luana Anders, Jan Englund

A pretty good film, originally released with *Rock around the World.* The story has lots of teen lingo, and bits of attempted rape, car theft, and hit-and-run death. The main plot centers around a girls reformatory, with innocent Gloria Castillo thrown in with a bunch of tough girls. ("A shocking *true* story of delinquent girls.") Of course with the help of love, understanding, and a caring male psychologist, Castillo is put on the right road. Byrnes is quite good as the bad delinquent, and Yvette Vickers also stands out as a tough hellcat. This was Byrnes's first film, and was later rereleased as "starring Edd Byrnes of '77 Sunset Strip.' " Also look for Sally Kellerman in a small role as one of the imprisoned teenagers. Bernds directed Blondie and Bowery Boys films in the forties and fifties, and later handled such teen topics as *Joy Ride* and *High School Hellcats.* Ronald Stein also did the music for *Runaway Daughters, Sorority Girl, Dragstrip Girl, Hot Rod Gang,* and others.

The Restless Years

Producer: Ross Hunter
Writer: Edward Anhalt
Director: Helmut Kautner
Music: Joseph Gershenson
Universal-International; 86 minutes
Released 12/58

Cast: John Saxon, Sandra Dee, Margaret Lindsay, Teresa Wright, James Whitmore, Luana Patten, Virginia Grey, Jody McCrea

A rather tame story of illegitimacy, newfound love, and reconciliation. "The story of a town with a 'dirty' mind—where evil gossip threatened disgrace to two decent youngsters in love." John Saxon made a career in teen movies starting with 1955's *Running Wild* and continuing with *The Unguarded Moment, Rock, Pretty Baby, Summer Love,* and *Cry Tough.* Luana Patten also graced *Rock, Pretty Baby,* and *The Young Captives.*

Rockabilly Baby

Producer: William F. Claxton
Writers: Will George, William Driskill

Music: Paul Dunlap
20th Century–Fox; 81 minutes
Released 10/57

Cast: Virginia Field, Douglas Kennedy, Judy Busch, Marlene Willis, Gary Vinson, Irene Ryan, Ken Miller, Cindy Robbins

A pretty tame movie that has about as much to do with rockabilly as does the appearance of Les Brown and His Band of Renown. Basically the story covers the mother (Field) and her problems with a conservative town. The kids are all supportive and helpful. "Dig this action, daddy-o—she's a 'rockabilly baby,' and mother was a showgirl." Look for Irene Ryan, later Granny on "The Beverly Hillbillies." Only for the dedicated.

Rock All Night

Producer: Roger Corman
Writer: Charles Griffith
Director: Roger Corman
Music: Buck Ram
American International; 63 minutes
Released 4/24/57

Cast: Dick Miller, Russell Johnson, Abby Dalton, Robin Morse, Richard Cutting, Bruno Ve Sota, Chris Alcaide, Jonathan Haze

This is a Corman quicky, made in a few days and on only two sets, and it went out with *Dragstrip Girl.* It's the story of gangsters who hold patrons of a rock bar hostage, and the drama that ensues. "Two killers with a grudge against the world with a thrilling musical background—some have to dance, some have to kill . . ." Dick Miller is quite good, and you can catch the Platters in one sequence. There's some good lines, and as writer Charles Griffith later recalled: "I once wrote a musical in twenty-four hours called *Rock All Night.* Lord Buckley was supposed to be in that. He was a friend of mine and I used to write material for him. Lord Buckley was a great character, and he was supposed to play 'Sir Bop' in that picture, but he was on the road somewhere, so they got somebody else."

Rock Baby, Rock It

Producer: J. G. Tiger
Writer: Murray Douglas Sporup
Director: Murray Douglas Sporup
Freebar/United; 77 minutes
Released 1957

Cast: Johnny Carroll, Don Coats, Kay Wheeler, Rosco Gordon, George Russell, Dave Miller, Phylliss Elzey, Sylvia Graves

This was an outtake from **Rock Baby, Rock It.** *Were they selling the girl, the car, or the film? Most probably, all three.*

Sal Mineo decides to sell his ID bracelet so that John Saxon **(left)** *can buy a new guitar. Rod McKuen* **(center)** *looks on in this scene from 1957's* **Rock, Pretty Baby.**

Rock, Pretty Baby *was a typical "mild-youth" teenage film.*

An obscure film shot totally in Dallas, and one which was distributed in very limited areas. The plot concerns a teen nightclub, gangsters, and a big benefit show. "The sizzling story of hot rock as you have never seen it before"—and indeed you haven't. The acting is wooden, the camera work somewhat amateurish, and the film is filled with local talent ranging from wild R 'n' B to howling rockabilly. But the film does have a certain charm to it, using real teenagers in real clothes and dancing real dances, while spouting tons of hip lingo. The film definitely captures a certain time and place, perhaps better than many Hollywood productions. And what an assortment of faces!

Rock, Pretty Baby

Producer: Edmond Chevie
Writer: Herbert Margolis, William Raynor
Director: Richard Bartlett
Music: Henry Mancini, Joseph Gershenson
Universal-International; 89 minutes
Released 12/56

Cast: Sal Mineo, John Saxon, Luana Patten, Edward Platt, Fay Wray, Rod McKuen, John Wilder, Alan Reed, Jr., Douglas Fowley

A 'good teen' movie: all these rambunctious kids want to do is get their rock 'n' roll combo off the ground—plus find the girls of their dreams. The flick moves along at an amiable pace, and mixed with some R 'n' R music are problems with parents, problems with money, and problems of young love. John Saxon is pretty wooden as the bandleader, but Mineo (although top-billed, he is really not the lead character) does an excellent and natural job. Bass player Rod McKuen is okay and even gets to croon a couple of numbers. Look for thirteen-year-old Shelley Fabares as Saxon's kid sister. "The whole wonderful story of today's rock 'n' roll generation! Told the way they want it told . . ." The sequel was *Summer Love.*

***Do these look like your typical high school students?* (Left to right): *Marla English, Mary Ellen Kaye, and Gloria Castillo get ready to leave home in 1956's* Runaway Daughters.**

Rumble on the Docks *(1956) took pains to explain that "rumble" is "juvenile delinquency lingo for gang war."*

Said one exhibitor: "Teenagers filled the house the first night. Half a house the second. They enjoyed it. Sorry, I'm an old fogey and go for harmony rather than 'beat.' "

Rumble on the Docks

Producer: Sam Katzman
Writer: Lou Morheim, Jack DeWitt
Director: Fred F. Sears
Music: Mischa Bakaleinikoff
Columbia; 82 minutes
Released 12/56

Cast: James Darren, Laurie Carroll, Michael Granger, Jerry Janger, Robert Blake, Edgar Barrier, Celia Lovsky

This is a Katzman quickie made to support *Don't Knock the Rock.* It's the story of a teen gang leader, a corrupt longshoremen's union, parental resentment, and the delinquent's ultimate maturity. "Authentic and terrifying—the juvenile delinquency story never told before—the most savage teenage terror of all—the teenage gangs on the waterfront." The producers put an asterisk after the title in many ads explaining *Rumble* as "juvenile delinquency slang for 'gang war.' " Fred Sears began directing in 1949, doing mostly low-budget westerns and crime movies, then locked into teen movies in the fifties, turning out *Teen-age Crime Wave, Rock around the Clock, Cha-Cha-Cha Boom!, Don't Knock the Rock, Calypso Heat Wave,* and *Going Steady.*

Runaway Daughters

Producer: Alex Gordon
Writer: Lou Rusoff
Director: Edward L. Cahn
Music: Ronald Stein
American International; 90 minutes
Released 11/56

THE STARK BRUTAL TRUTH ABOUT TODAY'S LOST GENERATION!

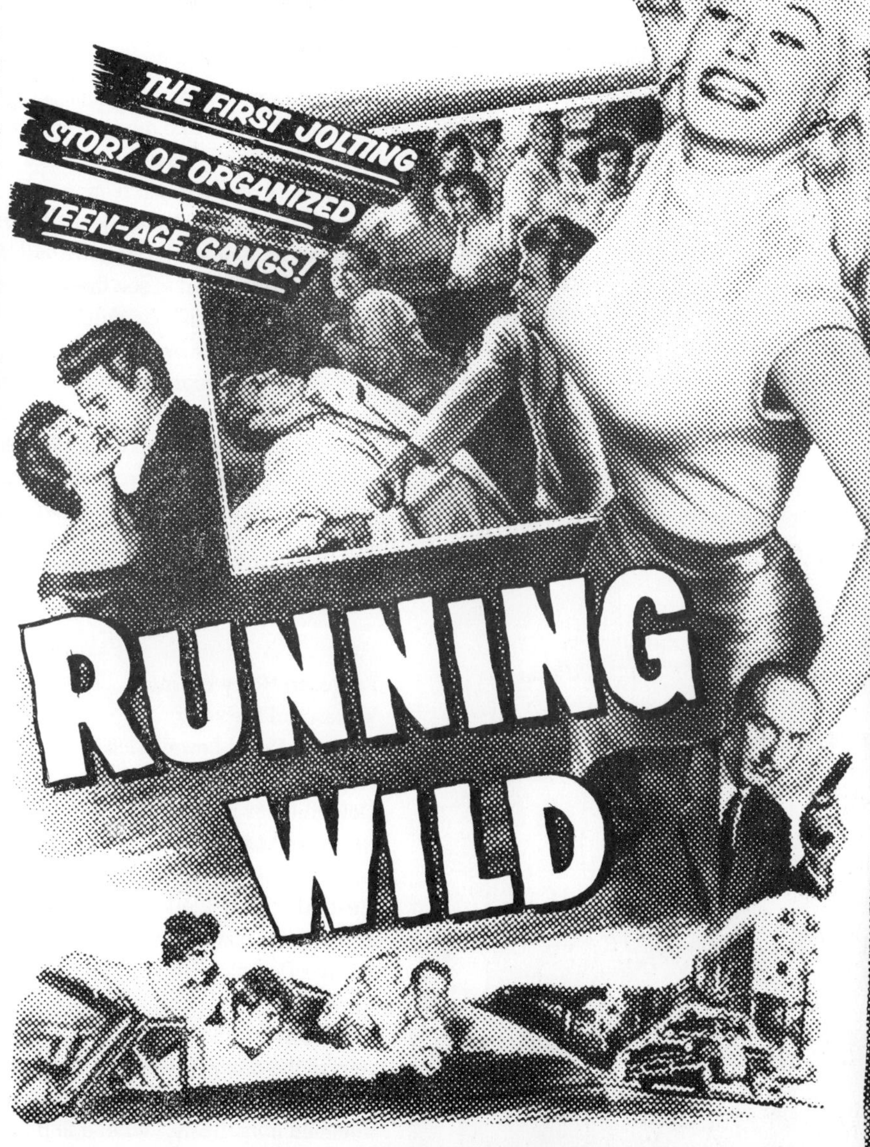

starring

WILLIAM CAMPBELL • MAMIE VAN DOREN
KEENAN WYNN • KATHLEEN CASE

with JAN MERLIN • JOHN SAXON • CHRIS RANDALL • WALTER COY

DIRECTED BY ABNER BIBERMAN • SCREENPLAY BY LEO TOWNSEND
PRODUCED BY HOWARD PINE • A UNIVERSAL-INTERNATIONAL PICTURE

Cast: Marla English, Anna Sten, John Litel, Lance Fuller, Adele Jergens, Mary Ellen Kaye, Gloria Castillo, Steve Tyrell

An early low-budget picture, which went out with *Shake, Rattle and Rock,* and was peppered with film stars of the thirties and forties as well as a bunch of new teen faces. It's a pretty dull story of bad parents and three girls who run away to L.A. to escape the trauma. Only trouble is, they don't run away until an hour into the picture, and then, after one death and two happy endings, the whole film wraps up rather quickly. "The shocking story of teenage girls in revolt against today's delinquent parents." There's a bit of light sex, one unmarried pregnancy, and some car theft, but overall this nine-day production is pretty crude and unintentionally humorous. Photographer's model Marla English looks good as a sexy Elizabeth Taylor lookalike, and Frank Gorshin camps it up in a bit part. One trade paper said: "Of a slightly better calibre and longer length than the regular twin-billed films turned out by American International, this has a capable cast with a few familiar players and an exploitable title and theme." Writer Lou Rusoff, who also penned *Motorcycle Gang, Hot Rod Gang, Girls in Prison,* and *Dragstrip Girl,* was Sam Arkoff's brother-in-law.

***Mamie Van Doren shows some leg in the early (1955) teenage film,* Running Wild.**

Running Wild

Producer: Howard Pine
Writer: Leo Townsend
Director: Abner Biberman
Music: Joseph Gershenson
Universal-International; 81 minutes
Released 12/55

Cast: William Campbell, Mamie Van Doren, Keenan Wynn, Kathleen Case, Jan Merlin, John Saxon, Chris Randall, Walter Coy

An early entry in the teen-delinquency cycle, *Running Wild* was the story of teens involved in hot-car rackets, romance, and general hoodlumism. "Stark savage truth stabs from the juke-box jungle! The first jolting story of organized teenage gangs. Hear the hit tune sensation 'Razzle-Dazzle' by Bill Haley and His Comets!" Said one exhibitor: "We can't seem to get the younger element out to see these pictures and they should. But ours have too much other business. Where they go is nobody's business, but it isn't the picture show. A good enough programmer and worth a date on any double bill, and priced at a minimum." Another said: "Very good mid-week picture for adults as well as teenagers. It drew above average business and showed some profit." On many bills, *Running Wild* was teamed with *Tarantula.*

Senior Prom

Producer: Harry Romm
Writer: Hal Hackady
Director: David Lowell Rich
Music: Morris Stoloff, Van Alexander, Gil Grau
Columbia; 82 minutes
Released 12/58

Cast: Jill Corey, Paul Hampton, Jimmie Komack, Barbara Bostock, Tom Laughlin, Frieda Inescort, Selene Walters, Francis De Sales

Very tame and dull picture which deals with young love at the prom. The film is filled with adult-type musical stars who have no youth appeal at all. One exhibitor summed it up nicely: "What a flop, what a bore. The sooner Columbia gives this to TV the sooner the public will return to the movie theaters and leave their little electronic monsters in the living room."

Sing, Boy, Sing

Producer: Henry Ephron
Writer: Claude Binyon
Director: Henry Ephron
Music: Lionel Newman

20th Century–Fox; 90 minutes
Released 1/30/58

Cast: Tommy Sands, Lili Gentle, Edmond O'Brien, John McIntire, Nick Adams, Diane Jergens, Jerry Paris, Regis Toomey

Pretty solid rags-to-riches story of a teen idol from the South—closely patterned after the story of Elvis Presley. Sands is quite good as the rock 'n' roll star who grows guilty for leaving his church roots, and O'Brien is the typical grab-the-money manager, but Nick Adams almost steals the film as the delivery boy who becomes part of the entourage. This stuff may seem pretty tame now, but it was somewhat revealing in its day—and Elvis and the "Colonel" weren't too happy about it. Tommy Sands was later married to Nancy Sinatra (1960–65).

***Sing, Boy, Sing** bore more than a passing resemblance to the real-life story of Elvis Presley's rise to fame.*

(Confessions of a) Sorority Girl

Producer: Roger Corman
Writer: Ed Walters, Leo Lieberman
Director: Roger Corman
Music: Ronald Stein
American International; 60 minutes
Released 10/22/57

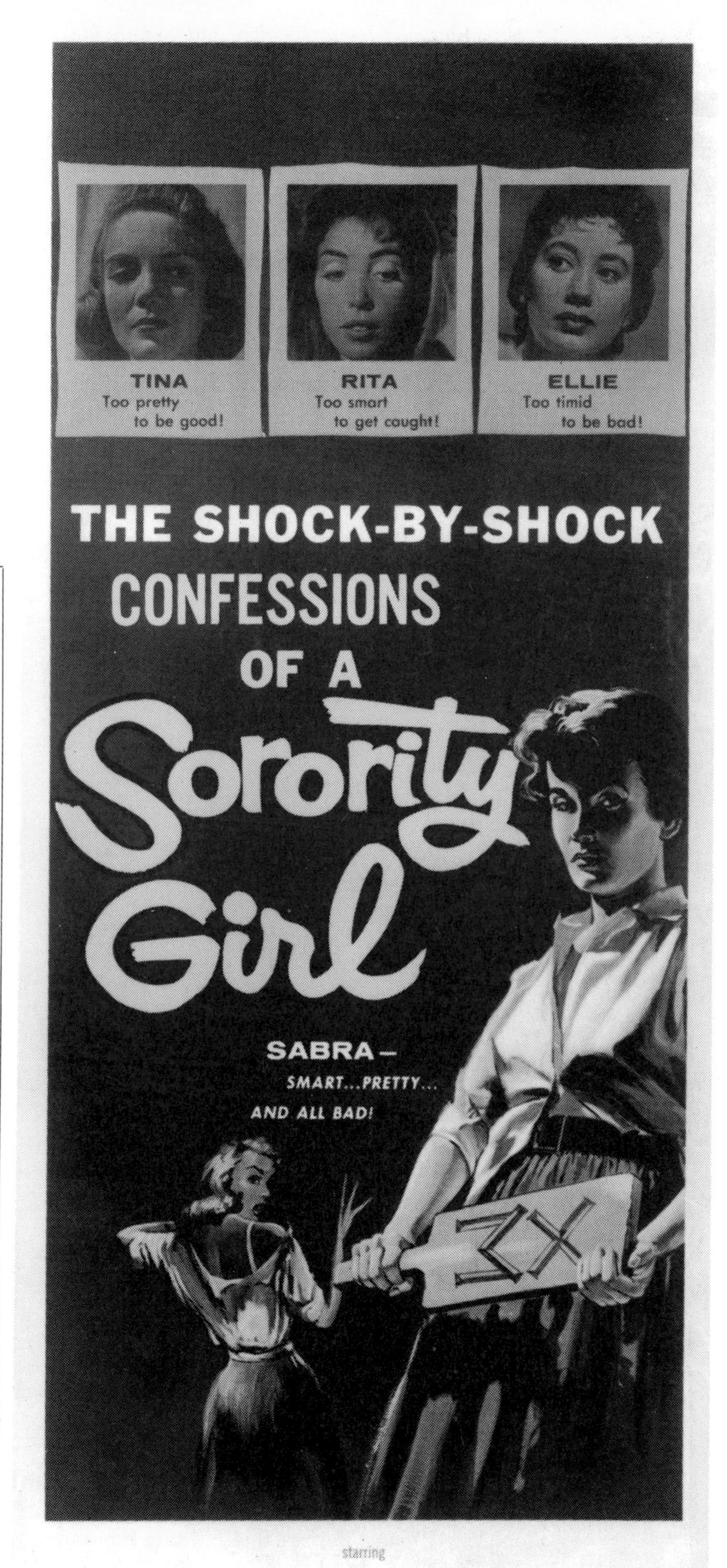

Cast: Susan Cabot, Dick Miller, Barboura O'Neill, June Kenney, Barbara Crane, Fay Baker, Jeane Wood

This one is almost over before you get your popcorn passed around. It's the story of a bad sorority girl who takes out her problems on the rest of the girls—her specialties are blackmail, catfights, and paddling—with the ever-popular sorority pledge board. Susan Cabot is quite good, and some of the scenes are pretty moody and atmospheric. Said one trade: "The film does not fulfill its promising premise, and what might have been a fresh plot with a wholesome influence turns out to be a somber, depressing depiction of a sadistic coed who is an exaggerated exception. Outstanding aspects of the movie are the young cast, notably Susan Cabot as the misfit sorority girl; Ronald Stein's music and photography by Monroe P. Askin." After this film, most girls would want to take a pledge—not to join a sorority. This was twin-billed with *Motorcycle Gang.*

***A moody scene from 1957's* (Confessions of a) Sorority Girl.**

Stakeout on Dope Street

Producer: Andrew J. Fenady
Writers: Irvin Kershner, Irwin Schwartz, Andrew J. Fenady
Director: Irvin Kershner
Music: Richard Markowitz
Warner Bros.; 83 minutes
Released 5/3/58

Cast: Yale Wexler, Jonathan Haze, Morris Miller, Abby Dalton, Allen Kramer, Herman Rudin, Philip Mansour, Frank Harding

This is a story of teenagers who find a pile of dope lost by gangsters, and have to decide what to do. There's a bunch of chases from gangsters and police, and, after much tension and in-fighting, the kids decide to do the "right thing." The film was financed by Roger Corman and came in at $30,000—they sold it to Warners for $150,000. "The screen's first blazing story of kids who go rumbling

Stakeout on Dope Street *was directed by Irvin Kershner, who later helmed* The Empire Strikes Back.

down dope streets . . ." This was Kershner's first directing job—he followed this with *The Young Captives* and *The Hoodlum Priest.* In 1980 he directed *The Empire Strikes Back.*

Summer Love

Producer: William Grady, Jr.
Writers: William Raynor, Herbert Margolis
Director: Charles Haas
Music: Joseph Gershenson
Universal; 85 minutes
Released 4/58

Cast: John Saxon, Judi Meredith, Rod McKuen, Molly Bee, Jill St. John, Shelly Fabares, Fay Wray, John Wilder, Edward Platt

This was the sequel to *Rock, Pretty Baby,* taking off from where the last one left off—the "combo's" two-week stint at a summer camp. There's more band problems, summer scenes, and light romance. Teamed with *The Big Beat,* this picture was geared toward the family—something both the kids and their parents could watch. Said the ad hype: "their kind of love keeps time to the beat of their very own music. The all-new story of teenage romance as told by those *Rock, Pretty Baby* kids—with their souped-up rhythm and their mixed-up notions about romance." The first one was better.

Taming Sutton's Girl

Producer: William O'Sullivan
Writers: Thames Williamson, Frederic Louis Fox
Director: Lesley Selander
Music: Gerald Roberts
Republic; 71 minutes
Released 9/15/57

Cast: John Lupton, Gloria Talbott, Jack Kelly, May Wynn, Verna Felton

"Seventeen and lonesome—he was her first love and she meant to keep him . . ." This was teamed with *The Wayward Girl* and filmed in "Naturama," and took teenage love to the back woods—there's a lot of drama, gunshooting, and really is more for voyeuristic adults than confused teenagers. One exhibitor tried to convince his fellow theater owners to give these pictures better playing time: "It's a good combination and one picture is about as good as another. As a rule I try to book an extra good picture on my Sunday-Monday-Tuesday change. . . . A picture with good stars and good production. However I find that these teenage double features will do a lot more business on the Sunday-Monday-Tuesday change than a picture of higher rating. If some of you are using these on your mid-week change, try something different and put one in on 'A' playing time. You won't be sorry."

Teenage Bad Girl

Producer: Herbert Wilcox
Writer: Felicity Douglas
Director: Herbert Wilcox
DCA; 100 minutes
Released (in U.S.A.) 1957

Cast: Anna Neagle, Sylvia Syms, Kenneth Haigh, Norman Wooland, Wilfred Hyde White, Julia Lockwood, Helen Haye

"Born good with a desire to be bad. She's a doll, she's a dish, she's a delinquent. Sylvia Syms—teen and terrific in an explosive role." This is a pretty good look at juvenile delinquency, British style. The story follows the familiar paths of crime, rebellion, death, and redemption, but Syms is quite good. This was originally released in England in 1956 as *My Teenage Daughter* and later rereleased here in 1959, simply as *Bad Girl.* It went out on a double bill here with the German import *Teenage Wolfpack.*

Teenage Caveman

Producer: Roger Corman
Writer: R. Wright Campbell
Director: Roger Corman
Music: Albert Glasser
American International; 65 minutes
Released 7/58

Cast: Robert Vaughn, Leslie Bradley, Darrah Marshall, Frank DeKova, Joseph H. Hamilton, Marshall Bradford, Robert Shayne, Beech Dickerson, Jonathan Haze.

This was originally shot as *Prehistoric World* but retitled by the teenhappy advertising people at American International. It's the story of a teen in a prehistoric world, which in the end turns out to be a post-nuclear war setting. It's a picture with a message, but that gets lost in the tedium and low-budget production. The ads cried: "Prehistoric rebels and prehistoric monsters." There's little of either. Originally sent out with *How to Make a Monster.*

***Robert Vaughn contemplates teenage life in a post-nuclear primitive society in 1958's* Teenage Caveman.**

Teenage Crime Wave

Producer: Clover Productions
Writers: Harry Essex, Ray Buffum
Director: Fred F. Sears
Music: Mischa Bakaleinikoff
Columbia; 77 minutes
Released 11/55

Cast: Tommy Cook, Mollie McCart, Sue England, Frank Griffin, James Bell, Ray Riehl, Guy Kingsford, Larry Blake

Excerpt from the prologue: "Over twenty-five percent of the crimes committed in this country are perpetrated by teenagers. Only an aroused public can put an end to this. We hope this picture will open your eyes. . . ." This is basically a low-grade crime film, this time substituting teenagers for the older gangsters of yore. There's the usual dosage of criminal activity, jail, catfights, murder, kidnapping, capture, and death. In a kind of teen Bonnie and Clyde epic, former child star Tommy Cook is okay as the vicious hood, with a bit of a John Garfield look about him. Girlfriend Mollie McCart is good as his tough girlfriend, and sports an interesting short hairdo, unique for its day. But overall the picture is still fairly routine and ultimately quite dull.

Teenage Doll

Producer: Roger Corman
Writer: Charles B. Griffith
Director: Roger Corman
Music: Walter Greene
Allied Artists; 68 and 71 minutes (two versions)
Released 9/22/57

Cast: June Kenney, Fay Spain, John Brinkley, Ziva Roden, Sandy Smith, Collette Jackson, Barbara Wilson, Barboura Morris

The ads proclaimed: "Tarnished, tempted, violently thrown aside—too young to be careful, too tough to care, now it's too late to say 'no'." *Teenage Doll* is an intense picture dealing with gangs, stabbings, violence, treachery, and—surprise—not a happy ending. This is one aspect of the film that made it controversial, and criticized by the straight media. Moreover, it was lit strangely, is often episodic in nature, and its action takes place in a single night. The movie is intense, moody, and atmospheric and is indeed a tour de force. Even so, many compromises were made to get the film past the censors, and to deliver a partially "happy" ending. Said screenwriter Griffith: "I hated some of the titles they put on the films. I did one called *Teenage Doll* where every page of the script was rejected by the censors, and I had to write it over again during the weekend." *Teenage Doll* was teamed with *Undersea Girl,* filmed in wide-screen, and released in various lengths—some of the violence was

Teenage Doll *was a classic teenage exploitation film, directed by Roger Corman.*

pruned for some showings. *Variety* said: "This low-budgeter is ostensibly directed toward the fight against juvenile delinquency. However, only real contribution in this direction is that it offers employment to a corps of juve actors and thus keeps them off the street. . . . The characters talk a stylized jargon and engage in continual brutality and violence, their motivations, delinquent or otherwise, bearing only the slightest resemblance to human beings." But *Boxoffice* was even more searing in its misguided review, almost an editorial diatribe: "A woefully meager programmer . . . still another entry in the apparently inexhaustible cycle of pictures dealing with juvenile delinquency. One may require a crystal ball to determine why it should ever have been produced. Accenting violence for violence's sake alone and viciousness without rhyme or reason, the picture is more episodic than narrative and seems to specialize in individual character analyzing of as unsavory a group of adolescents as was ever assembled. The overall result is that a batch of would-be dramatic screen tests made in some acting school for aspiring young troupers were thrown together with but scant regard for continuity, consistency, or believability. Sure, there are new faces—nothing else but—and probably some of them possess promising talent. But handicapped as they are herein by outlandishly extreme situations and dialog, all that they succeed in projecting is a veritable marathon of unmitigated mugging. Even the venturesome teenagers—it certainly should not be shown to children—will find the picture difficult to stomach." Catch it if you can.

Teen-age Menace

Producer: Bill Free
30 minutes
Released 1953/54

This was a hard-hitting film on the evils of drug addiction. The producers wanted to make a realistic film that would scare teenagers away from drugs. There were scenes of pot use, heroin, lies, cheating, and stealing. Ultimately there's a batch of bad heroin, a death, and in the end the dealer goes to the electric chair. But the New York State censors refused to let the film be released—they said it tended to corrupt morals and incite to crime. They called it "a how to—not a not to." The graphic film featured Mark Rydell and Martin Newman. It played around the country for a while, but was often banned, and now seems to have disappeared from circulation.

Teenage Monster

Producer: Jacques Marquette
Writer: Ray Buffum
Director: Jacques Marquette
Music: Walter Greene
Howco; 65 minutes
Released 1957

Cast: Anne Gwynne, Stuart Wade, Gloria Castillo, Charles Courtney, Gilbert Perkins

Dull and slow science fiction set in the old west of the 1800s. "Man—beast—or demon! A titan of terror . . ." After being exposed to a meteor a young boy becomes a kind of werewolf monster—not really much to do with teenagers, but they figured the title would sell it. The TV title, *Meteor Monster,* was more applicable. Watch at your own risk. Said *Variety:* "Imbecile killer protected by Mother. Stirs up little interest. For low-IQ audiences only." On many bills this was teamed with *The Brain from Planet Arous.*

Teenage Rebel

Producer: Charles Brackett
Writers: Walter Reisch, Charles Brackett
Director: Edmund Goulding
Music: Leigh Harline, Lionel Newman
20th Century-Fox; 94 minutes
Released 11/56

Cast: Ginger Rogers, Michael Rennie, Betty Lou Keim, Mildred Natwick, Rusty Swope, Lili Gentle, Louis Beavers, Warren Berlinger, Diane Jergens

Taken from the stage play *A Roomful of Roses,* the contemporary title was conveniently added by the studio. It's a tame story of a divorced mom (Rogers) trying to keep her teenage daughter on the straight and narrow. Said one exhibitor: "One of the finer motion pictures to deal with our teenagers and one that did not draw the vandal type crowd. General consensus was 'expertly done.' "

Teenage Thunder

Producer: Jacques Marquette
Writer: Rudy Makoul
Director: Paul Helmick

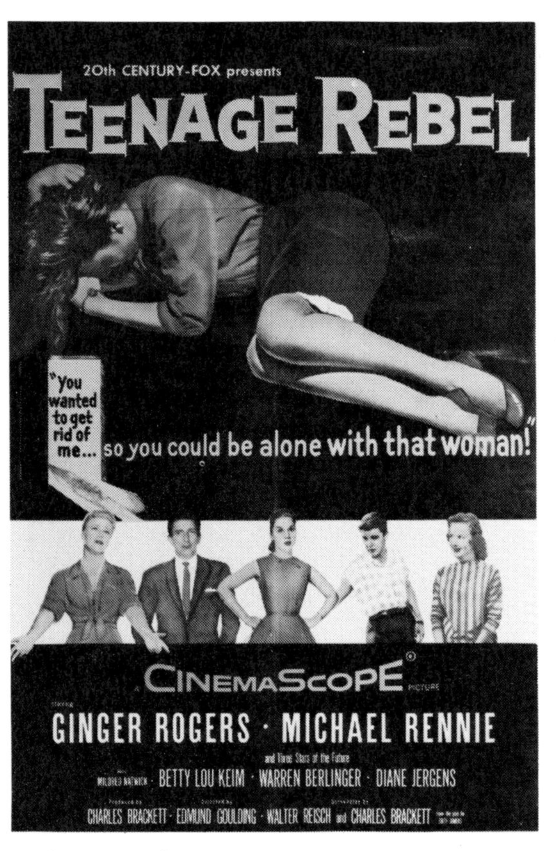

Music: Walter Greene
Howco
Released 1958

Cast: Charles Courtney, Melinda Byron, Robert Fuller, Tyler McVey, Paul Bryar, Helene Heigh

"Revved-up youth on a thrill rampage—How can you tell them to be good—they've too many reasons to be bad . . ." Low-budget teen flick that went out with *Carnival Rock.* It's the story of hot rods, speeding, drag races, runaways, victory, and reconciliation. Its prediction "featuring the stars of tomorrow" was not exactly prophetic. Hard to find, but don't try too hard.

Teenage Wolfpack

Producer: Wenzele Ludecke
Writers: Will Tremper, Georg Tressler
Director: Georg Tressler
Music: Martin Boettcher
DCA; 89 minutes
Released 1957

Cast: Henry Bookholt, Karen Baal, Christian Doermer, Jo Herbst, Victoria von Ballarko, Stanislaw Ledinik, Mario

Henry Bookholt, star of this 1957 German juvenile delinquent film, later became better known to U.S. audiences as Horst Bucholz, but the promise of becoming the new James Dean was less than prophetic.

Ahrenz, Manfred Hoffman

"Think of a law—they've broken it. Think of a crime—they've committed it!" This German film first went to England and then came to the United States on a double bill with *Teenage Bad Girl*. Henry Bookholt was the number-one boxoffice star in Germany, and later became well known in the States as Horst Buchholz ("Nothing like him has hit the screen since James Dean!"). It's a tough story of teen gangs, robbery, violence, murder, and arrest, all dubbed into English. A good look at juvenile delinquency in Germany, this feature shows some of the atmosphere the Beatles soaked up when they first went to Germany in the early sixties. Not bad.

The Tijuana Story

Producer: Sam Katzman
Writer: Lou Morheim
Director: Leslie Kardos
Music: Mischa Bakaleinikoff
Columbia; 73 minutes
Released 10/57

Cast: Rudolfo Acosta, James Darren, Robert McQueeney, Jean Willes, Joy Stoner, Paul Coates, Paul Newlan, George E. Stone

"Selling drugs to teenagers was their business—until one man dared to fight them. The story of the most notorious sucker-trap in the Western Hemisphere." Based on a true story and filmed entirely in Tijuana, this is the story of gangs, love, marijuana, death, a crusading newspaperman, and partial salvation. *Boxoffice* said: "Exhibitors should be more than passingly interested in this drama of intrigue south of the border, for its ingredients hold equal appeal for adults and younger generation ticket buyers, guaranteeing reasonably profitable returns." Look for Robert Blake in a supporting role.

The Unguarded Moment

Producer: Gordon Kay
Writers: Herb Meadows, Larry Marcus
Director: Harry Keller
Music: Herman Stein, Joseph Gershenson
Universal International; 95 minutes
Released 11/56

Cast: Esther Williams, George Nader, John Saxon, Edward Andrews, Les Tremayne, Jack Albertson, Edward Platt

Based on a story by Rosalind Russell, this film is the tale of attempted love between a well-meaning teacher and a warped student whose father is the real pervert. In the end there's a convenient death for the dad, and a stint in the army for Saxon. Edward Platt played an authority figure in many teen movies, most notably *Rebel Without a Cause, Rock, Pretty Baby,* and *Summer Love.* This film is okay, but nothing more.

Unwed Mother

Producer: Joseph Justman
Writers: Anson Bond, Alden Nash
Director: William A. (aka Walter) Doniger
Allied Artists; 74 minutes
Released 11/23/58

Cast: Norma Moore, Robert Vaughn, Diana Darrin, Billie Bird, Jeanne Cooper, Ron Hargrave, Kathleen Hughes, Ken Lynch

A story of teen romance and petty crime. These kids sure are confused, and who wouldn't be with all these crazy movies they go to see? Robert ("The Man From U.N.C.L.E.") Vaughn also graced such teen epics as *No Time to Be Young* and *Teenage Caveman.* Doniger first

gained notice for his prison films like *The Steel Cage, The Steel Jungle,* and *House of Women,* and later directed a few years of "Peyton Place" for television.

Untamed Youth

Producer: Aubrey Schenck
Writer: John C. Higgins
Director: Howard W. Koch
Music: Les Baxter
Warner Bros.; 80 minutes
Released 5/18/57

Cast: Mamie Van Doren, Lori Nelson, John Russell, Eddie Cochran, Lurene Tuttle, Don Burnett, Yvonne Lime, Michael Emmet

"Youth turned 'rock n roll' wild and the 'punishment' farm that makes them wilder. . . . Starring the girl built like a platinum powerhouse—Mamie Van Doren." A classic story of a corrupt prison farm and the goings on there, an unnecessary death, public help, and finally freedom for the kids. Some great lines, and don't miss the cavorting of Mamie Van Doren and the work of Eddie Cochran. Said one exhibitor: "Did better than average business on this because it appealed to the teenagers who make up ninety percent of my business." Another theater owner was almost ecstatic: "Man, oh man! This is

Mamie Van Doren struts her stuff in this scene from the classic* Untamed Youth. *And check out those expressions on the guys!

a show right down the alley for the young folks. A real gone thing, they told me. It held its own with the homecoming football game. It pulled a few extra bucks, but I sent them on to WB to take care of the extra rental on this one." *The New York Times* was less enthusiastic: "Miss Van Doren sings . . . to a variety of torrid gyrations that are guaranteed to keep any red-blooded American boy awake. Nothing else in this picture can make that claim." Recommended.

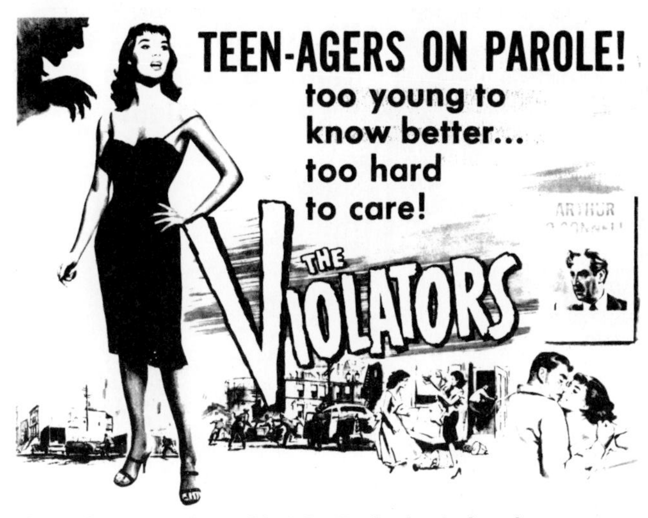

The Violaters ***was directed by John Newland, who later became better known as the eerie host of*** **One Step Beyond.**

The Violators

Producer: Himan Brown
Writer: Ernest Pendrell
Director: John Newland
Music: Elliott Lawrence
Universal-International; 76 minutes
Released 12/57

Cast: Arthur O'Connell, Nancy Malone, Clarice Blackburn, Fred Beir, Bill Darrid, Henry Sharp, Frank Maxwell, Mary Michael

"Teenagers on parole! Too young to know better . . . to hard to care!" From a story by the great juve author Wenzell Brown, *The Violators* is a story of probation officers, parole violators, a teenage daughter involved in fraud, and final reconciliation. Said one trade paper: "An honest, realistically dramatic program—far above the usual program film and is excellently acted, particularly Nancy Malone as O'Connell's teenage daughter and Fred Beir as the girl's opportunist boyfriend." Director Newland later became a successful director of TV movies—could you forget *Don't Be Afraid of the Dark* and *The Legend of Hillbilly John?* Besides acting and directing in many TV shows, he is probably best known as the eerie host of "One Step Beyond."

The Violent Years

Producers: O'Camp and A. O. Bayer
Writer: Ed Wood, Jr.
Director: William M. Morgan
Music: Manuel Francisco
Headliner Productions
Released 1956

Cast: Jean Moorhead, Barbara Weeks, Arthur Milan, Theresa Hancock, JoAnne Cangi, Gloria Farr, Glenn Corbett, Lee Constant, I. Stanford Jolley

Another entry in the Ed Wood pantheon, *The Violent Years* is a tough and graphic story of female gangs, robbery, vandalism, murder, and a hot pajama party thrown in for good measure. The ads promised: "Untamed girls of the pack gang—thrill girls of the highway—see what actually happens behind the locked doors of a pajama party." The film is a grainy, murky, low-grade enterprise with touches of fetishism utilized for the raincoat crowd. This film is even too weird for teenagers, and actually leaves a bit of a bad taste in your mouth. Two classic moves: a teen gang girl almost gets to destroy an American flag before she is shot by the police; and the unrepetant leader's "So what?" before she dies during illegitimate childbirth. Beyond camp, and rather depressing.

"Hey you, is that a gun in your pocket or are you just glad to see us?" From **The Violent Years** ***written by Ed "Plan Nine From Outer Space" Wood, Jr.***

Just another typical teenage party, in this scene from* Young and Dangerous *(1957).

The Wayward Girl

Producer: William J. O'Sullivan
Writers: Houston Branch, Frederic Louis Fox
Director: Lesley Selander
Music: Gerald Roberts
Republic; 71 minutes
Released 9/22/57

Cast: Marcia Henderson, Peter Walker, Katherine Barrett, Whit Bissell, Rita Lynn, Peg Hillias, Tracey Roberts

Filmed in fabulous "Naturama" and teamed with *Taming Sutton's Gal, The Wayward Girl* was a quick exploitation feature that dealt with prison, rackets, and redemption, with the obligatory hair-pulling scene thrown in for good measure. Look for Barbara Eden in a small role. One trade review: "Lithesome Marcia Henderson, whose ability to project logical pre-teenage portrayals has been evidenced in past major studio ventures, is now grown to young womanhood. Exploitation possibilities are unlimited with this type of attraction, and enterprising showmen should have a field day." The tireless Selander directed his first feature in 1936, and went on to make over 150 movies *and* 150 shows for television!

The Wild One

Producer: Stanley Kramer
Writer: John Paxton
Director: Laslo Benedek
Music: Leith Stevens
Columbia; 79 minutes
Released 12/31/53

Cast: Marlon Brando, Mary Murphy, Robert Keith, Lee Marvin, Jay C. Flippen, Jerry Paris, Bruno Ve Sota, Peggy Haley

Trendsetting biker film which established many styles that followed. Brando squeezed this in between *Julius Caesar* and *On the Waterfront,* and the film caused a torrent of controversy. Said *The New York Times:* "An ugly, debauched, and frightening view of a small but particularly significant and menacing element of modern youth." The film is solid until the cop-out ending where Brando is won over by young love, but the characterizations and lingo ("Hey Johnny whatya rebelling against?" "Whatya got?") set the tone for many teen jive films that followed. It played well in the cities, but in small towns it caused problems as evidenced by this theater owner's note to *Boxoffice:* "The reports of some of the grosses it was chalking up let a little greed enter my heart and I sort of sidestepped my obligation as a small-town theater owner. It made me sick at the soul to see how the teenagers and little folks laughed at this rank hoodlumism. I couldn't look the mothers in the eye when they tore the picture apart as they left the theater. I deserved the beating I took at the box office for allowing this time on my screen. The acting is fine but it should be limited to adults of twenty-five or over." Don't miss it.

Young and Dangerous

Producer: William F. Claxton
Writer: James Landis
Director: William F. Claxton
20th Century–Fox; 78 minutes
Released 10/57

Cast: Lili Gentle, Mark Damon, Edward Binns, George Brenlin, Jerry Barclay, William Stevens, Dabbs Greer, Ann Doran, Connie Stevens

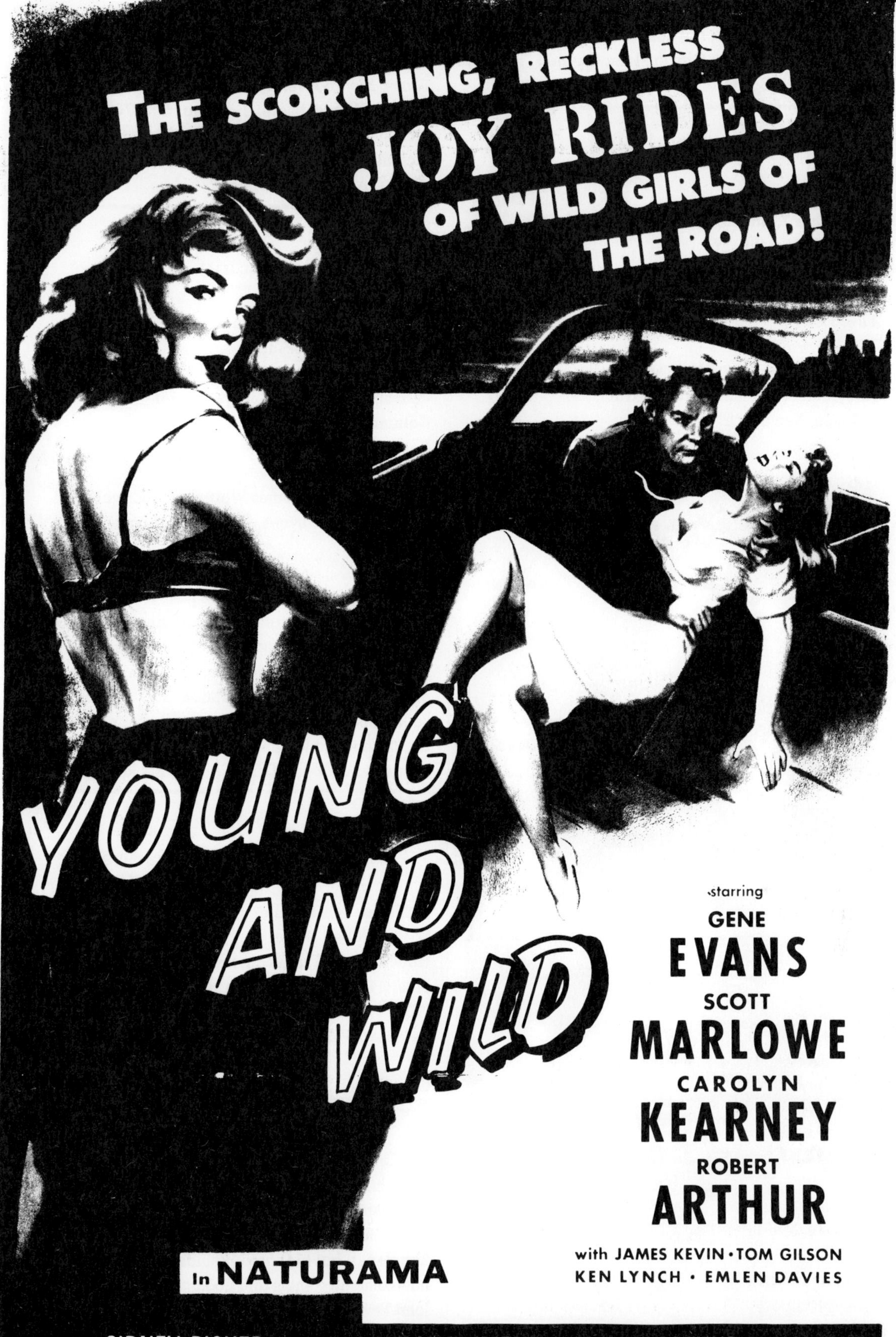
THE SCORCHING, RECKLESS
JOY RIDES
OF WILD GIRLS OF
THE ROAD!
YOUNG
AND
WILD
starring
GENE
EVANS
SCOTT
MARLOWE
CAROLYN
KEARNEY
ROBERT
ARTHUR
with JAMES KEVIN • TOM GILSON
KEN LYNCH • EMLEN DAVIES
In NATURAMA
Produced by SIDNEY PICKER • Directed by WILLIAM WITNEY • Written by ARTHUR T. HORMAN
REPUBLIC PICTURES Presents An ESLA Production

"We've got a right to live our own lives. Hot rod gangs tangling over juke box cuties!" Average programmer of hot rods and young love. The ads were quite a bit better than the picture. William Claxton later directed "The High Chaparral" and "Bonanza."

Young and Wild

Producer: Sidney Picker
Writer: Arthur T. Horman
Director: William Witney
Music: Gerald Roberts
Republic; 69 minutes
Released 4/24/58

Cast: Gene Evans, Scott Marlowe, Carolyn Kearney, Robert Arthur, Morris Ankrum, James Kevin, Tom Gilson, Ken Lynch

Originally sent out with *Juvenile Jungle* (and filmed in "Naturama"), *Young and Wild* told the story of hot cars, teen gangs, violence, death, and police capture. Marlowe also appeared in *The Young Guns, The Cool and the Crazy, Riot in Juvenile Prison,* and *The Subterraneans.* William Witney began directing in 1937 and turned out almost seventy films, mostly westerns. His teen films include *Juvenile Jungle, The Cool and the Crazy,* and, in 1965, *The Girls on the Beach.*

The Young Don't Cry

Producer: Philip A. Waxman
Writer: Richard Jessup
Director: Alfred L. Werker
Music: Ernest Gold, George Antheil
Columbia; 89 minutes
Released 8/57

Cast: Sal Mineo, James Whitmore, J. Carrol Nash, Roxanne, Gene Lyons, Paul Carr, Thomas Carlin, Leigh Whipper

"Explosive youth—a little past 17—nearly past saving." For once, truth in advertising—Mineo was only eighteen when he made this film, and as usual he gives a natural, confident performance. The story concerns an orphanage, violence, corruption, and freedom. Rather sentimental, but not bad. Alfred Werker began directing in 1929 and made almost fifty films, mostly quick B movies. *The Young Don't Cry* was his last film.

The Young Stranger

Producer: Stuart Miller
Writer: Robert Dozier
Director: John Frankenheimer
Music: Leonard Rosenman
RKO; 84 minutes
Released 5/57

Cast: James Macarthur, Kim Hunter, James Daly, James Gregory, Marian Seldes, Whit Bissell, Jeff Silver

Originally a TV drama, *The Young Stranger* was a thoughtful teen drama revolving around violence, parental tensions, arrests, and reconciliations. Macarthur, Helen Hayes's son, drew some good notices for this, his film debut, but his career foundered after that. The film had some nice shots and good performances. This was John Frankenheimer's first feature film, after several years as a TV director. He followed this with a tough hoodlum picture, *The Young Savages,* before going on to direct such classics as *Birdman of Alcatraz, The Manchurian Candidate, Seven Days in May,* and *Seconds.*

7. 1959-1962
The Lost Years

***A production still from* College Confidential*, with* Albert Zugsmith*, (center, in T-shirt),* Steve Allen, Mamie Van Doren, Conway Twitty, and Jayne Meadows.**

By 1959, most of the teen exploitation field was left to fast-buck entrepreneurs who had been late getting into the cycle and only churned out mediocre imitations of what had gone before. Some producers tried to create a trend out of beatnik themes—*The Beatniks, The Beat Generation, Beat Girl, The Rebel Set*—but most kids didn't seem to identify with the beat milieu. And anyway, the beatniks as portrayed onscreen were little more than lowlife scum—lazy, corrupt, degenerate, cruel, and overall rejects from society. The title song from *The Beat Generation,* sung by Mamie Van Doren, summed up the exploitation producers' attitude toward the beats: "Now your lives don't have any meaning/ Though you're living up a storm/ You'll do anything at all except conform/ You don't have much ambition/ You're just aimless and depressed/ You think you're really with it/ But you're missing all the best."

Albert Zugsmith, sensing an opening, produced some pictures where general teenage themes were sublimated in favor of sex and violence, and his pictures—*The Beat Generation, Girls Town, College Confidential, Platinum High School,* and *Sex Kittens Go to College*—did spice things up considerably; but he couldn't carry the whole field on his back. Roger Corman formed Filmgroup Pictures, which churned out supercheap teen flicks for awhile *(The Wild Ride, The Girl in Lover's Lane, T-Bird Gang, High School Big Shot),* but they were later eaten up by AIP, more to save the industry from embarrassment than anything else.

Most of the impetus from pop culture had dissipated by 1959. Many original rock 'n' rollers were dead, in the army, in jail, or banished by scandal. In an attempt to clean up their image, ward off complaints from parents, and soften the impact of the payola scandal, the music business and teen publications began to roll out an assembly line of cute, clean, and safe teen idols—Frankie Avalon, Paul Anka, Fabian, Bobby Rydell, and so on—and because of their all-American image, for the most part these artists steered clear of teen exploitation pictures. Without stars, and without new, wild, or exciting trends to capitalize on, the exploitation business was clearly adrift. In 1959, there were about twenty-five exploitation films distributed, and by 1960 that number had fallen to twenty. In 1961 and 1962, only ten teen-oriented pix hit the market, and many of these were merely low-budget, obscure, and regionally distributed films. The big wave of the mid fifties had definitely ended, and even AIP, the trendsetter and leader in the field, abandoned the market for a while. They bided their time with gladiator pictures, many bought from Europe and dubbed clumsily into English. This carried the company until Roger Corman came up with the Edgar Allan Poe series, which was very successful at the box office. These obviously had little to do with teenage culture, and the only trend that was deemed worthy for quicky films was the twist, a fad which was soon co-opted by adults, leaving the teens to try to find something else.

There were only a handful of teen-oriented films which made box-office noise between 1959 and 1962, and several of these also had strong adult audiences: *Blue Denim, Where the Boys Are, The Young Savages, Twist around the Clock, Hey, Let's Twist!,* and a few Presley vehicles. Most of the rest came and went and were barely noticed. Very few classics were released, with only *Girls Town* and *The Young Savages* rating high. Not only were the producers in trouble, the whole world of teen culture was in danger of disappearing. After making such an impact in the fifties, the early sixties were years of boring teen idols, and of the sublimation of real teenage life.

Among the few highlights of these years were the screen appearances of Mamie Van Doren. Many thought she was a third-in-line blond bombshell following Marilyn Monroe and Jayne Mansfield, but she was really in a different category. Monroe wanted to be taken seriously, and played roles exclusively in adult-oriented pictures. Mansfield was an incessant publicity hound and exhibitionist whose gift for satire was turned into a freak show. But Mamie seemed to relish the role of teen sexpot, and she set the style for all of the imitators that followed her in teen films. Her style walked the fine line between seriousness and camp, although her looks alone were enough to get the male audience into the theaters—even the stodgy *New York Times,* in their scathing review of *Untamed Youth,* said: "Miss Van Doren sings . . . to a variety of torrid gyrations that are guaranteed to keep any red-blooded Ameri-

***Just some good clean sing-a-long fun in this still from* College Confidential.**

can boy awake. Nothing else in this picture can make that claim." She had made three teen exploitation films in the fifties, *Running Wild* and two certified classics of the genre, *Untamed Youth* and *High School Confidential!,* and in the early sixties was teamed almost exclusively with producer Albert Zugsmith, who starred her in a long series of films—including the teen-styled *Girls Town, College Confidential,* and *Sex Kittens Go to College.* Zugsmith was a master of publicity, and Mamie soon became a household name, not only in America, but around the world as well. Her films with Zugsmith were meant to draw both adults and adventurous teens, and for the most part they succeeded in that goal. To adults she was just a sexpot; to teens she was probably some kind of wild fantasy figure.

By this time Mamie was in her upper twenties, and it was pretty impossible to get by as a teenager anymore, but she threw herself into these parts with abandon. Her acting skills may not have won her any awards, but she seemed to have a screen charisma that helped her steal every scene she was in. She was certainly sexy—and often posed scantily clad in men's magazines to drive home that point—but it was more than that. She seemed to be saying, "I know what I'm doing—I'm no dummy—I'm just having a lot of fun—so why don't you come along for the ride?" Her films were funny, campy, racy, silly, melodramatic, and sexy all wrapped together. She was a star when teen films had no stars, and lived a free-spirit life without embarrassment. She made a lot of money, but as she got older she hankered for a bit more. "It got so

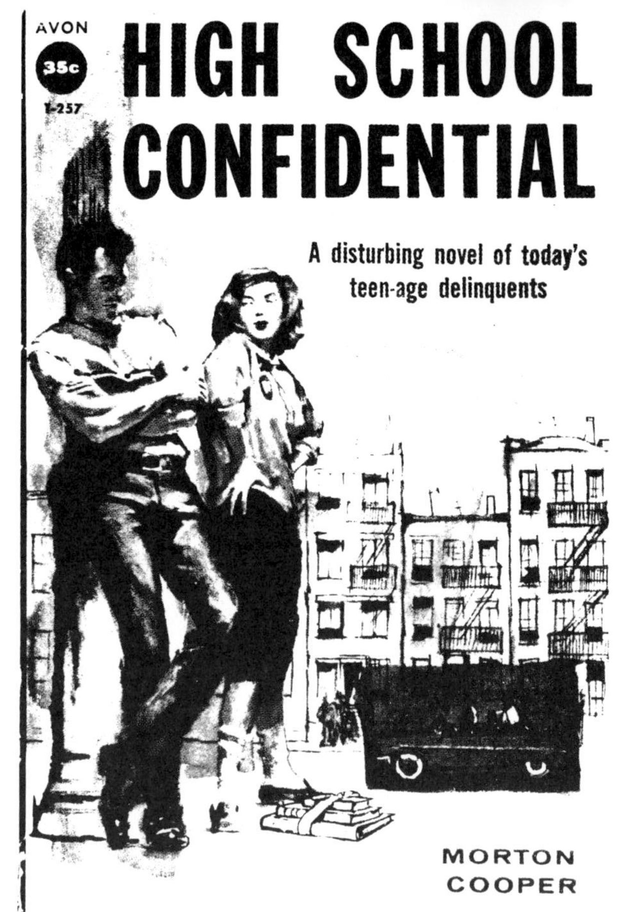

Novelizations of teen movies, even for some of the more obscure releases, were popular in the late fifties.

that everybody started calling you a dumb blonde onscreen and in magazines," she told me, "and it was really the ultimate put-down. And after a while you begin to think, 'Hey maybe I am dumb.' " As she neared thirty, although she still looked much younger, the parts stopped coming. The producers were on the prowl for new, less costly talent: "If you were thirty years old back then, your career was over. They'd rather find some eighteen-year-old to play these parts, and then dress them up with a lot of makeup to look older. It was easier for them to find someone young, dumb, and with the mind of an adolescent." Moreover, her name and image were locked into the fifties thing, and with the coming of the sixties generation, she seemed to be quickly forgotten. It's true, perhaps, that some laughed at Mamie Van Doren, and others, perhaps, lived vicariously through her, but I think the most winning way to appreciate her is to laugh and live with her, figuratively speaking.

Mamie Van Doren helps steam up the censors in this scene from **Untamed Youth.**

What is the real appeal of teen exploitation flicks? The answer to this is a bit different for each fan of the genre. It's often a bit disconcerting to find someone who appreciates something you like because you often find that they see something you don't see, or like it for different reasons than you do. In short, all fans are not created equal, and teen flicks work on many levels. For one, there is the pure camp value—the bad productions, the wooden acting, the unintentionally funny lines,

One of Mamie's sexiest films was* Girls Town, *which the producers described as "the fast-paced action-packed story of girls who have reached the age of decision — the age where they are physically mature, but emotionally immature — the age of the teens." Mamie played the part to the hilt.

and so on. The whole it's-so-bad-it's-good routine. This is undeniable. Then you have the examination of teen subculture from hair to lingo to clothes to music to image. There's reality, there's Hollywood, and there's much in between. These films mirror and often capture the teen culture of their era, as much as they helped to influence it. It's the old chicken-or-the-egg story. Did these films create and mass-market these trends, or were they merely a reflection of their times? The spectrum of teen films is so wide that there is not one simple answer. They surely did both at times, although they were usually somewhere in the middle. They certainly helped popularize personalities and trends, but they were hardly created in a void: they were exploiting the trends as well. Teen exploitation movies were well named because they exploited the fears, dreams, problems, loves, isolation, and confusion of the teen years. In a way, though, they were a safety net, because teens could see the pictures and say to themselves, "Gee, someone else has the same problems, fears, and hang-ups as I do," or, probably more

often, "Gee, I'm glad that my life isn't as bad off as the lives of the kids onscreen."

The teen flicks also provide a pure nostalgia element; like the darker side of *Grease* or "Happy Days," they remind us of our growing-up years, and offer a vision of a stark world with its own rules and regulations. Then of course there's the fun of seeing the faces of those who would later become famous stars in these early, tentative performances. That adds a historical perspective that many fans crave. And finally, there is the amazement that these films got made in the first place. Upon first seeing a teen exploitation film, many viewers think it to be an abberation or novelty. But when one looks at the wild advertising campaigns, and then realize that, with rock 'n' roll movies included, there were almost three hundred of these films produced in roughly fifteen years, the knowledge is staggering. I think it's best if one can appreciate these films on many levels—the camp, the nostalgia, the history, the famous faces, the genre plots, the cults, and the serious merits of some of the films. To merely appreciate them on a one-note basis, or to lump them together as all simple or the same, is a disservice to both the films and the viewer.

Filmography '59–'62

The Beat Generation

Producer: Albert Zugsmith
Writer: Richard Matheson
Director: Charles Haas
Music: Albert Glasser
MGM; 95 minutes
Released 7/3/59

Cast: Steve Cochran, Mamie Van Doren, Ray Danton, Fay Spain, Maggie Hayes, Jackie Coogan, Jim Mitchum, Cathy Crosby

As usual Albert Zugsmith latched on to a popular media phrase, but never really understood what it actually meant. This is basically a cops-and-robbers story with a "beat" background, centering around a psychopath, assaults, murder, a beat bar, and detectives. Besides the stellar main players, you can also catch Ray Anthony, Louis Armstrong, Dick Contino, Irish McCalla, Vampira, Billy Daniels, Maxie Rosenbloom, and Charles Chaplin, Jr. The film never really lived up to its billing: "Behind the weird, 'way out' world of the beatniks!" *The New York Times* called it "excruciating and tasteless—contrived and downright embarrassing. . . . These greasy little characters are seen sitting around, writhing to 'noise' records or noisier music, and raptly listening to what passes for poetry." Severe camp at best.

Beat Girl

Producer: George Willoughby
Writer: Dail Ambler
Director: Edmond T. Greville
Music: John Barry
Renown/Victoria; 85 minutes *(Beat Girl)*/91 minutes *(Wild for Kicks)*
Released 1960 *(Beat Girl)*, 10/20/61 *(Wild for Kicks)*

Cast: David Farrar, Noelle Adam, Gillian Hills, Adam Faith, Christopher Lee, Shirley Ann Field, Peter McEnery, Claire Gordon, Oliver Reed

A British import, released first as *Beat Girl* and then in a slightly racier version as *Wild for Kicks.* It's an involved story of a rebellious teen daughter, beatniks' clubs, stripteasers, wild parties, murder, and reconciliation. British pop star Adam Faith acts and sings, with a strong score by John Barry. Pretty adventurous and not bad. As the ads put it: "A story of todays lost generation." This was marketed more toward the Forty-second Street crowd than to teenagers, and is worth catching.

The racy British import,* Beat Girl, *also released as* Wild for Kicks *featured U.K. pop sensation, Adam Faith.

The Beatniks

Producer: Ron Miller
Writers: Arthur Julien, Paul Frees
Director: Paul Frees
Barjul International; 78 minutes
Released 1959

Cast: Tony Travis, Peter Breck, Karen Kadler, Joyce Terry, Charles Delaney

"A pulsating story of modern youth—defiant—explosive. Their password was mutiny against society!" A pretty obscure flick about singers, talent scouts, teen gangs, robbery, and miscellaneous mayhem. But really, not much about beatniks at all. Ginsberg and Kerouac probably couldn't believe what they had wrought—this certainly wasn't it.

Starring

STEVE COCHRAN · MAMIE VAN DOREN · RAY DANTON · FAY SPAIN

MAGGIE HAYES · JACKIE COOGAN and LOUIS ARMSTRONG AND HIS ALL-STARS

Guest Stars CATHY CROSBY · RAY ANTHONY · DICK CONTINO · IN CINEMASCOPE

Written by RICHARD MATHESON and LEWIS MELTZER · Directed by CHARLES HAAS

In this trade magazine advertisement for The Beat Generation, producer Albert Zugsmith ballyhooed the fact that "beatniks" were in, and, as usual, Zugsmith declared that he was first with their story.

As usual with exploitation films, the real story of "the beatniks" was lost between the sex, violence, and fantasy.

Because They're Young

Producer: Jerry Bresler
Writer: James Gunn
Director: Paul Wendkos
Music: Johnny Williams
Columbia; 102 minutes
Released 4/60

Cast: Dick Clark, Michael Callan, Tuesday Weld, Victoria Shaw, Roberta Shaw, Warren Berlinger, Doug McClure, Linda Watkins

Taken from the John Farris novel, *Harrison High,* this film is a tame and sappy story of a helpful teacher, tough students, fights, romance, and reconciliation—wimpy all the way. *Boxoffice* said: "With Clark plugging the picture, which also boasts innumerable record and merchandising tieups, it's a box office smash. Everything is handled in good taste . . . James Darren and Duane Eddy will have the youngsters squealing . . . Michael Callan, Warren Berlinger, and Linda Watkins are outstanding. . . ." As you can see, cross-promotion is nothing new.

The Big Night

Producer: Vern Alves
Writer: Ric Hardman
Director: Sidney Salkow
Music: Richard La Salle
Paramount; 74 minutes
Released 2/60

Cast: Randy Sparks, Venetia Stevenson, Dick Foran, Jesse White, Dick Contino, Frank Ferguson, Paul Langton, House Peters, Jr.

"For these two teenagers this was *The Big Night* until passions exploded into a nightmare of violence. . . ." Well, not exactly. This film tells the story of teens who find $200,000 and fight over it; teen confusion, chases, and death. But in the end they do the right thing and everything ties up nicely. Co-star Venetia Stevenson was a highly sought-after photographer's model (once voted "most beautiful model" by shutterbugs) and was also married to Don Everly for awhile. She also appeared in *Island of Lost Women, Studs Lonigan,* and *Horror Hotel,* among others.

The Bloody Brood

Producer: Julian Roffman
Writers: Elwood Ullman, Ben Kerner, Des Hardman
Director: Julian Roffman
Sutton/Allied Artists/Astor
Released 1959 (Sutton), 10/60 (Allied Artists), 1962 (Astor)

Cast: Jack Betts, Ronald Hartmann, Peter Falk, Barbara Lord, Robert Christie, William Brydon, Michael Zenon

This Canadian-made film features Peter Falk as a crazed gang leader who goes around with his beatnik pals and does things like feed people hamburgers with ground-up glass in them. This low-budget wonder played for many years under several different distributors wherever unsuspecting movie audiences could be found. Good thing this guy didn't know about Tylenol.

***Blue Denim* was a "sensitive" story about teen pregnancy and possible abortion. Adults and kids both flocked to see it.**

Blue Denim

Producer: Charles Brackett
Writers: Edith Sommer, Philip Dunne
Director: Philip Dunne
Music: Bernard Herrmann
20th Century–Fox; 89 minutes
Released 8/59

Cast: Carol Lynley, Brandon de Wilde, Macdonald Carey, Marsha Hunt, Warren Berlinger, Buck Class, Nina Shipman, Vaughn Taylor

Carol Lynley repeated her role from the successful stage play of the same name. It's a tale of delinquent parents, youthful pregnancy, almost abortion, reconciliation with parents, and happy marriage. Opinions varied on this "controversial" film. From *Boxoffice:* "It will be among the most discussed films of the year and build favorable word of mouth. This is a natural to attract the younger fans . . . tender, true, tremendously moving, compassionate film. . . ." *The New York Times,* on the other hand, called it "a situation exploited in a shamefully clumsy and artificial way. . . ." In some places, this was released as *Blue Jeans.*

Born to Be Loved

Producer: Hugo Haas
Writer: Hugo Haas
Director: Hugo Haas
Music: Franz Steininger
Universal; 82 minutes
Released 7/59

Cast: Carol Morris, Vera Vague, Hugo Haas, Dick Kallman, Jacqueline Fontaine, Billie Bird, Pat Goldin, Robert C. Foulk

Hugo Haas, the B-movie mogul with an Orson Welles complex, did everything in this movie except play the female lead. That was left to Miss Universe of 1957, Carol Morris, who is cast against type, playing, as *Motion Picture Herald* put it, "a plain, bespectacled Miss Nobody who wants a boyfriend." Hugo wants a new piano. "Who should she turn to in the city's crowded jungle? The eager middle-aged man who wanted to 'help'? The wise girls who knew all the ropes? Or the boy with a promise in his eyes?" In the end everybody gets what they want and more.

This trade magazine advertisement stressed the family values of* Born to be Loved*; other ads were more sensationalistic.

control should be exercised over after-school activity by activity-prone teenagers. . . ." This film was produced in 1959, but not released until 1961—perhaps they were waiting for the world to catch up with the vocalizing of Arch Hall, Jr.—he sings "Konga Joe" and "Monkey in My Hatband."

Mamie Van Doren gets cozy with Conway Twitty in **College Confidential.**

College Confidential

Producer: Albert Zugsmith
Writer: Irving Shulman
Director: Albert Zugsmith
Universal; 91 minutes
Released 8/60

Cast: Steve Allen, Jayne Meadows, Mamie Van Doren, Walter Winchell, Mickey Shaughnessy, Cathy Crosby, Herbert Marshall, Randy Sparks

"Actually based on a true story that shocked the nation," this film documents the woes of a well-meaning college professor who takes a student sex survey. The whole matter ends up in court and both sides get to air their views. Not very realistic (does that really matter here?), and as the *Times* remarked: "The students seem even more adolescent, apparently never touch a book, continually grasp each other instead, or slither around mouthing a kind of steamy, beatnik jargon. This is movie claptrap, best described as punk." But it sure is fun.

The Choppers

Producer: Arch Hall, Sr.
Writer: Arch Hall, Sr.
Director: Leigh Jason
Music: Al Pellegrini
Fairway-International; 66 minutes
Released 11/30/61

Cast: Arch Hall, Jr., Marianne Gaba, Robert Paget, Tom Brown, Rex Holman, Mickey Hoyle, Chuck Barnes, Bruno Ve Sota

You may think this is a motorcycle flick from its title, but the "Choppers" refers to a teen gang, not a biker club. This is a story of teens, hot-rod thefts, "chop shops," murder, and capture. From *Boxoffice:* "A modern teenage tragedy wherein a 'typical' American youth, receiving just about everything he wants in life from a 'typical' American family, proceeds to steal hubcaps, eventually stripping everything removable from automobiles. The path to inevitable tragedy is accompanied by dramatics the likes of which teenagers in the audience will readily identify themselves [sic]. There's a poignant lesson imparted via the perceptive Arch Hall screenplay, namely that parental

Crime and Punishment U.S.A.

Producer: Terry Sanders
Writer: Walter Newman
Director: Denis Sanders
Music: Herschel Burke Gilbert
Allied Artists; 78 minutes
Released 11/1/59

Cast: Mary Murphy, Frank Silvera, Marian Seldes, John Harding, Wayne Heffley, Eve McVeagh, Toni Merrill, Lew Brown, and introducing George Hamilton

"From the passion-twisted lives of today's lost generation," promised the ads, but believe it or not, this one was based on Fyodor Dostoyevski's *Crime and Punishment,* this time transplanted to Santa Monica's beat scene. All the essentials are there—robbery, murder, romance, blackmail, suicide, and confession. George Hamilton isn't bad in his big-screen debut, and even the *Times* had some nice things to say: "a commendable, interesting, if not entirely gripping drama . . . set in our current 'beat' milieu . . ." Denis Sanders later directed *Shock Treatment, Elvis—That's the Way It Is, Soul To Soul,* and *Invasion of the Bee Girls.*

Crime and Punishment U.S.A. "introduced" George Hamilton to the screen public — the rest is history.

Cry Tough

Producer: Harry Kleiner
Writer: Harry Kleiner
Director: Paul Stanley
Music: Laurindo Almeida
United Artists; 83 minutes
Released 8/59

Cast: John Saxon, Linda Cristal, Joseph Calleia, Arthur Batanides, Paul Clarke, Joe De Santis, Don Gordon, Perry Lopez, Harry Townes

Based on a story by Irving Shulman, this is a violent story of prison, robbery, murder, family discontent, police, and death. *Motion Picture Herald* said: "The appearance of John Saxon in the starring role will have undoubted appeal for teenagers, among whom he is very popular. Otherwise, the film will have to be sold on the basis of lurid action plus the sexy acting of Linda Cristal in the role of a tart. Action fans will like it . . . downbeat in the extreme, the backgrounds are depressing. . . ." The *Times* said: "Starts out as a promising picture about poor Puerto Ricans in N.Y. . . . but ends up as a routine gangster melodrama. John Saxon does such an obvious Marlon Brando imitation that the ethnic factor is completely confused. Linda Cristal's flashy, fierce eccentric nature is the most consistent point in the film." This was Paul Stanley's first feature film. He was also a successful TV director, working on such shows as "Then Came Bronson," "Mission Impossible," "The Untouchables," "Naked City," "Route 66," and many others. He later directed several TV movies.

The ads for Cry Tough exaggerated slightly when they called John Saxon and Linda Cristal "the hottest teenage stars on the screen today!"

Daddy-O

Producer: Elmer C. Rhoden, Jr.
Writer: David Moessinger
Director: Lou Place
Music: John Williams
American International; 74 minutes
Released 5/59

Cast: Dick Contino, Sandra Giles, Bruno Ve Sota, Gloria Victor, Ron McNeil, Jack McClure, Sonia Torgeson, Kelly Gordon

"Meet the 'beat'—daring to live, daring to love!" A quick little flick revolving around sports cars, drag racing, rock 'n' roll singers, the underworld, romance and triumph over evil. *Motion Picture Herald* offered: "Action and conversation are strictly in accordance with the modern day concept of the teenage and post-teen element, and it's to this segment of the audience that the producer has aimed the dramatic emphasis. Rating—Fair." Music by John Williams, who later struck megabucks with his themes for films including the *Star Wars* sagas. *Daddy-O* was also released as *Out on Probation,* and in the UK was issued as *Downbeat.* It was teamed here with *Road-Racers.*

Daddy-O *featured music by John Williams, later the creator of all the* Star Wars *themes.*

Another quickie from the Filmgroup Company,* Date Bait *promptly fled into obscurity.

Date Bait

Producer: O. Dale Ireland
Writer: Robert Slaven, Ethel Mae Page
Director: O. Dale Ireland
Filmgroup; 71 minutes
Released 1960

Cast: Gary Clarke, Marla Ryan, Richard Gering

"Too young to know; too wild to love; to eager to say I will. At 16 a girl learns about love—one way or the other!" Co-billed with *High School Caesar,* this quicky reveled in the problems of teenagers, parents, and boyfriends, with a bit of dope thrown in. All in all it's pretty wild, and not too bad. Don't miss "Date Bait Baby," sung by Reggie Perkins.

Diary of a High School Bride

Producer: Burt Topper
Writers: Burt Topper, Mark and Jan Lowell
Director: Burt Topper
Music: Ronald Stein
American International; 72 and 80 minutes (two versions)
Released 7/59

Cast: Anita Sands, Ronald Foster, Chris Robinson, Wendy Wilde, Louise Arthur, Barney Biro, Richard Gering, Peggy Miller.

"Does she get her lunch money from her husband or her daddy? I don't understand why you can't control yourself—you're only seventeen. You can't live in two houses—make up your mind—books or babies." Such are the problems of a seventeen-year-old girl who elopes with a twenty-four-year-old guy. Then follow the problems with parents, housekeeping struggles, other suitors, fights, and death. But finally, the happy lovers are reunited. This is not a classic flick. *Motion Picture Herald* said: "The film tells, within the confines of 80 minutes running time, of modern day teenage problems, entertainingly enough, without too much stress or sociological implications. It figures, with the aid of intelligent exploitation, to take care of apparent audience receptiveness." One exhibitor complained: "We do business on these kind, but honestly I think the average intelligence rate has dropped below the 14-year-old level." This went out with *Ghost of Dragstrip Hollow,* and Tony Casanova sings "The Diary Of A High School Bride."

Eegah!

Producer: Nicholas Merriwether
Writer: Bob Wehling
Director: Nicholas Merriwether
Fairway-International; 90 minutes
Released 6/8/62

Cast: Arch Hall, Jr., Marilyn Manning, Richard Kiel, William Watters, Ray Dennis Steckler, Carolyn Brandt

This wild low-budget film tells the unbelievable story of a teen girl and a discovered giant: giant loves girl, and police kill giant. As awful as it is, one exhibitor had some kind words: "Picture is fairly good, and the color and photography are excellent. This is good double-bill material and did excellent business here." *Eegah!*

The Explosive Generation

Producer: Stanley Colbert
Writer: Joseph Landon
Director: Buzz Kulik
Music: Hal Borne
United Artists; 89 minutes
Released 9/21/61

Cast: William Shatner, Patty McCormack, Lee Kinsolving, Billy Gray, Steve Dunne, Arch Johnson, Virginia Field, Phillip Terry

This moralistic film tells the story of a teacher who offers sex-education in school—a tale of parental uproar, school freedom, a student strike, and final victory for students and teachers. Pretty tame, but fun to see the familiar faces. Besides the stars listed above, you can see Edward Platt, Jocelyn Brando, and Beau Bridges. This was Buzz (Seymour) Kulik's first feature film—he later did *Warning Shot, Riot,* and almost two dozen TV movies.

Force of Impulse

Producer: Peter Gayle
Writer: Francis Swann
Director: Saul Swimmer
Music: Joseph Liebman, Lionel Hampton
Sutton; 84 minutes
Released 11/1/61

Cast: Robert Alda, J. Carrol Naish, Tony Anthony, Jeff Donnell, Jody McCrea, Brud Talbot, Lionel Hampton, Christina Crawford

Filmed in and around Miami Beach, this low-budget film dealt with class conflicts and teen love, hot rods, robbery, parental problems, and final reconciliation. *Boxoffice* said: "A hard hitting, ever realistic study of modern-day American teenage problems . . . played out spiritedly by Tony Anthony and a bright new ingenue Teri Hope . . . rousing entertainment. . . ." This was the battle of movie-star offspring—Jody McCrea was the son of Joel McCrea, while Christina *Mommie Dearest* Crawford was the daughter of Joan. Jody later had a running role in the AIP beach-movie series, while Saul Swimmer later directed *Mrs. Brown, You've Got a Lovely Daughter* and *The Concert for Bangladesh.*

Ghost of Dragstrip Hollow

Producer: Lou Rusoff
Writer: Lou Rusoff
Director: William Hole Jr.
Music: Ronald Stein
American International; 65 minutes
Released 7/59

Cast: Jody Fair, Martin Braddock, Russ Bender, Leon Tyler, Elaine Dupont, Henry McCann, Sanita Pelkey, Dorothy Neumann

This was a sequel to *Hot Rod Gang,* unfortunately minus Gene Vincent. It's the story of a teen car club, drag racers, a haunted house, funny cars, and the solving of the big creature mystery. It's all pretty light stuff. *Ghost of Dragstrip Hollow* was released on a double bill with *Diary of a High School Bride,* and featured some early music by Nick Venet and one song ("I Promise You") by Bruce Johnston, later to become a member of the Beach Boys. You can hear Venet's twangy instrumentals "Charge" and "Geronimo" about four times each—coincidentally they were both on American International records. This film has some okay special effects, lots of jive lingo, and a female pajama party for the guys. Jody Fair also appeared in *High School Confidential, Attack of the Giant Leeches, Hot Rod Gang,* and *The Brain Eaters.* William Hole, Jr., directed over 150 TV shows, including forty episodes of "Peyton Place."

For Diary of a High School Bride, *another ad campaign that was more adventurous than the finished product.*

Girls Town ***was a pretty wild and classic teen flick, featuring a host of name talent.***

The gang takes time out for a soda while figuring out what scam to run next in this scene from **High School Big Shot.**

The Girl in Lover's Lane

Producer: Robert Roark
Writer: Jo Heims
Director: Charles R. Rondeau
Music: Ronald Stein
Filmgroup; 78 minutes
Released 1960

Cast: Brett Halsey, Joyce Meadows, Lowell Brown, Jack Elam, Selette Cole, Emile Meyer

This low-budget film, teamed with the equally cheesy *The Wild Ride,* was a story of runaways, romance, murder, confession, and salvation. Even the trade magazine *Boxoffice,* which usually found something worthwhile in any release, said: "Only the unimaginative and naive of audiences are going to swallow all that transpires on the screen . . . hackneyed, heavy handed, and a slow crawl. . . ." Said the ads: "Too young to know, too reckless to care . . ." And, probably, too bored to watch. Director Rondeau directed a dozen features and 350 hours of TV.

Girls Town

Producer: Albert Zugsmith
Writer: Robert Smith
Director: Charles Haas
Music: Van Alexander
MGM; 92 minutes
Released 10/9/59

Cast: Mamie Van Doren, Mel Torme, Paul Anka, Ray Anthony, Maggie Hayes, Cathy Crosby, Gigi Perreau, Elinor Donahue

"Anything goes in *Girls Town*—last stop on the road to nowhere." It's also the last stop for Mamie Van Doren, as she is framed and sent up for a crime she didn't commit. There's a lot of tease in this film, and it's fun watching the famous names go through their paces. Besides the stars listed above, you can spot Gloria Talbott, Sheilah Graham, Jim Mitchum, Dick Contino, Harold Lloyd, Jr., Charles Chaplin, Jr., and the Platters. What were *they* doing in girls town? A benefit? Director Haas was also responsible for *Summer Love, The Beat Generation,* and *Platinum High School.* On TV he directed "Man from U.N.C.L.E.," "Alfred Hitchcock Presents," "The Outer Limits," "Route 66," "Leave It to Beaver," and much more. *Girls Town* was rereleased in 1961 as *The Innocent and the Damned.* At the time of its original release, *Variety* said: "At a time when Hollywood is facing a rising storm of opposition about films with adult themes and adult treatment, it cannot help but be ammunition for the opposition. In the case of *Girls Town* there is not a mitigating ounce of artistry or the pretense of it." Sounds right to us.

High School Big Shot

Producer: Stan Bickman
Writer: Joel Rapp
Director: Joel Rapp
Filmgroup; 70 minutes
Released 7/59

Cast: Tom Pittman, Virginia Aldridge, Howard Viet, Malcolm Atterbury, Stanley Adams

"The kid who showed the big-time how!" This went out on a bill with *T-Bird Gang*, and cost about as much as a T-Bird. It's the tale of a high school brain and how he ultimately executes a heist that "dazzles the underworld." But not for long, and all sorts of mayhem erupts. Roger Corman was executive producer, which means he skipped lunch one day to oversee this flick. You can also catch Pittman in *The Young Stranger, No Time to Be Young,* and *Bernadine.*

High School Caesar

Producer: O. Dale Ireland
Writers: Robert Slaven, Ethel Mae Page
Director: O. Dale Ireland
Filmgroup; 63 minutes
Released 1960

Cast: John Ashley, Lowell Brown, Steve Stevens, Judy Nugent, Gary Vinson, Daria Massey

"Mob rule in a high school—he had more rackets than Al Capone!" John Ashley works all sorts of scams, instead of studying—but eventually good triumphs over his evil. Ashley was one of the few actors who made the transition from delinquent movies into the beach-party romps of the sixties, and was still going in the late sixties in biker and horror films. *High School Caesar* went out on a double bill with *Date Bait.* Don't miss hearing the title tune sung by Reggie Perkins. There's nothing quite like it.

Jacktown

Producer: William Martin
Writer: William Martin
Director: William Martin
Music: Aldo Provenzano
Pictorial International; 62 minutes
Released 8/1/62

Cast: Patty McCormack, Richard Meade, Douglas Rutherford, Mike Tancredi, Johanna Douglas, John Anthony, Gordon Grant, Alice Gordon

An obscure film shot on location at South Michigan Prison in Jackson, Michigan—hence the title *Jacktown.* It's the story of a juvenile delinquent, a robbery, a statutory rape charge, a prison, a riot, an escape, love with the warden's daughter, and eventual voluntary return to prison—all in sixty-two minutes. A rare but classic Patty McCormack role as the warden's daughter. After this film, McCormack made mostly guest spots on TV shows, until she returned to films in the late sixties—this time with a vengeance—in *Maryjane, The Mini-Skirt Mob, Born Wild, The Young Runaways,* and others.

Juke Box Racket

Producers: Jim Geallis, George Barris
Director: Barry Mahon
Music: Steve Karmen, Peter Szabo
Brenner Films; 62 minutes
Released 5/60

Cast: Arlene Corwin, Lou Anne Lee, Beverly Nazarow, Seymour Cassel, Peter Clune, Steve Karmen

A cheap and quick little film concerning teens, mobsters, and juke boxes. Steve Karmen later became a successful jingle writer, while Barry Mahon became king of the nudie-sexploitation boom in the sixties. From 1961 to 1970, he wrote, produced, or directed over forty films. Some of the highlights were: *Hollywood Nudes Report, Nudes, Inc., Confessions of a Bad Girl, Fanny Hill Meets Lady Chatterly,* and *Forbidden Flesh.* A true artiste.

Dennis Hopper was one of the young "punks" in this 1960 story of intimidation, directed by cult star Phil Karlson.

Key Witness

Producer: Kathryn Hereford
Writers: Alfred Brenner, Sidney Michaels
Director: Phil Karlson
Music: Charles Wolcott
MGM; 82 minutes
Released 10/6/60

Cast: Jeffrey Hunter, Pat Crowley, Dennis Hopper, Joby Baker, Susan Harrison, Johnny Nash, Corey Allen, Frank Silvera

This is the tough story of a teen gang who try to force a family not to testify in a criminal case. "The young punks . . . and Ruby was their girl." A good group of character actors do a fine job with their roles, and Phil Karlson's direction is taut and often violent. Karlson began directing in 1944, and after two dozen quickies for Monogram and Columbia he became known for his hard-hitting and violent films. Some of his classics include: *Kansas City Confidential, The Phenix City Story, The Brothers Rico,* and *Hell to Eternity.* In the 1970s, when Karlson was in his mid-sixties, he was still at it, turning out *Ben, Walking Tall,* and *Framed.*

Married Too Young

Writer: Nathanial Tanchuck
Director: George Moskov
Music: Manuel Francisco
Headliner; 80 minutes
Released 5/22/62

Cast: Harold Lloyd, Jr., Jana Lund, Anthony Dexter, Marianna Hill, Trudy Marshall, Brian O'Hara, Nita Loveless, Lincoln Demyan

A story of elopement, career, and parental problems, stolen cars, police capture, and the inevitable happy ending. Harold Lloyd, Jr., was a fixture in such teen films as *Girls Town* and *Platinum High School,* but here he finally gets to play the lead, opposite B juvenile-delinquent star Jana Lund. This low-budget production didn't do them justice, however.

Night of Evil

Producers: Richard Galbreath, Lou Perry
Writer: Louis Perino
Director: Richard Galbreath
Music: Arnold Holop
Astor/Sutton; 88 minutes
Released 1/27/62

Cast: Earl Wilson (narrator), Lisa Gaye, William Campbell, Lynn Bernay, Remo Pisani, George Dietsel, Joseph Garri, Don De Leo, Burtt Harris

This is a busy story concerning teen attacks, reform school for girls, beauty pagents, a criminal husband, strippers, attempted suicide, arrest, and prison. Said *Boxoffice:* "Together, they serve as forceful and penetrating a study of teenage misdirection and casual disregard for parental respect as has been viewed in many months. . . . Brisk paced, taut, and sometimes tearful melodrama . . . It adheres, more or less, to what has gone before in attractions of this genre. The quality of emoting is compact and convincing enough to make this dramatic entertainment." William Campbell also graced *Running Wild, Love Me Tender, Eighteen and Anxious,* and *The Young Racers,* among others.

Platinum High School

Producer: Red Doff (an Albert Zugsmith Production)
Writer: Robert Smith

Director: Charles Haas
MGM; 93 minutes
Released 5/13/60

Cast: Mickey Rooney, Terry Moore, Dan Duryea, Yvette Mimieux, Conway Twitty, Jimmy Boyd, Harold Lloyd, Jr., Richard Jaeckel, Warren Berlinger

Another Zugsmith exploitation wonder, this one placing the emphasis on violence rather than sex (though there's some of that too). It's the tale of a boys' military school, the murder of a student in a hazing, a cover-up, a murderous riot, and final correction. Said *Boxoffice:* "If one cares to overlook the implausibility of the basic plot idea and the several unbelievable situations it develops, there's plenty of entertainment in this photoplay—action, violence, suspense, mystery, and touches of sex. The teenage ticket buyers, who as a class are not too critical of story inconsistencies, are almost certain to be enthusiastic about all the derring-do, most especially since the yarn revolves around youngsters of their own age group. That should add up to substantial grosses with emphasis on drive-ins and subsequent situations. . . ." But those fuddy-duddies at the *Times* didn't see it that way: "A shoddy and obviously inexpensive exploitation melodrama. On the sidelines a pair of rock 'n' roll singers, Conway Twitty and Jimmy Boyd, are seen, but fortunately not heard as delinquent students, while Yvette Mimieux, a bikini clad blonde, inexplicably residing at the all-male school, provides ample scenic decoration. . . ." We like watching Rooney beat up guys twice his size—only in the movies.

EXPOSING THE TRUTH
about a very "Exclusive" Private School where money can buy everything...*even MURDER!*

METRO-GOLDWYN-MAYER Presents
MICKEY ROONEY · TERRY MOORE · DAN DURYEA
in AN ALBERT ZUGSMITH PRODUCTION

Co-Starring YVETTE MIMIEUX · Introducing CONWAY TWITTY
Screen Play by ROBERT SMITH · Based On a Story by HOWARD BRESLIN · Directed by CHARLES HAAS · Produced by RED DOFF

A strange and violent melodrama from the house of Albert Zugsmith,* Platinum High School *almost made 1960 worthwhile.

The Prime Time

Producer: Hershell Gordon Lewis
Writer: Robert Abel
Director: Hershell Gordon Lewis
Music: Marty Rubenstein, Buddy Frye
Essanjay; 76 minutes
Released 3/60

Cast: Jo Ann LeCompte, Frank Roche, Ray Gronwold, James Brooke, Maria Pavelle, Betty Senter, Karen Black, Robert Major

This is a pretty racy film, probably not marketed to teenagers, concerning a teen girl acting adult, beatnik clubs, attacks, attempted murder, death, blackmail, and some seminude sequences. Filmed in Chicago, this was Hershell Gordon Lewis's first film; later he delved into the world of blood feasts and the like and became known as "The Wizard of Gore." *The Prime Time* also features Karen Black's first screen appearance, this at age seventeen.

The Proper Time

Producer: Tom Laughlin
Writer: Tom Laughlin
Director: Tom Laughlin
Music: Shelly Manne
Lopert
Released 1960

Cast: Tom Laughlin, Nira Monsour, Richard Shannon, Norma Quine

Another morality play from Tom Laughlin, wherein he battles seduction and the confusion of life in general. Laughlin was only twenty-two at the time of this film, and he later went on to make *The Born Losers* and the fantastically successful series of Billy Jack films. As the ads blared: "The no-punches-pulled story of a generation that has torn the word 'morals' out of the dictionary—they just couldn't wait for the 'proper time.' " This one's hard to find.

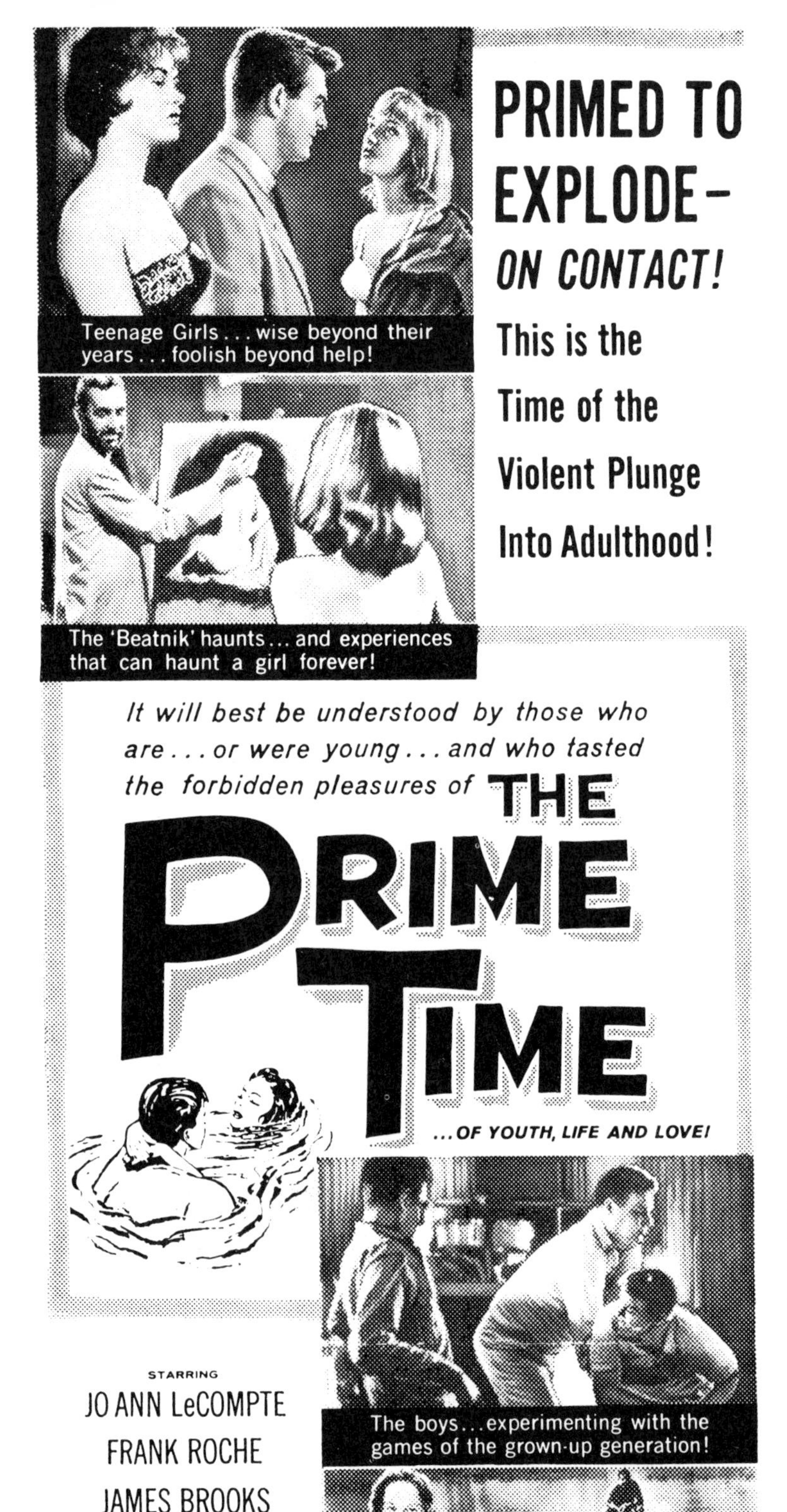

***The Prime Time* was directed by Hershell Gordon Lewis, who later became famous for his low-budget blood and gore pictures.**

This obscure Tom Laughlin extravaganza featured music by Shelly Manne and his band of jazz all-stars.

The Pusher

Producers: Gene Milford, Sidney Katz
Writer: Harold Robbins
Director: Gene Milford
Music: Raymond Scott
United Artists; 81 minutes
Released 12/59

Cast: Kathy Carlyle, Felice Orlandi, Douglas F. Rodgers, Sloan Simpson, Robert Lansing, Sara Aman, Jim Boles

Teamed with *Vice Raid, The Pusher* is a tough, realistic drama for the action fan, with a lot of on-site Manhattan street footage. It's a tale of police problems dealing with drug addiction, murder, addicts, confusion, a policeman's daughter hooked on dope and later cured, and a final reconciliation with Dad. "The shock-packed story of today's young addicts." Said *Boxoffice:* "A topical action programmer . . . realistic, documentary like quality and the use of unfamiliar faces adds to the authenticity. There is no attempt to gloss over close-ups of the hypodermic needle or the addicts delirious struggles. . . . Felice Orlandi is fascinatingly evil in the title role. . . ." Screenplay by trash king Harold Robbins, from a novel by Evan *Blackboard Jungle* Hunter.

Rebel Angel

Producer: James J. Gannon
Writer: Denny Ross
Director: Lamont Douglas
Music: The Stardusters
Hoffman Distributors; 96 minutes
Released 6/62

Cast: Patricia Manning, Richard Flynn, Tom Falk, Denny Ross

This is an obscure film about confused teen love, child murder, and abandonment. If you can find it, you deserve what you get.

The Rebel Set

Producer: Earle Lyon
Writers: Louis Vittes, Bernard Girard
Director: Gene Fowler, Jr.
Music: Paul Dunlap
Allied: Artists; 72 minutes
Released 6/28/59

Cast: Gregg Palmer, Kathleen Crowley, Edward Platt, Ned Glass, John Lupton, Don Sullivan, Vikki Dougan, I. Stanford Jolley

"The screens' big jolt about the Beatniks—the drifters, the hipsters, and the hot sisters." Once again Hollywood portrays the beats as a bunch of lazy criminals . . . well, at least they were wrong on one count. This is a story of beats, rackets, armored car theft, murder, and capture. *Motion Picture Herald* said: "Good action, suspense, and surprise developments make this worthy of better than average program picture attention." Features a rare screen appearance by Vikki "the Back" Dougan, who became famous in the late fifties for the daring plunges in her dresses—only hers were in the back, rather than in the front like most of the fifties sex symbols. Director Fowler also turned out *I Was a Teenage Werewolf, Gang War,* and *I Married a Monster from Outer Space.* For TV he directed many shows, including "Rawhide," "Perry Mason," and "Gunsmoke." *The Rebel Set* was also released as *Beatsville.*

Riot in Juvenile Prison

Producers: Robert E. Kent, Edward L. Cahn
Writers: George O'Hanlon, Tommy Noonan
Director: Edward L. Cahn
Music: Emil Newman
United Artists; 71 minutes
Released 4/59

Cast: Jerome Thor, Marcia Henderson, Scott Marlowe, John Hoyt, Dick Tyler, Virginia Aldridge, Dorothy Provine, Jack Grinnage

"The wildest dolls, the toughest guys thrown together in a co-ed reform school—delinquent and damned!" This is the story of a state training school, politics, inhumane treatment, coed rehabilitation, full-scale riot, and a caring psychiatrist who has his way. Scott Marlowe is good, and writer Tommy Noonan gained fame for either

***The Pusher** was written by Harold Robbins, whose career could only decline after this masterwork.*

Another look into the weird, way-out world of the Beatniks — accuracy in media hadn't been invented yet.

acting with or directing the three major sex symbols of the fifties—Marilyn Monroe, Jayne Mansfield, and Mamie Van Doren. Tough job, but somebody's got to do it.

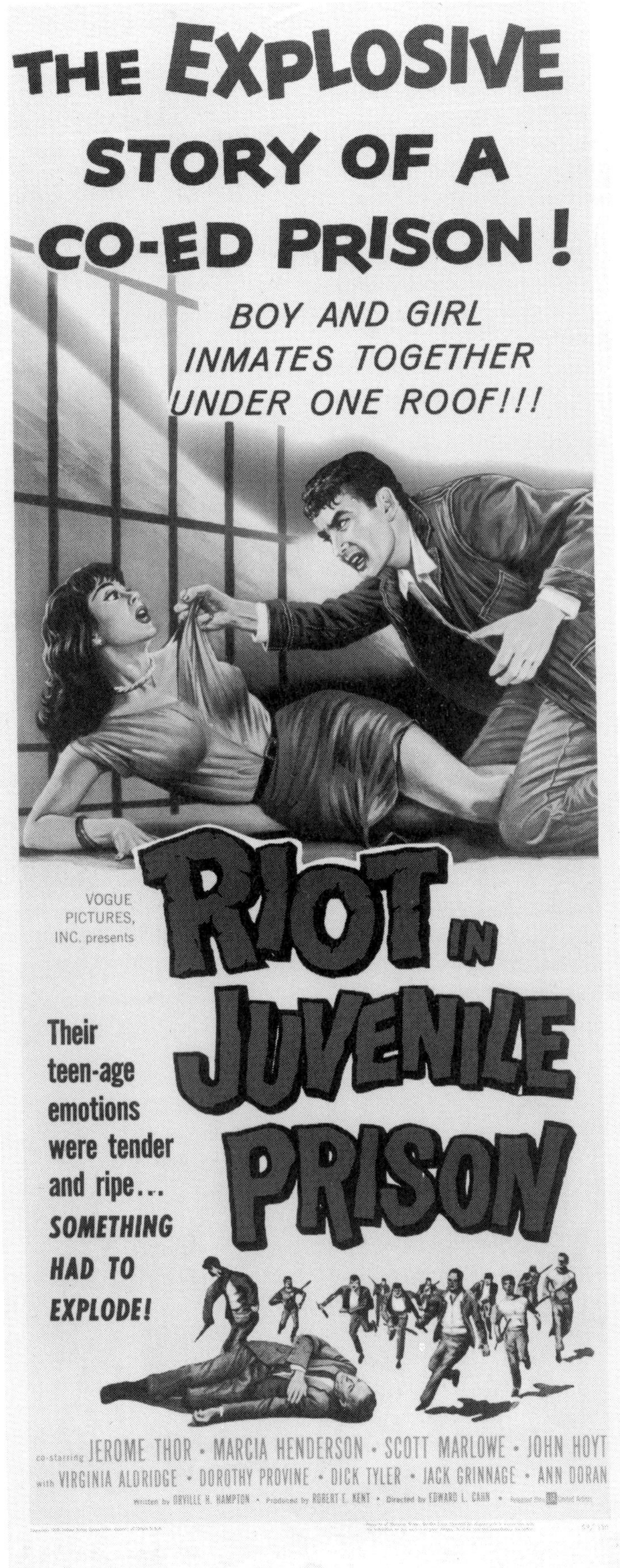

Another teens in prison flick — weren't there any good teens in the fifties?

Road-Racers

Producer: Stanley Kallis
Writers: Ed Lakso, Stanley Kallis
Director: Arthur Swerdloff
Music: Richard Markowitz
American International; 78 minutes
Released 5/59

Cast: Sally Fraser, Alan Dinehart, Jr., Skip Ward, Joel Lawrence, Marian Collier, Irene Windust, John Shay, Michael Gibson

A cheap little film about race drivers, reckless conduct, death, girlfriend problems, and a happy ending. "Screeching hell on wheels—is it sport or murder?" Or is it worth watching? Only for the dedicated. Director Swerdloff later did some highly respected documentaries for television.

Runaway

Producer: Elliot H. Kone
Writer: Joseph Caldwell
Director: Elliot H. Kone
Group 9; 76 minutes
Released 1960

Cast: Ludwig Salem, Marge Andrews, Stuart Stoddard, Brandon Stoddard, Estelle Owens, Eulalie Noble

This started out as a school project for professor Kone's film class. It turned into a feature film shot in New Haven and featuring all local talent. It's a story of parental neglect, hooky playing and petty theft, a boy kicked out of his home, his drifting, and parental reconciliation. *Boxoffice* was quite taken with the film: "It delves adroitly into the whys and wherefores of juvenile delinquency. Stuart Stoddard displays a refreshing grip on an adolescent's confused gropings for maturity and understanding in a hostile world. Given the benefit of extensive promotion, Stoddard can be built as a new James Dean." Trying to find this film would probably be as hard as trying to find Stoddard.

Sex Kittens Go to College

Producer: Albert Zugsmith
Writer: Robert Hill
Director: Albert Zugsmith

Is there a metaphor in this graphic that we're missing?

Mamie Van Doren poses with co-star in one of 1960s dumbest films — Sex Kittens Go to College.

Music: Dean Elliott
Allied Artists; 94 minutes
Released 8/60

Cast: Mamie Van Doren, Tuesday Weld, Mijanou Bardot, Mickey Shaughnessy, Louis Nye, Pamela Mason, Marty Milner, Conway Twitty

Zugsmith strikes again! This time with a really lame story about strippers, robots, and college. The film is packed with famous faces like the ones listed above, (Mijanou was Brigitte's younger sister, by the way), but also peppered with Jackie Coogan, John Carradine, Vampira, Charles Chaplin, Jr., and Harold Lloyd, Jr. The final title was toned down from the prerelease hoopla of *Sexpots Go to College* and *Teacher Was a Sexpot.* Theater owners were mixed on this one. One said: "Used for late show on Saturday night for the teenagers. They loved it!" Another one reported: "The poorest picture we have had since *Top Banana* several years ago. Eighteen walked out the first hour, all teenagers, and five of them asked for their money back." For the dedicated only.

Speed Crazy

Producer: Richard Bernstein
Writers: Richard Bernstein, Georg Waters
Director: William Hole, Jr.
Music: Dick La Salle
Allied Artists; 75 minutes
Released 6/28/59

Cast: Brett Halsey, Yvonne Lime, Charles Wilcox, Slick Slavin, Jacqueline Ravell, Baynes Barron, Regina Gleason, Keith Byron

"From juke-joint to dragstrip . . . it's the livin' end." Here's a story of a cruel sports car racer who's crazy for girls, fights, murder, and ultimate death. Said *Motion Picture Herald:* "There is action aplenty in this story of a youthful psychopathic soldier of misfortune who seeks escape from a complex of being crowded and pushed around by people—a psychosis which he attributes personally to a bad experience with some older boys during his childhood at an orphanage. Brett Halsey's star potential is wide, and Yvonne Lime shows much promise in her co-starring role." Not bad, and don't miss comic rock 'n' roll singer Slick Slavin warbling "Speed Crazy" and "Ghost Town Rock." Halsey continued onward in a series of less than inspiring films, but, sadly, this was Lime's last screen role, after a run of strong teen films.

One of the more serious teen films, the executive producer of* Take a Giant Step *was Burt Lancaster.

Swingin' Along

Producer: Jack Leewood
Writer: Jameson Brewer
Director: Charles Barton
Music: Arthur Morton, Lionel Newman
20th Century–Fox; 74 minutes
Released 2/62

Cast: Tommy Noonan, Peter Marshall, Barbara Eden, Connie Gilchrist, Carol Christenson, Alan Carney, Mike Mazurki, Tommy Farrell

A silly story, allegedly a comedy, about a bumbling delivery boy, song sharks, a songwriting contest, and final victory. You can catch Ted Knight as a priest, but more importantly, Bobby Vee and Ray Charles performing some tunes. Otherwise, a pretty painful experience.

Take a Giant Step

Producer: Julius J. Epstein
Writers: Louis S. Peterson, Julius J. Epstein
Director: Philip Leacock
Music: Jack Marshall
United Artists; 100 minutes
Released 12/59

Cast: Johnny Nash, Estelle Hemsley, Ruby Dee, Frederick O'Neal, Ellen Holly, Pauline Meyers, Beah Richards, Royce Wallace

"Here's the real rage behind today's tormented 'blue jeans' generation! Here's what makes them tough . . . what makes them tremble . . . what makes them take a giant step!" Another film of teen turbulence, this time with a racial angle. Executive producer was Burt Lancaster. The *Times* said: "Some interesting and possibly poignant problems of an intelligent, sensitive Negro lad, growing up in a socially strained environment of a middle-class white community, are handled in a shoddy, clumsy fashion in the unworthy film that has been made from Louis Peterson's play, *Take a Giant Step.* Weak motivations and jerky transitions in the script. . . . The picture is driven by its director at a wobbly, senseless pace, and is so full of angry shouting characters that it almost leaves one deaf." Philip Leacock made seventeen features and over a dozen TV movies.

T-Bird Gang

Producer: Stan Bickman
Writers: John Brinkley, Tony Miller
Director: Richard Harbinger
Music: Shelley Manne
Filmgroup; 75 minutes
Released 7/59

Cast: Ed Nelson, John Brinkley, Pat George, Beach Dickerson, Tony Miller

Released on a twin bill with *High School Big Shot, T-Bird Gang* was a cheap little film about a youngster avenging his father's death, featuring gang syndicates, the gang's demise, and revenge for the son. Said *Motion Picture Herald:* "It has to do with that element of restless American youth not long out of high school and not certain of career resolvement. . . . Of promotion value is the fact that jazzdom's own Shelley Manne was responsible for the musical score. Rating—Fair." Filmgroup was the poor man's AIP, and their films showed it.

Teenage Millionaire

Producer: Howard B. Kreitsek
Writer: H. B. Cross (Harry Spalding)
Director: Lawrence F. Doheny
United Artists; 84 minutes
Released 8/17/61

Cast: Jimmy Clanton, Rocky Graziano, ZaSu Pitts, Diane Jergens, Joan Tabor, Sid Gould, Maurice Gosfield, Eileen O'Neill

A pretty bad film which tells the story of an inheritance, a teen idol, hit records, the army, and future plans. "Dig this deal—a free record of Jimmy Clanton singing the title song to every teenager who buys a ticket." Does that mean that they didn't have to *see* the movie? The film is saved by guest appearances by Jackie Wilson, Chubby Checker, Dion, and Marv Johnson. Filmed in "Musicolor."

Teenage Zombies

Producer: Jerry Warren
Writer: Jacques Le Cotier
Director: Jerry Warren
Music: Erich Bromberg
Governor Films; 73 minutes
Released 4/60

Cast: Katherine Victor, Chuck Niles, Don Sullivan, Steve Conte, Jay Hawk

This low-budget oddity was shot in 1957, but not released until 1960. It's the story of a crazed female doctor, a desert island, nerve gas, and zombiefied teenagers. Hey, their parents thought they were zombies *before* the nerve gas. But this was pretty tame stuff for Jerry Warren, who later gave us such epics as *Invasion of the Animal People, The Violent and the Damned, Curse of the Stone Hand,* and *The Wild World of Batwoman.*

Teen-Agers from Outer Space

Producer: Tom Graeff
Writer: Tom Graeff

Teenage Zombies — just a bunch of nice kids out for a day of fun.

Teen-agers From Outer Space — *hey, is that a pin-cushion or what?*

Director: Tom Graeff
Warner Bros.; 86 minutes
Released 6/20/59

Cast: David Love, Dawn Anderson, Harvey B. Dunn, Bryant Grant, Tom Lockyear, King Moody, Helen Sage, Frederic Welch

"Teenage hoodlums from another world, on a horrendous raygun rampage—before, a beautiful girl—one moment later, a skeleton!" This low-budget film was picked up by Warner Bros., probably so they could have a teen-horror film like all the other companies. But this one was so embarrassing that I'm sure they only bought the exploitable title, and figured they'd make a few quick bucks. Said one exhibitor: "Poorest picture we have played in this theatre since it opened 15 years ago. I can't understand why they make a cheap picture like this. It's even worse than a black and white 60-minute western. Acting, photography (terrible), direction, are all very poor. Biz was average. I can only say to leave it in the cans." Young triple threat Tom Graeff was not heard from again.

This Rebel Breed — *I said I wanted a Coke, not Pepsi, you idiots!*

This Rebel Breed

Producer: William Rowland
Writer: Morris Lee Green
Director: Richard L. Bare
Music: Ronald Stein
Warner Bros.; 90 minutes
Released 3/19/60

Cast: Rita Moreno, Mark Damon, Gerald Mohr, Jay Novello, Eugene Martin, Tom Gilson, Richard Rust, Douglas Hume

"With blazing impact the screen looks squarely into the face of today's wild teenage emotions caught in the crossfire of love and hate!" Another entry in the interracial teen-gang sweepstakes, this time throwing in violence, sex, dope, and more violence. Said the *Times:* "Narcotics, rock 'n' roll, interracial love and war, and assorted forms of competative violence . . . substitutes action for insights but maintaining enough excitement to place it a cut or two above the usual sensationalized products of the genre." Although Bare had directed about a dozen features, he moved over to television after this film, working on "77 Sunset Strip," "The Twilight Zone," "Green Acres," "Petticoat Junction," "The Donna Reed Show," and many others. After roles in almost two dozen films, Rita Moreno won an Oscar for her role in her next film, *West Side Story.*

Too Soon to Love

Producer: Richard Rush
Writers: Laszlo Gorog, Richard Rush
Director: Richard Rush
Music: Ronald Stein
Universal; 85 minutes
Released 3/60

Cast: Jennifer West, Richard Evans, Warren Parker, Ralph Manza, Jack Nicholson, Jacqueline Schwab, Billie Bird, William Keen

This is a pretty obscure film, featuring Jack Nicholson's second screen appearance. It is the story of youthful pregnancy, attempted abortion, petty theft, and police chases, with a happy ending. This was Richard Rush's first feature—he later became successful doing biker and hippie films like *Hell's Angels on Wheels, Psych-Out,* and *The Savage Seven,* before moving on to more mainstream Hollywood movies.

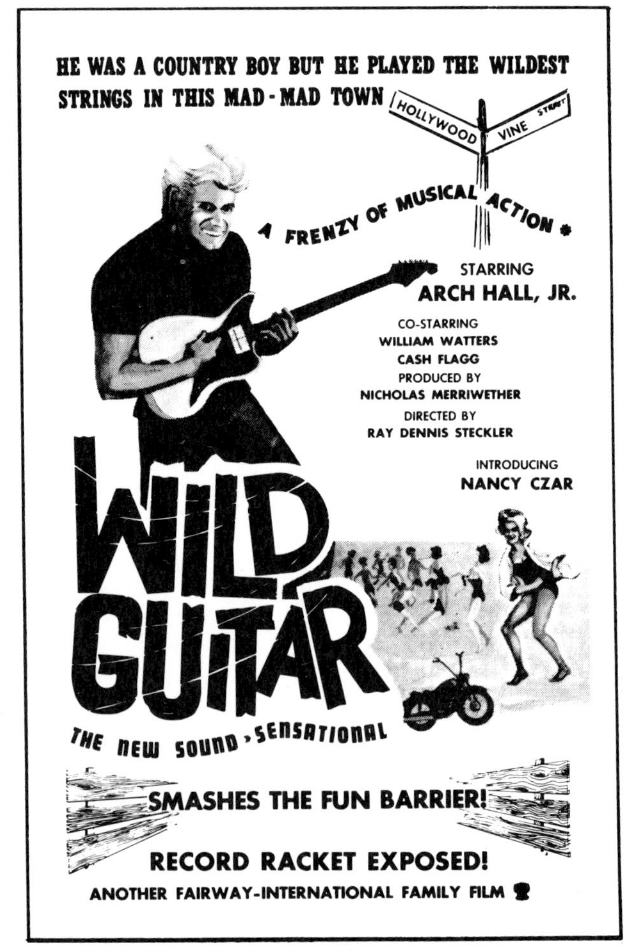

One of the many Arch Hall, Jr. classics — and they only cost $1.98 each to make.

Wild Guitar

Producer: Nicholas Merriwether
Writer: Nicholas Merriwether
Director: Ray Dennis Steckler
Music: Alan O'Day
Fairway-International; 87 minutes.
Released 11/6/62

Cast: Arch Hall, Jr., Nancy Czar, William Watters, Cash Flagg, Marie Denn, Bob Crumb, Bill Lloyd, Mike Kannon

Arch Hall strikes again! Another strange one concerning a motorcyle-driving aspiring rock 'n' roll star, a corrupt promoter, riches, retirement, abduction, and the victory of a fair contract. Cash Flagg is Ray Dennis Steckler, and William Watters and Nicholas Merriwether are Arch Hall, Sr. Nancy Czar was a teenage Olympic ice-skating champion. *Boxoffice:* "This low-budget rock 'n' roll entry featuring a youthful, mostly non-professional cast, will find a suitable audience on double-bill programs primarily for teenagers. . . ." I guess the principals figured if they used pseudonyms they'd be taken more seriously. They weren't.

The Wild Ride

Producer: Harvey Berman
Writers: Ann Porter, Marion Rothman
Director: Harvey Berman
Filmgroup; 63 minutes
Released 8/60

Cast: Jack Nicholson, Georgianna Carter, Robert Bean

This was Nicholson's fourth feature release, teamed with Filmgroup's *The Girl In Lover's Lane.* This is a supercheap story of hot rods, the death of a policeman, drag racing, more death, a tour of hot spots, and police capture. *Boxoffice:* "Weak, weak sister to the upteen beatnik yarns that, for one illogical reason or another, finally reach the screen, only to play off before dwindling audience reaction. This is weirdly rambling, humdrum, standard and anticipated. One redeeming factor, perhaps, is the obvious presence of beat talk, which may, or may not, appeal to the teen and post-teen element said to be enthralled with the unconventional method of communication." Yeah, uh, like wow, man!

Wild Youth

Producer: John Bushelman
Writers: Robert J. Black, Jr., Lester William Berke, Dean Romano

***Jack Nicholson grapples with Georgianna Carter in this scene from Filmgroup's 1960 low-budget quickie* The Wild Ride.**

Director: John Schreyer
Music: Richard La Salle
Cinema Associates; 73 minutes
Released 9/8/61

Cast: Robert Hutton, Carol Ohmart, Jan Brooks, Clancy Cooper, Steve Rowland, John Goddard, Robert Arthur

This is a fast-paced and not bad film about an honor farm, romance, drug addicts, a dope-filled doll, smuggling, a gun battle, and death. "The 'way out' guys and the 'make-out' gals . . . what is their latest kick?" *Wild Youth,* filmed in New Mexico, was also known as *Naked Youth,* and rereleased in 1966. The title song was sung by Steve Rowland, who later became a very successful songwriter and producer in England in the mid and late sixties.

John Frankenheimer directed this vivid look at teenage gangs and violence, which was quite successful at the box office in 1961.

The Young Captives

Producer: Andrew J. Fenady
Writer: Andrew J. Fenady
Director: Irvin Kershner
Music: Richard Markowitz
Paramount; 66 minutes
Released 2/59

Cast: Steven Marlo, Tom Selden, Luana Patten, Joan Granville, Ed Nelson, Dan Sheridan, Jim Chandler

This is a quick picture about teen elopement, a hitchhiking killer, knifings, attempted rape, and final capture. *Boxoffice:* "This is sure-fire entertainment for the teenagers, and male adults, but it will run the risk in some areas of being labeled too sensational. It is certainly not for the kiddies and not for many women . . . but the action will glue viewers to their seats. Steven Marlo excels as the wild-eyed kidnapper-killer. Tom Selden is satisfactory as the eloping youth, but Luana Patten occasionally seems to disregard the fact that a knife is pointed at her throat. She is, however, very pretty." Irvin Kershner also directed *Stakeout On Dope Street, The Hoodlum Priest,* and some more mainstream Hollywood films, before striking it big with *The Empire Strikes Back.*

The Young Savages

Producers: Pat Duggan, Harold Hecht
Writers: Edward Anhalt, J. P. Miller
Director: John Frankenheimer
Music: David Amram
United Artists; 100 minutes
Released 5/23/61

Cast: Burt Lancaster, Dina Merrill, Shelley Winters, Edward Andrews, Vivian Nathan, Larry Gates, Telly Savalas, Pilar Seurat

Taken from Evan Hunter's novel *A Matter Of Conviction* (1959), this well-meaning film concerns Puerto Rican and Italian gangs, murder, a trial, intimidation, violence, and a correct verdict. "Here is the raw truth . . . nailed to the screen!" Said one exhibitor: "Another bleeding-heart flop about the poor hoodlum teenagers from UA. Does Lancaster really believe this stuff?" Music by avant-garde composer David Amram, and some excellent shots and direction from John Frankenheimer—a hint of what was to come.

Glamor Girls and Muscle Boys Exhibit Their Talents for 'Muscle Beach Party'

This is a scene at the Milwaukee airport showing the muscle men assembled for a reception for Darlene Lucht, a former Miss Milwaukee beauty contest winner who has a part in "Muscle Beach Party." Note the half dozen or so girls behind Darlene—each one is also a former Miss Milwaukee.

Candy Johnson of the "Bikini Beach" cast demonstrating the swim dance at a promotion party held at the Peppermint Tree Lounge in San Francisco. The event was covered by a local television station.

John Ashley, AIP Star, Adds Two P.A. Stops

HOLLYWOOD—American International Pictures contract star John Ashley moves to bolster his claim to the title of "Hollywood's Most Traveled Personal Appearance Personality" with the acceptance of another extensive p.a. tour, it was announced Wednesday (17) by AIP ad-publicity chief Milton I. Moritz.

Ashley's new tour will be highlighted by special appearances at the Texas Drive-In Theatre Owners Convention in Dallas, February 23-25, and at the Heart of America Theatre Owner's "Show-A-Rama" convention in Kansas City, March 1-4, according to Moritz. James H. Nicholson and Samuel Z. Arkoff, AIP chief executives, will receive Show-A-Rama's "Producers of the Year" award.

Ashley, who had twice previously toured the Texas and midwestern areas for AIP, was specifically requested by the two theatre owners' groups because of the splendid impression he had made. They said his work, and the results thereon, should be an example of showmanship to other Hollywood stars.

The young actor, who is married to Deborah Walley, another AIP star, also will plug his latest film, "Beach Blanket Bingo" on his p.a. tour.

American International Picture's Stars of "Beach Party" recently got together at a luncheon with director William Asher and AIP toppers James H. Nicholson and Samuel Z. Arkoff. Seen, left to right, seated, are Harvey Lembeck, Dorothy Malone, Asher, Eva Six, producer Nicholson, executive producer Arkoff, Annette Funicello, and Frankie Avalon. Standing are, from left, David Landfield, Delores Wells, Jody McCrea, John Ashley, and Morey Amsterdam. Missing is Robert Cummings, unable to attend.

This group visited downtown Milwaukee and all the shopping centers in plugging the Riverside Theatre's "Beach Blanket Bingo" playdate.

RIGHT, BOTTOM: "Beach Party" was screened at an apartment building pool in Baltimore. During a long intermission, the Dick Dale combo continued the soundtrack thunder, bringing complaints from the surrounding fashionable area. In the photo Dale is seated with Vicki Webb, swim-suited hostess. Standing are the Del Tones, two Capitol Records men and Jerry Sandy, AIP publicist.

1963-1966
Beach Blanket Boffo

In a 1971 interview, Sam Arkoff, looking back over his years at AIP said, "I look upon my movies as being merchandise, just as Woolworth's has a line of merchandise. The fact that many of my acquaintances wouldn't buy Woolworth's merchandise doesn't keep it from being perfectly good merchandise. Many people in this business feel that merchandise not aimed at them must be shoddy." Arkoff and Company felt little need to compete with the major studios over big-name casts or serious films. They each had their own turf. AIP was still aiming squarely at the teen exploitation market. AIP had been successful in the years 1959 to 63 with gladiator pictures and Roger Corman's Poe films, but they had not yet come up with a new cycle totally geared to teenagers.

In 1963 they had a script floating around about bad kids, marijuana, and delinquents, and thought the time might be right for that cycle again. They called in director William Asher, who had directed feature films from 1948 to 1956, but who had spent the last six years or so as a very successful director of television shows, most notably on many episodes of "I Love Lucy" and "Make Room For Daddy." Asher wanted to get back into feature films, but felt that AIP was off-base and that their new film should be about clean-cut kids who just wanted to have fun. After much discussion, AIP went along with Asher, with much trepidation—they just weren't quite sure about this one.

But who should the lead cast members be? They already had been working with Frankie Avalon, whose last two pictures had been for AIP, 1961's *Alakazam The Great* and 1962's *Panic in the Year Zero.* His career was going nowhere. Disney Studios had Annette Funicello, but didn't know what to do with her. She had made *The Shaggy Dog* in 1959, and *Babes in Toyland* in 1961, and nothing since. Her career was going nowhere. But they were recognizable names and faces. They were perky. They were clean and wholesome. They were good-looking. Despite their years in the business, they both looked young—though Avalon was twenty-four and Funicello was twenty-one—and, surprise of all surprises, when they got together, there was actually some chemistry between them. So together they formed the core of the picture, and they were surrounded by a campy group of oldsters (not parents), a parody of motorcycle gangs led by Harvey Lembeck, a bunch of silly regulars, and a slew of beautiful California-tanned beach bodies—both male and female, but with the accent on female. When the picture, now dubbed *Beach Party,* was set for release, AIP was still unsure of what they had, and spent a small fortune on a media blitz and advertising campaign. And when the picture opened

Master of ceremonies Sam Riddle of KHJ-TV's Ninth Street West show interviews AIP star Annette Funicello. In the background are AIP music coordinator Al Simms and ad-pub director Milt Moritz, along with the Bikini girls.

PATTI CHANDLER (above), American International star, was the official hostess for Clarise Sportswear which welcomed buyers to New York to view their brand new "It's Annette" line which will be tied in with every "beach" picture produced by AIP. The first film Clarise is featured in is "Beach Blanket Bingo," an Easter release.

Seven AIP 'Beach' Pictures Shown at Mexican Festival

MEXICO CITY—Mexico's Producciones Sotomayor staged a seven-day Festival honoring American International heads, James H. Nicholson and Samuel Z. Arkoff, with daily screenings of AIP beach pictures at The Metropolitan Theatre here starting July 29. Arkoff and Frankie Avalon, who stars in six of the seven AIP pictures, were special guests from the U.S.A.

The pictures shown were "Beach Party," "Muscle Beach Party," "Bikini Beach," "Pajama Party," this one starring Tommy Kirk; "Beach Blanket Bingo," "Ski Party" and "How to Stuff a Wild Bikini," all of them in color and Panavision and all "boxoffice record-breakers," according to Mexican exhibitors. The seven pictures were also shown simultaneously at the Juarez, new theatre in Monterey City.

Giant TV Dance Party Attracts 5,000 To Shop Center on Eve of 'Bikini'

The Canoga Park parking lot of Zody's department store in Los Angeles was the scene of a giant TV dance party telecast on KHJ in the hour-long time slot of the station's Ninth Street West teenagers show. The spectacular, on TV from 6 to 7 p.m., attracted over 5,000 youngsters to the parking lot. It took place on the day preceding the opening by a week of "Bikini Beach" in 30 Los Angeles theatres.

American International Pictures had stars Annette Funicello, Harvey Lembeck and his Rat Pack, Jody McCrea and six bikini-clad beauties who came direct from the studio where AIP is filming "Pajama Party." The girls danced the twist with six lucky spectators.

The giant TV dance party was presold by Zody's with single and double page ads in 12 suburban newspapers and in the metropolitan dailies, plus more than 40 radio spots and 20 TV spots.

Zody's advertising director Harry Spitzer described the event as "one of the biggest promotional successes in Zody's history." The company operates seven giant discount stores in southern California. Eight teenagers won trips via PSA Super Electra jet to San Francisco where they were guests at Rickey's Hyatt House. No purchases were necessary. Coupons were available at all Zody's stores. In addition, record albums of the "Bikini Beach" soundtrack and single records of the picture's hit songs were given away.

"Bikini Beach" chalked up a summertime record gross in its multiple during the first seven days in Los Angeles and was held over for a third week's showings.

It was a fine co-op promotion.

Lots of Twist, Muscles, Squeals and Glamor at 'Muscle Beach' Premiere

American International Pictures concentrated its management, star and promotion brigades in San Francisco for the world premiere of "Muscle Beach Party" at the big Fox Warfield Theatre and Mission Drive-In. With James H. Nicholson and Samuel Z. Arkoff on hand to provide top generalship, the premiere was proclaimed on numerous fronts and in all media.

Picture at left shows star Annette Funicello, greeting a crowd of teenagers, estimated at 5,000, who gathered at the Hillsdale Shopping Center. Jody McCrea and Frankie Avalon also were there, with Morey Amsterdam, the comedian who appears in the picture, doing the emcee chores.

In the next photo, Annette admires the muscles of Stan Brice, winner of the Mister Muscle Beach contest which was featured at a press cocktail party held in the Garden Room of the Jack Tar Hotel. The winner received a surfboard, a Sea & Ski year-around tanning kit, record albums and passes to see the film.

There were other promotions at the party.

The next picture shows Galaxie dancer Jody Mac, originator of the Swim dance, teaching Avalon the steps, and at extreme right, another Galaxie dancer, Joni Lyman demonstrates the dance with Jody McCrea.

Other activities included a party for the "Muscle Beach Party" visitors by Steve Yamamoto, manager of Nikko's Sukiyaki restaurant. Leading San Francisco motion picture editors also were guests.

Rose Marie models displayed beachwear from H. Liebes & Co. at a Beachwear Fashion Show held at the Jack Tar Hotel press party. Nicholson, Arkoff and the "Muscle Beach Party" stars and promotion men were guests of the San Francisco Variety Club at the first of Tent 5's Celebrity luncheons.

. . . the theater was flooded with kids. In many cases house records were set, and new AIP gross records were also secured. All of a sudden, theaters began clamoring for prints of *Beach Party.* A new cycle had begun.

Over the next two years there would be a total of five pure AIP beach pictures released—*Beach Party, Muscle Beach Party, Bikini Beach, Beach Blanket Bingo,* and *How to Stuff a Wild Bikini*—alongside two others that were offshoots of the genre, *Pajama Party* and *Ski Party.* These, as far as the public was concerned, were just more of the same. But William Asher directed all five of the beach flicks, and his steady hand and professionalism gave them a continuity and a vivid look. Why were the pictures so successful? Well, they moved fast and were escapist fun. There were no parents. They were ridiculous. They were, despite AIP's claims of cleanliness, sexy. All those bodies and bikinis churning away to twangy rock 'n' roll offered a fantasy vision of life without serious problems. And with the mid-sixties real world bringing youth such problems as assassinations, the Vietnam war, racial unrest, radical changes in clothes and hairstyles, drugs, and the like, these pictures were a safe haven for a retreat to the status quo. They were great drive-in pictures, colorful, quick-cut, and perhaps sexually stimulating.

Adults were split on the issue. *The New York Times* waged a continuing campaign against their "idiocy . . . their moronic intellectual level . . . and their sexual leering and suggestiveness." Others agreed, but another portion felt the movies were clean-cut fun, without overt sex, drugs, or rebellion. In fact, national magazines such as *Life* and *Look* published extensive pro–beach movie pieces centering in on the new faces and new bodies. And although many adults found the films to be all noise and stupidity, grown-ups did form a significant portion of the audience. This allowed the pictures to gross even more money, and AIP didn't complain. And unlike other series or sequels, where the plot changed and the participants grew older, the beach pictures were a fantasyland where no one talked about jobs, or divorce, or money problems. It was, as director Asher later put it, "the longest summer on record." And it didn't hurt that surfing and hot-rod groups like the Beach Boys and Jan and Dean were propagating their "summer means fun" lifestyle with hit records and a fun image.

The films themselves started at a cost of about $500,000, and by the end of the series had risen to a budget of almost a million dollars per picture. About the same amount was spent on advertising. But they each grossed several million dollars, and were booked over and over again in various combinations. The other studios, of course, tried to compete, but *their* films made sense, and often had parents and problems in them. No one wanted that. There was no real competition; of the numerous beach films made in answer to AIP, only *For Those Who Think Young* and *Ride the Wild Surf* were significant grossers. But, because their costs were higher, they barely made money for their producers. That's not to say that the others didn't make some change, but not the megabucks that the AIP films did. All of a sudden there were *Palm Springs Weekend, Get Yourself a College Girl, The Lively Set, A Swingin' Summer, Beach Ball, The Girls on the Beach, Wild on the Beach, Winter a Go-Go, Out of Sight,* and *Wild, Wild Winter.* Some concentrated on beaches and bikinis. Some centered in on hot rods.

Some took place in ski settings. Some concentrated on rock 'n' roll. But no one could match the pure zaniness of AIP's films, and their wild cast of regulars. They were filled with pure fantasy characters, and there was safety for the audience in repetition. AIP was smart to get out in 1965 with the final film, *How to Stuff a Wild Bikini,* as most of 1966 was the final year of the cycle—filled mainly with dull, repetitive, low-budget imitations that barely found an audience. But AIP had created and milked another cycle to the tune of several million dollars' profit. AIP had not only zealously followed their own theory on three-year cycles, they had also geared their beach films to their corporate motto, which was dubbed the Peter Pan syndrome. It went something like this:

1. A younger child will watch anything an older child will watch.
2. An older child will not watch anything a younger child will watch.
3. A girl will watch anything a boy will watch.
4. A boy will not watch anything a girl will watch.
5. Therefore, to catch your greatest audience, you zero in on a nineteen-year-old male.

Not exactly on the level of Albert Einstein, perhaps, but in the exploitation filmmaking business, and for AIP in particular, it was pure genius, and money in the bank.

The beach pictures were unique in the fact that except for Frankie and Annette, the films were filled with fresh faces. Very few of the actors and actresses who had made names for themselves in previous cycles got any parts at all. Adults may have been attracted by the small parts and cameos by older-generation personalities: Buster Keaton, Don Rickles, Paul Lynde, Bob Cummings, Morey Amsterdam, Vincent Price, Mickey Rooney, Buddy Hackett, Peter Lorre, and Dorothy Lamour. For ther most part they didn't interfere with the kids' fun, because their roles were really quite silly, not serious at all. The youthful players interchanged new faces with television and recording stars known mainly to teens: Pamela Tiffin, Chad Everett, Linda Evans, Dwayne Hickman, James Darren, Doug McClure, Jackie DeShannon, Tommy Kirk, Toni Basil, Troy Donahue, Connie Stevens, Fabian, Shelly Fabares, Tab Hunter, Barbara Eden, Deborah Walley, James Stacy, Raquel Welch, Johnny Crawford, and Sherry Jackson. There were some ministars made, who seemed born for beach pictures and little else: Donna Loren, Patti Chandler, Joy Harmon, Chris Noel, and Candy Johnson. And finally, the beach pictures were utilized to introduce much of second-generation Hollywood to the public: Jody McCrea, Lana Wood, James Mitchum, William Wellman, Jr., Tisha Sterling, Beau Bridges, Tim Rooney, Nancy Sinatra, and Meredith MacRae. Together they formed an up-and-coming group of young Hollywood on the scene. Good-looking. Photogenic. Sexy. And, as portrayed onscreen, not very deep. Perhaps that's what the times demanded, but it probably trapped some good people in some straitjacket images.

In a sense it was strange, with so much turmoil going on in the real world, and with so much fast-moving change and loosening of morals,

Touring RKO neighborhood theatres in New York on behalf of Embassy Pictures' "Village of the Giants" are (l-r) producer-director Bert I. Gordon, dancer Kathy Karr, emcee Murray the K, and film's stars Mike Clifford, Tisha Sterling, Tim Rooney and Tommy Kirk.

Hollywood titled a picture after Pepsi's theme: "For Those Who Think Young." It's like getting a whole feature-length commercial aimed at the young movie-going crowd!

Here a jam-packed audience awaits the start of the Hollywood Theatre's first Hullabaloo, featuring local amateur talent. Ron Olson, manager of the Montevideo, Minn., house, coupled "Get Yourself a College Girl" with the show and had an overflow crowd.

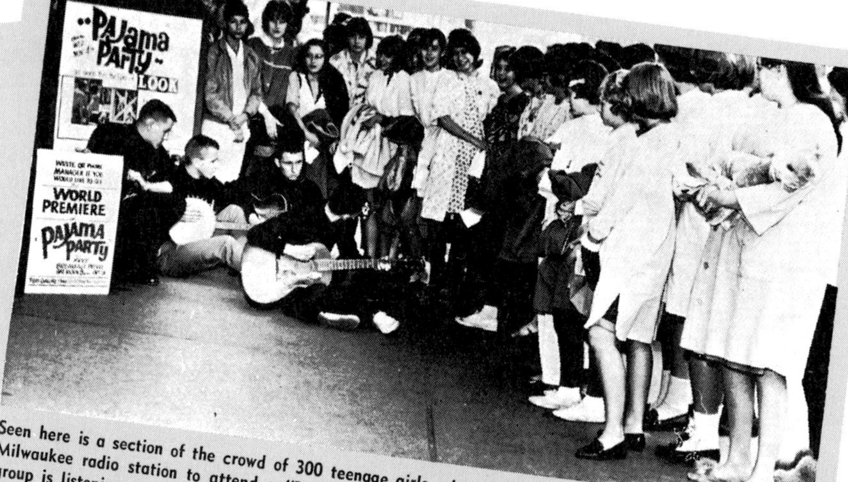

Seen here is a section of the crowd of 300 teenage girls selected from more than 800 letters sent in to a Milwaukee radio station to attend a "Pajama Party" at the Warner Theatre and nearby cafeteria. The group is listening to the Three Lads in front of the theatre. The group was picked up for the event at a USO. There was a beauty contest on the Warner stage, then a screening of "Pajama Party."

Carol Bradley, manager of the New Mission Theatre in San Francisco, starts checking vital statistics of four girls entered in a Miss Bikini contest conducted for "Operation Bikini," at the New Mission and the Geneva Drive-In. Bradley reports the measurements of Cathy Carver: 125 lbs., 5' 6", 36-24-36.

In all, Bradley had 15 dancers, secretaries, students, salesgirls and cashiers in the contest. The main prize was an expense-paid trip to Hollywood with a bit part in American International's "Beach Party," plus $100 for her appearance in the film. Other prizes included cash, gift certificates, hairdos, record albums and theatre passes.

Judges were Bill Hall, San Francisco Examiner; Roger Grimsby, KGO-TV; Ira Blue, KGO; Ken Knox, KEGW, and Gene Nelson, KYA. The winner was Gayle Richardson, a Polynesian dancer, 35-22-35.

that the beach pictures were so clean. But for millions of kids this worldly change was threatening and confusing, and though a large percentage of youth was caught up in these changes, another significant group fought steadfastly to hold onto what was safe, fun, and familiar. By the end of 1966, however, the tide had turned considerably, and the increasing popularity of drugs, looser sex, strange clothes and hairstyles, protests, hippies, and progressive rock music were becoming the predominant forces. The beach pictures became anachronisms without an audience, and AIP and others were loading the cannons for the next cycle. The production code had been virtually dismantled by this point, and filmmakers were let loose to tackle any subject in almost any manner they chose. And with 1967 fast approaching, it was again time for a major change—a new cycle and a new style of filmmaking. Sex, drugs, and rock n roll—they were all right around the corner, and there was no turning back.

FILMOGRAPHY '63–'66

Beach Ball

Producer: Bart Patton
Writer: David Malcolm
Director: Lennie Weinrib
Music: Frank Wilson
Paramount; 83 minutes
Released 10/13/65

Cast: Edd Byrnes, Chris Noel, Robert Logan, Gale Gilmore, Aron Kincaid, Mikki Jamison, Don Edmonds, Brenda Benet.

Another beach frolic, this time about a rock n roll group, surfers, hot rods, money problems, dropouts, and the essential happy ending. The story isn't much, but you can catch the Supremes, the Four Seasons, the Righteous Brothers, the Hondells, and the Walker Brothers. Said one exhibitor: "Paramount's *Beach Ball* is the usual teen picture, but as we played it ahead of our closest theater, we did real well with it. One of the better grossing teen pictures, topping the *Gidget* pictures. A teen ball." Lennie Weinrib also had his hand in *Out of Sight, Wild, Wild Winter, Good Times,* and the unforgettable TV special "Minis and Bikinis."

Beach Blanket Bingo

Producers: James H. Nicholson, Samuel Z. Arkoff
Writers: William Asher, Leo Townsend
Director: William Asher
Music: Les Baxter, Al Simms
American International; 98 minutes
Released 4/65

Cast: Frankie Avalon, Annette Funicello, Deborah Walley, Harvey Lembeck, John Ashley, Jody McCrea, Donna Loren, Marta Kristen

This was the fourth in the series of AIP beach pictures, the usual tale of frolic, skydiving, motorcycle gangs, mermaids, and a happy tie-up. Said *Motion Picture Herald:* "Aimed squarely at the teen market, and likely to be on target, *Beach Blanket Bingo* features youthful players, exciting color photography, and rousing contemporary tunes that are pleasant to see and hear. The young audience can probably be depended on to overlook the fact that the film has no central plot and is largely concerned with parading skydivers, mermaids, juvenile delinquents, and press agents before the cameras in a series of unrelated romantic and comic sequences . . . but some of the characters are quite funny and give a lift to the film." Said the stuffy *Times:* "We simply can't believe, no matter what the reports say, that teenagers buy such junk. It's for morons!" Besides the leading cast members you can spot Linda Evans, Patti Chandler, the Hondells, Don Rickles, Paul Lynde, Buster Keaton, and a bevy of *Playboy* playmates.

The BEACH PARTY gang goes SKY DIVING!
BEACH BLANKET BINGO
AN AMERICAN INTERNATIONAL PICTURE
IN COLOR AND PANAVISION®
STARRING
FRANKIE AVALON · ANNETTE FUNICELLO · DEBORAH WALLEY · HARVEY LEMBECK
JOHN ASHLEY · JODY McCREA · DONNA LOREN · MARTA KRISTEN · LINDA EVANS
CO-STARRING
BOBBI SHAW · DON RICKLES · PAUL LYNDE
as "BIG DROP" as "BULLETS"
AND CAMEO STARS
BUSTER KEATON · EARL WILSON
written by
WILLIAM ASHER & LEO TOWNSEND
directed by
WILLIAM ASHER
produced by
JAMES H. NICHOLSON & SAMUEL Z. ARKOFF
co-producer
ANTHONY CARRAS
65/156

tone for what was to follow. It's basically the story of a professor studying the sex play of teenagers, with the usual light romance, comedy, parodies, and music. Said the *Times:* "It's harmless, eyefilling and disarming, until the entrance of Mr. Cummings, when the picture tilts archly, sniggering and wide-eyed, suggestively and dully. The cast emerges as the dullest bunch ever, with the old folks even sillier than the kids. We suspect that the youngsters in the audience may find it all pretty laughable. A clanging group called Dick Dale and the Deltones look like praying mantises." Besides the lead players, you can catch Eva Six, Candy Johnson, Yvette Vickers, Brian Wilson, Meredith MacCrea, Peter Falk, Roger Christian, Gary Usher, and Vincent Price.

This is a still from* The Beach Girls and the Monster. *Can you spot the monster?

The Beach Girls and the Monster

Producer: Edward Janis
Writer: Joan Gardner
Director: Jon Hall
Music: Frank Sinatra, Jr., Chuck Slagle
U.S. Films; 70 minutes
Released 9/15/65

Cast: Jon Hall, Sue Casey, Walker Edmiston, Arnold Lessing, Elaine DuPont, Read Morgan, Clyde Adler, Gloria Neil.

This is a cheap and unintentionally funny story of surfing, death, monsters, murder, and a "surprise" ending. The real surprise is that people paid to see it. This was also distributed as *Monster from the Surf* and *Surf Terror.*

Beach Party

Producers: James H. Nicholson, Lou Rusoff
Writer: Lou Rusoff
Director: William Asher
Music: Les Baxter, Al Sims
American International; 101 minutes
Released 8/7/63

Cast: Bob Cummings, Dorothy Malone, Frankie Avalon, Annette Funicello, Harvey Lembeck, Jody McCrea, Morey Amsterdam, John Ashley

The very first of the AIP beach films, this one set the

Annette Funicello and Frankie Avalon in* Bikini Beach, *the third of AIP's beach ball series.

Bikini Beach

Producers: James H. Nicholson, Samuel Z. Arkoff
Writers: William Asher, Leo Townsend, Robert Dillon
Director: William Asher
Music: Les Baxter, Al Simms

American International; 100 minutes
Released 7/22/64

Cast: Frankie Avalon, Annette Funicello, Martha Hyer, Harvey Lembeck, Don Rickles, John Ashley, Jody McCrea, Candy Johnson

The third of AIP's beach series *Bikini Beach* has Frankie Avalon playing two parts—one is his usual role, and one is a British pop star, where he gets to make fun of the British Invasion. There's the usual gaggle of beach frolics, disapproving adults, a campy motorcycle gang, drag races, and a happy ending. The *Times,* continuing their war on beach films, called it "a horrible, birdbrained comedy in which surfers fight cyclists and convert their elders to the pleasures of the bronzed physique." One theater owner, however, knew which side his bread was buttered on: "Here is a picture that the young folks will go to see and it will make any theater money. All theaters should play AI pictures. They have made many films that have kept small-town theaters in business. If you haven't been using their films, you should get in touch with them immediately and start making money." Also look for Meredith MacRae, Donna Loren, Little Stevie Wonder, the Pyramids, the Exciters, and Boris Karloff.

Daytona Beach Weekend

Producer: Robert Welby
Director: Robert Welby
Dominant; 87 minutes
Released 4/14/65

Cast: Del Shannon, Houston and Dorsey, Rayna, Sue Skeen, Don Jackson, the Offbeets.

Originally filmed in sixteen-millimeter at Daytona Beach, this regional quicky was only notable for the appearance of Del Shannon, amid the usual gaggle of teens, vacation fun, and drag racing. The sales pitch tried to make it much more: "Pre-sold to the hundreds of thousands of high school and college students from every state that come to the world's most famous beach every year for their Spring Easter vacation . . . and to the millions of others that have been reading and hearing about the wall-to-wall ball had by all during these way-out weekends. Also the all-new perfect drive-in bill—the wildest ride of all—Featurette: *Ride in a Wild Pair of Bikini Pajamas!* Dominant Pictures also brought us *Six Shes and a He, Blast-Off Girls,* and *The Girl, the Body, and the Pill.*

Daytona Beach Weekend *featured an appearance by Del Shannon. Try and find this movie today.*

Feelin' Good

Producer: James A. Pike
Writers: James A. Pike, Mildred Maffei
Director: James A. Pike
Music: Arthur Korb
Pike; 85 minutes
Released 10/26/66

Cast: Travis Pike, Patricia Ewing, Judi Reeve, Leslie Burnham, Ron Stafford, Frank Dolan

Filmed in Boston, this vanity production was put together by television-industry education and public-affairs filmmaker James A. Pike. It's a story of a rock group, roommates, romance, a battle of the bands, dances, reconciliation, and a happy ending. There's music by Brenda Nichols, the Brattle Street East, and the Montclairs, the real-life winners of the Massachusetts Jaycees' battle of the bands. Said *Boxoffice:* "Pike has photographed his footage in metropolitan Boston, a town with which he is obviously well acquainted, pacing out an essentially simple story of a boy-girl relationship amid musical atmosphere. Travis Pike, the producer-director's son, is credible enough as the male lead, while Patricia Ewing blends an impressive personality with a wistful smile. The film should be embraced by the teen audience, for which this attraction has been lovingly geared." For regional fans only.

***The sultry Pamela Tiffin, who starred in* For Those Who Think Young.**

***The gang does the Watusi in* Get Yourself a College Girl.**

For Those Who Think Young

Producer: Hugh Benson
Writers: James and George O'Hanlon, Dan Beaumont
Director: Leslie Martinson
Music: Jerry Fielding
United Artists; 96 minutes
Released 6/3/64

Cast: James Darren, Pamela Tiffin, Woody Woodbury, Paul Lynde, Tina Louise, Nancy Sinatra, Bob Denver, Claudia Martin

More college hijinks—students, surfing, nightclubs, romance, disapproving professor, and a happy ending. This movie had massive tie-ins with Pepsi, as this was their marketing slogan. Squeaky clean and pretty dull. Bob Denver and Tina Louise were stranded together again on "Gilligan's Island." Director Martinson made a handful of fifties JD flicks, and later such epics as *Batman* (the movie, 1966), and the TV film *Rescue from Gilligan's Island* (1978).

Get Yourself a College Girl

Producer: Sam Katzman
Writer: Robert E. Kent
Director: Sidney Miller
Music: Fred Karger
MGM; 87 minutes
Released 11/9/64

Cast: Mary Ann Mobley, Chad Everett, Joan O'Brien, Nancy Sinatra, Chris Noel, Willard Waterman, Fabrizio Mioni, James Millhollin

Here's another romping tale of songwriters, conservative schools, vacations, senators, election, and a happy ending. Said one exhibitor: "This film is a natural for teenage trade and that means good business to my small-town deluxe theater. It did excellent business." Another added: "Used this one for a mid-week change and added record giveaways to boost interest. We did very well with this one and here is a picture your teenage patrons will really enjoy. A good picture, nice color, and clean fun." Also look for the Animals, the Dave Clark Five, Stan Getz, and the Standells.

The Girls on the Beach

Producer: Harvey Jacobsen
Writer: David Malcolm
Director: William Witney
Music: Gary Usher, Nick Venet
Paramount; 80 minutes
Released 5/12/65

Cast: Martin West, Noreen Corcoran, Peter Brooks, Arnold Lessing, Linda Marshall, Steve Rogers, Anna Capri, Aron Kincaid

Executive producer Gene Corman moved into beach pictures with this film, a story of a sorority beach house, nightclubs, money problems, Beatle impersonations by the girls, and the requisite tie-up at the end. Also with the Beach Boys, the Crickets, Lesley Gore, and Lana Wood. William Witney began directing in 1937. Some sixty films later, at age sixty-five, he directed this epic. His fifties JD films *Juvenile Jungle, The Cool and the Crazy,* and *Young and Wild* were pretty good.

The Horror of Party Beach

Producer: Del Tenney
Writer: Richard L. Hilliard
Director: Del Tenney
Music: Bill Holmes
20th Century–Fox; 82 minutes
Released 4/1/64

Cast: John Scott, Alice Lyon, Allen Laurel, Eulabelle Moore, Marilyn Clark, Agustin Mayer, Damon Klebroyd, Monroe Wade

Released on a double bill with *Curse of the Living Corpse,* this laughable film concerned radioactive waste, teenagers, monster murders, scientists, and the ultimate death of the monster. *Boxoffice* said: "Modestly mounted and is significant only in its unprecedented incorporation of musical sequences amid horror setting, and where the teenage crowd seeks something offbeat this may be a drawing card of encouraging box-office take. Credibility is too often lacking and the introduction of teenage music into the familiar framework of a monster clan loose against humanity soon wears thin. Del Tenney's directorial prowess here doesn't seem to blend the proceedings into a cohesive package." The *Times,* always on top of such matters, asked the relevant question: "The most curious aspect of the film is why, after the first couple of homicides, the rest of the victims linger around the disaster area. Audiences lured into the theater may ask themselves the same thing." But perhaps the final word goes to this theater owner: "The critics can pan this all they want to but, somehow or other, this has definite appeal for the teenagers that make up ninety percent of my patrons. So who am I to complain if this pulled above average for me, which it did." Del Tenney also brought us *Violent Midnight* and *The Curse of the Living Corpse.* Whatta guy.

Hot Rod Hullabaloo

Producers: Martin L. Low, William T. Naud
Writer: Stanley Schneider
Director: William T. Naud
Music: Elliot Lawrence

"Please, please don't make us watch* The Horror of Party Beach *again!"

Allied Artists; 81 minutes
Released 11/30/66

Cast: John Arnold, Arlen Dean Snyder, Kendra Kerr, Ron Cummins, Val Bisoglio, Marsha Mason, William Hunter, Gene Bua

With the motto "Speed's their creed," the gang in *Hot Rod Hullabaloo* go through their paces. It's a story of hot rods, demolition derbys, dirty tricks, death, and the now-familiar happy endings. The trouble with most of the beach and hot-rod films of the mid-sixties was that they always had happy endings, so it was hard to build up any suspense or interest in the characters. This was unlike many of juvenile-delinquent films of the fifties, where it often wasn't clear what would happen to whom. This film is rather dull and uninteresting, although it did perform okay at many drive-ins.

How to Stuff a Wild Bikini

Producers: James H. Nicholson, Samuel Z. Arkoff
Writers: William Asher, Leo Townsend
Director: William Asher
Music: Les Baxter, Al Simms
American International; 93 minutes
Released 8/11/65

Cast: Annette Funicello, Dwayne Hickman, Brian Donlevy, Harvey Lembeck, Beverly Adams, Jody McCrea, John Ashley, Marianne Gaba

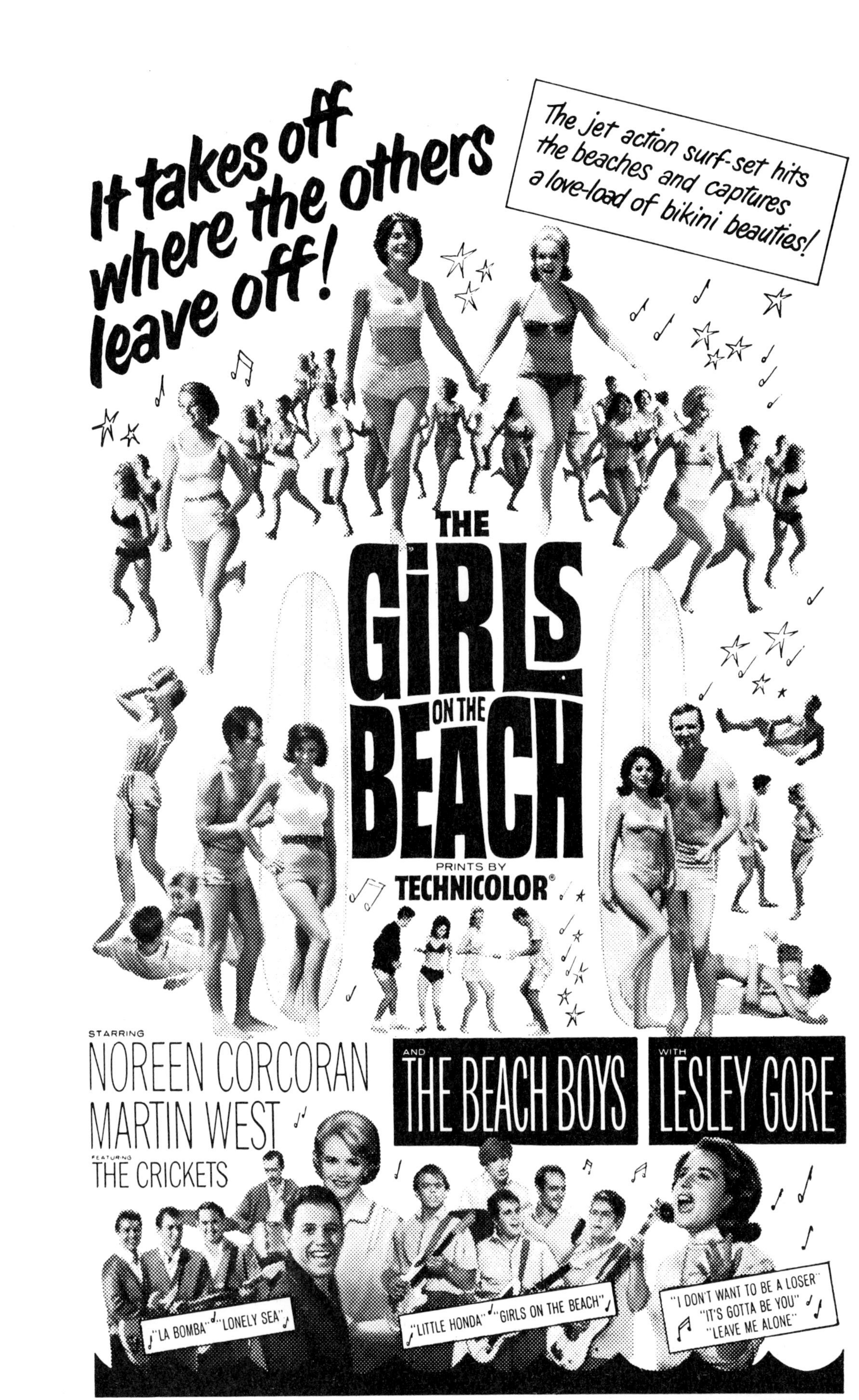
It takes off where the others leave off!
The jet action surf-set hits the beaches and captures a love-load of bikini beauties!
THE GIRLS ON THE BEACH
PRINTS BY TECHNICOLOR®
STARRING
NOREEN CORCORAN
MARTIN WEST
FEATURING
THE CRICKETS
AND
THE BEACH BOYS
WITH
LESLEY GORE
"LA BOMBA" "LONELY SEA"
"LITTLE HONDA" "GIRLS ON THE BEACH"
"I DON'T WANT TO BE A LOSER"
"IT'S GOTTA BE YOU"
"LEAVE ME ALONE"
Produced by HARVEY JACOBSON · Directed by WILLIAM N. WITNEY · Screenplay by DAVID MALCOLM

A PARAMOUNT RELEASE

At last, the fifth and final flick of AIP's beach-party series. This one was done without Frankie Avalon, who was "away on naval reserve duty," and only manages a cameo. It's another tale of witch doctors, advertising men, motorcycle gangs, beach frolics, and the happy finale. Said one exhibitor: "All of these types of movies do excellent business. Good color, excellent print. I don't know how they make them so fast. Seems like we average one a month. Keep them coming. Book it." AIP had already realized that they'd come to the end of another cycle, as one exhibitor hinted at here: "AI, the small company which grew large through the years, deserves another big bouquet of roses on the best yet of the beach pictures, *How to Stuff a Wild Bikini.* It had somewhat of a better story, the color was excellent, and it had an especially good job of acting from Buster Keaton. Business was only average due to the fact that our teenagers here have seen about all the beach films they want to see. When you see this one, you have seen them all." But *The New York Times,* almost without much energy left, still contributed their closing diatribe: "For here, finally and in color, is the answer to a moron's prayer—the squealing young cuties, their gawking male counterparts, and the usual 'guest stars.' The young folk cheerfully yelp the worst musical score since 1925 (the year before sound movies)." Also look for Patty Chandler, Brian Wilson, Salli Sachse, Mickey Rooney, and the Kingsmen.

In the early seventies, AIP reissued all five beach movies on one bill. The campy ads concentrated on nostalgia and silliness.

The Incredibly Strange Creatures Who Stopped Living and Became Crazy Mixed-Up Zombies

Producer: Ray Dennis Steckler
Writer: Gene Pollack
Director: Ray Dennis Steckler
Music: Henry Price
Fairway-International; 82 minutes
Released 3/64

Cast: Cash Flagg, Brett O'Hara, Carolyn Brandt, Atlas King, Sharon Walsh, Madison Clarke, Erina Enyo, Jack Brady

Another bizarro production from Ray Dennis Steckler—aka Cash Flagg. An unbelievable romp, with carnival freaks, fortune tellers, murder, beatniks, hypnotism, and capture. This was also released as *Teenage Psycho Meets Bloody Mary.* There's so much to wonder about here, it's hard to pick out a highlight, but be sure not to miss "The Mixed-Up Zombie Stomp." All this and only midway in Steckler's career. He later gave us *Scream of the Butterfly, The Thrill Killers,* and *Rat Pfink and Boo Boo.*

Kitten with a Whip

Producer: Harry Keller
Writer: Douglas Heyes
Director: Douglas Heyes
Music: Joseph Gershenson
Universal; 83 minutes
Released 11/4/64

Cast: Ann-Margret, John Forsythe, Peter Brown, Patricia Barry, Richard Anderson, James Ward, Diane Sayer, Ann Doran

This is a wild little picture, and coming after her role in *Bye Bye Birdie,* it certainly must have stunned some of Ann-Margret's fans. It's an involved story of a detention home, knifings, arson, blackmail, runaways, wild parties, delinquents, a car crash, and, believe it or not, salvation. Said the *Times:* "A lurid little exploitation picture—but Ann-Margret demonstrates enough untrained talent to suggest interesting dramatic possibilities in better films." What, better than this?

WORLD'S WEIRDEST MOVIE
TEENAGE PSYCHO
MEETS
BLOODY MARY
NOT FOR SISSIES!
DON'T COME IF YOU'RE CHICKEN!
FIRST FULL-LENGTH FEATURE IN
A
BLOODY-VISION
AND BLOODY-COLOR!
MOVIE OF WEIRD BEAUTIES AND Shocking MONSTERS Together
AND YOU ARE IN IT!
NOT 3-D but real FLESH and BLOOD monsters ALIVE! in the audience
YOU ARE SURROUNDED BY MONSTERS!
SHE KEEPS monsters IN CAGES FOR PETS!
NO ONE WILL BE SAFE! THEY MIGHT GET YOU!
1001 WEIRDEST SCENES EVER!
WE DARE YOU TO REMAIN SEATED WHEN MONSTERS INVADE AUDIENCE!
WARNING!
UNLIKE ANYTHING BEFORE
DO NOT CONFUSE WITH LITTLE SHORTS OR "SPOOK SHOWS
HE PREYS ON WILD GO-GO GIRLS!

The Leather Boys

Producer: Raymond Stross
Writer: Gillian Freeman
Director: Sidney J. Furie
Music: Bill McGuffie
Allied Artists; 108 minutes
Released 11/8/65 (in U.S.A.)

Cast: Rita Tushingham, Colin Campbell, Dudley Sutton, Gladys Henson, Avice Landon, Lockwood West, Betty Marsden, Martin Mathews

This is a good, serious British film centering on a London teenage marriage, motorcycle clubs, mixed-up romance, and a bit of homosexuality. The *Times* said: "They are not tackling new problems, in *The Leather Boys,* but the actors and director have given them sincerity, reality, and pathos of truth." Sidney Furie later directed *The Ipcress File, Lady Sings the Blues,* and many others. *The Leather Boys* was originally released in England in January 1964.

(opposite)
Teenage Psycho Meets Bloody Mary *aka* The Incredibly Strange Creatures Who Stopped Living and Became Crazy Mixed-Up Zombies. *What more can we say?*

The Lively Set

Producer: William Alland
Writers: Mel Goldberg, William Wood
Director: Jack Arnold
Music: Bobby Darin
Universal; 95 minutes
Released 10/24/64

Cast: James Darren, Pamela Tiffin, Doug McClure, Joanie Sommers, Marilyn Maxwell, Charles Drake, Peter Mann, Carole Wells

Another of the hot-rod flicks made as companion pieces to beach films, only usually with slightly older and more "mature" characters. Once again it's the usual story of racing cars, romance, and the neat tie-up. But they seemed to sell tickets. Said one theater owner: "If you need a hypo at the boxoffice, play *The Lively Set.* It made up for one of Universal's high rental pictures that didn't gross. This is a honey." And another: "Teenagers really dig pictures like *The Lively Set.* They love them. We had a very good crowd. I found the picture all right myself and I cannot see why it should not be enjoyed by adults also. It is very informative concerning car racing." But the *Times* wrote: "By the fade-out everyone up there on the screen is positively beaming with joy. Before congratulating them on their acting ability, though, remember that they, unlike their helpless customers, were paid." Useful trivia: there are songs by Bobby Darin, Randy Newman, and Terry Melcher; the Surfaris sing "Boss Barracuda"; Pamela Tiffin was married to publishing magnate Clay Felker from 1962 to 1971.

Muscle Beach Party

Producers: James H. Nicholson, Robert Dillon
Writer: Robert Dillon
Director: William Asher
Music: Les Baxter, Al Simms
American International; 94 minutes
Released 3/25/64

Cast: Frankie Avalon, Annette Funicello, Luciana Paluzzi, John Ashley, Don Rickles, Peter Turgeon, Jody McCrea, Dick Dale

Only the second in AIP's beach-party series, but already the format was getting fixed, and not much changed afterward. Here's a tale of musclemen, surfers, European nobility, and teen romance. The *Times* almost died: "Never, anyway seldom, has so much idiocy cluttered a perfectly beautiful strip of California beach as in this dum-dum, another one of those twitch and twist musicals . . . a tangle of vigorous young people with beautiful bodies and empty heads." William Asher directed all five in this series—mixed in between his vast TV work, from "I Love Lucy" to "Bewitched" and many more. He was also married to Elizabeth Montgomery (from 1963 to 1974), and won an Emmy for "Outstanding Directorial Achievement in Comedy" for "Bewitched" in 1966. In *Muscle Beach Party* most of the songs were by Roger Christian, Gary Usher, and Brian Wilson, while onscreen you can also spot Candy Johnson, Stevie Wonder, Morey Amsterdam, Buddy Hackett, Donna Loren, Salli Sachse, and Peter Lorre.

***By 1966, the sixties mod influence had penetrated teen films, as in this shot from* Out of Sight.**

One Way Wahine

Producer: William O. Brown
Writer: Rod Larson
Director: William O. Brown
Music: Jo Hanson
United Screen Arts; 80 minutes
Released 10/65

Cast: Joy Harmon, Anthony Eisley, Adele Claire, David Whorf, Edgar Bergen, Lee Krieger, Ken Mayer, Harold Fong

Filmed in Hawaii, this low-budget film concerned runaways, stolen money, violence, robbery, and had a bittersweet ending. This picture substituted breast size for a deeper plot. From *Boxoffice*: The plot has enough action to keep audiences interested, as well as the two girls whose measurements will be enough to attract male viewers. Joy Harmon boasts a 42–22–35 figure and is appearing currently in *The Loved One*. Adele Claire, as a cocktail waitress willing to be talked into bigger things, is equally good to look at. Both girls are adept at comedy and with David Whorf, perform adequately." Joy Harmon was also perfectly cast in *Village of the Giants*, the same year.

Out of Sight

Producer: Bart Patton
Writer: Harry Hovis
Director: Lennie Weinrib
Music: Al De Lory, Fred Darian, Nick Venet
Universal; 87 minutes
Released 5/12/66

Cast: Jonathan Daly, Karen Jensen, Carole Shelyne, Robert Pine, Forrest Lewis, Wende Wagner, Maggie Thrett, Deanna Lund

Another beach frolic, this time with the addition of a secret-agent subplot. There's a lot of beach, a rock n roll fair, and the happy finale. You can also catch Gary Lewis and the Playboys, Freddie and the Dreamers, Dobie Gray, the Turtles, the Astronauts, the Knickerbockers, and Bob Eubanks. Bart Patton also appeared in or produced *Gidget Goes Hawaiian, Dementia 13, Beach Ball, Blood Bath, Wild Wild Winter,* and several others. Said one trade review: "This combination of a beach girl picture and a spoof on secret-agent films proves that American International has no copyright on such nonsense. It is fairly entertaining with its little known cast, including the bikini-clad bathing beauties, who perform their capers nicely. In to please the rock n roll devotees are some specialists in this art. Each performs one number, most of which sound alike. This should please the youngsters."

Pajama Party

Producers: James H. Nicholson, Samuel Z. Arkoff
Writer: Louis M. Heyward
Director: Don Weis
Music: Lee Baxter, Al Simms
American International; 85 minutes
Released 11/11/64

Cast: Tommy Kirk, Annette Funicello, Elsa Lanchester, Harvey Lembeck, Jesse White, Jody McCrea, Ben Lessy, Donna Loren

A variation on the beach pictures, this time comedy about a teenage martian, a planned invasion of Earth, robbery, a motorcycle gang, a pajama party, and a predictable happy ending. Said *Boxoffice:* "Aimed at teenage patrons, as were the tremendously successful beach party pictures, this musical is once again a lively song and dance light entertainment which should clean up at the boxoffice. Sorely missed however is Frankie Avalon—his replacement Tommy Kirk, a Walt Disney regular, lacks Avalon's singing ability and exuberance. The story is completely ridiculous but the younger set will love it." Theater owners were firmly behind AIP: "All these 'beach party' pictures have done real well here. The teenagers and kids flock to them—and lots of adults too. The scenery is terrific! The story, dialogue, and acting are terrible, but you'll make a few bucks." Said another: "While thumbing through a recent issue of *Boxoffice,* I ran across an exhibitor's comment stating that AI's *Pajama Party* did above average business, but he didn't know why. I think it's a shame that a person will criticize a company that goes out of its way to make pictures that will do above average business for both large- and small-town exhibitors. I appreciate AIP's showmanship and fair dealings with both large and small. Keep those money-makers rolling, AIP! I'm behind you all the way. We played *Pajama Party* to above average business despite stiff competition." Also featuring Susan Hart, Candy Johnson, Buster Keaton, Dorothy Lamour, Patti Chandler, and Toni Basil.

Palm Springs Weekend

Producer: Michael A. Hoey
Writer: Earl Hamner, Jr.
Director: Norman Taurog
Music: Frank Perkins
Warner Bros.; 100 minutes
Released 11/5/63

Cast: Troy Donahue, Connie Stevens, Ty Hardin, Stefanie Powers, Robert Conrad, Andrew Duggan, Jack Weston, Carole Cook

More schlock about high school and college kids at Easter week—romance, cars fights, parents, and the rest. The *Times* said: "Say this for the young people in *Palm Springs Weekend*—they're one heck of a lot more palatable than those braying, wiggling adolescents in the recent *Beach Party*—mercifully the kids here are older. The dialogue is tartly persuasive some of the time, with its briskly sensible coverage of youthful drinking and premarital flings." Sensible? Who wants that! Norman Taurog spent most of the sixties directing eight Elvis Presley flicks.

Rat Fink

Producer: Lewis Andrews
Writer: James Landis
Director: James Landis
Music: Ronald Stein
Cinema Distributors of America; 80 minutes
Released 12/22/65

Cast: Schuyler Hayden, Hal Bokar, Warrene Ott, Judy Hughes, Don Snyder, Eve Brenner, Alice Reinheart, Jack Lester

This is an interesting low-budget drama sabatoged by a horrible title. It's the story of a ruthless and violent rock n roll singer working his way to the top. It's filled with sex, robbery, adultery, teen abortion, corruption, and ultimate death. The movie trades went ga-ga over the performance of Schuyler Hayden. Here's some excerpts. First *Variety:* "A remarkably effective low-budget film, *Rat Fink* suffers from only one thing, its title. It's apparent from this fact that distributor has decided to pitch pic for the teenage market, but this dandy little psychological drama deserves a wider showing. . . . In the last analysis *Fink* depends on actor Schuyler Hayden who is in almost every frame and who sustains an underpinning of title role with a rare and real acting ability. The first film role for the 24-year-old unknown actor (he is reported to have personally put up a substantial amount of the $200,000 budget), he comes across with total believability. . . . Direction gives pic a suspenseful vertigo . . . but it remains for Hayden to make it come to life and he does, in what is one of the best hunks of acting by an unknown actor to be viewed in years." *Motion Picture Herald:* "A sizzling new talent is launched in the person of young Schuyler Hayden who carries along the rather thin plot with the sheer force of his portrayal. Although his versatility has yet to be tested in other roles, it would seem, on the basis of this impressive performance, to be nearly unlimited. . . . A powerful picture indeed." In 1967 Schuyler Hayden was ninth-billed in *Riot on Sunset Strip*—that's the last we heard of him.

Cast: Georgia Lee, Robert Sampson, Johnny Crawford, Kim Darby, Jean Engstrom, Billy Graham, Jerome Courtland, Lurene Tuttle

With all the negative images of youth rampant on the screen, it was left to Billy Graham to bring us something more uplifting and spiritual. This was a Billy Graham Associates production, and it concerned a teenage drunken driver, scriptwriters, runaways, teen pregnancy, attempted suicide, and final salvation through conversion to Christianity. Graham was always in the forefront in the usage of mass media, but we don't know how many converts he got from this regionally distributed film.

Ride the Wild Surf

Producers: Jo and Art Napoleon
Writers: Art and Jo Napoleon
Director: Don Taylor
Music: Stu Phillips
Columbia; 101 minutes
Released 7/1/64

Cast: Fabian, Shelley Fabares, Tab Hunter, Barbara Eden, Peter Brown, Susan Hart, James Mitchum, Anthony Hayes

Another beach movie, this time with some of the oldest teenagers around. The usual story of surfers, Hawaii, romance, and a happy tie-up . . . with the accent on surfing. One good thing is Shelley Fabares, we always like her, and she looks especially spiffy here with her blond hair. Jan and Dean sing the hit title tune.

Rat Fink and Boo Boo

Producer: Ray Dennis Steckler
Writer: Ronald Haydock
Director: Ray Dennis Steckler
Music: Henry Price
Craddock; 72 minutes
Released 9/66

Cast: Vin Saxon, Titus Moede, Carolyn Brandt, George Caldwell, Mike Kannon, James Bowie, Keith Wester, Mary Jo Curtis

Ray Dennis Steckler strikes again! Another bizarre trash epic, this one is a parody of the Batman and Robin craze that swept the nation. It's the story of a rock n roll singer and his bumbling friend (Rat Pfink and Boo Boo), their daring deeds, and the happy ending. Craddock Films also brought us *The Legend of Blood Mountain, The Gold Guitar, Mondo Daytona,* and *Passion in Hot Hollows,* among others.

The Restless Ones

Producer: Dick Ross
Writer: James F. Collier
Director: Dick Ross
Music: Ralph Carmichael
World Wide; 103 minutes
Released 12/2/65

The Sadist

Producer: L. Steven Snyder
Writer: James Landis
Director: James Landis
Music: Rod Moss
Fairway-International; 94 minutes
Released 4/63

Cast: Arch Hall, Jr., Helen Hovey, Richard Alden, Marilyn Manning, Don Russell

Another Arch Hall, Jr., masterwork, this time about teenage psychos terrorizing stranded teachers. There are murders, shootings, emotional terror, and a surprise death by rattlesnakes—take that, Steven Spielberg! Fairway-International also blessed us with *The Choppers, Eegah!, Wild Guitar,* and *The Incredibly Strange Creatures Who Stopped Living and Became Crazy Mixed-Up Zombies,* among others.

Ski Party

Producer: Gene Corman
Writer: Robert Kaufman
Director: Alan Rafkin
Music: Gary Usher
American International; 90 minutes
Released 6/30/65

Cast: Frankie Avalon, Dwayne Hickman, Deborah Walley, Yvonne Craig, Robert Q. Lewis, Bobbi Shaw, Aron Kincaid, Steve Rogers

Another beach movie, this time at a ski lodge. It's a tale of college kids, ski vacation, female impersonation, chases, and the happy ending. Exhibitors have their way: "More of the same 'beach party' stuff. A lot of people seem to like them. Played during holiday vacation, so I thought I'd try one of these on Sunday. This was a bad mistake. Strictly a Friday-Saturday movie. Worth playing." And another: "It did it again. I don't know why, but this type of movie really pulls them in. Good teenage entertainment." Also: "What would we small-towners do without AIP? Another perfect picture that we would have liked a lot more people to have seen, but everybody was out buying for Santa Claus." Also look for Patti Chandler, Salli Sachse, the Hondells, James Brown, Lesley Gore, and Annette Funicello. Music by Gary Usher, Roger Christian, Bob Gaudio, and Marvin Hamlisch.

Some People

Producer: James Archibald
Writer: John Eldridge
Director: Clive Donner
Music: Ron Grainer
American International; 93 minutes
Released 6/64

Cast: Kenneth More, Ray Brooks, Annika Wells, David Andrews, Angela Douglas, David Hemmings, Timothy Nightingale, Frankie Dymon, Jr.

A British import, pretty solid, concerning teenage factory workers, motorcycles, rock 'n' roll, romance, gangs, and reconciliation. This was originally released in Britain in 1962, so by the time it came here it was pretty outdated, culturally speaking. Clive Donner also directed *What's New Pussycat?, Luv, Here We Go 'round the Mulberry Bush,* and many others.

A Swingin' Affair

Producer: Gunther Collins
Writer: Gunther Collins
Directory: Jay O. Lawrence
Emerson; 85 minutes
Released 5/23/63

Cast: William Wellman, Jr., Arline Judge, Dick Dale and the Deltones, Sandra Gale Bettin, Baynes Barron, Susan Sturtridge

A cheap little film about prizefighting, college, and a waitress girlfriend. Dick Dale sings the title tune. Emerson Film Enterprises later evolved into a busy (thirty-six films in eight years) company specializing in sex and violence. Some of their classics included: *Two Living, One Dead, The Doctor and the Playgirl, Mondo Hollywood, Wild Ones on Wheels, Aggie—The Diary of a Nymph,* and *The Sexterminators.*

Surf Party

Producer: Maury Dexter
Writer: Harry Spalding
Director: Maury Dexter
Music: Jimmie Haskell
20th Century–Fox; 68 minutes
Released 1/64

Cast: Bobby Vinton, Patricia Morrow, Jackie DeShannon, Kenny Miller, Lory Patrick, Richard Crane, Jerry Summers, Martha Stewart

The major companies could never seem to get these beach movies right. Either the casting was dull, the music generic, or the story too serious—sometimes all of the above. This one has serious problems on all accounts, but we like watching Jackie DeShannon, the Astronauts, and the Routers. Said *Boxoffice:* "This light drama with music is geared to the teenage craze for surfboard riding, with numerous musical numbers of jukebox caliber to add interest. There are no well-known names in the cast, but they handle their roles adequately. . . . Little about it can be taken seriously, but the fun capers amuse and it will fill out the lower half of a double bill. Surfing scenes are interspersed with romantic ones, the latter kept to a fairly low boiling point, but the girls' beach costumes are provocative." And the *Times* added: "They bounce into passionless love affairs, take reckless surfboard risks in pointless tests of courage, and display an alarming lack of inhibitions and not a trace of social responsibility." Okay, so it isn't *Citizen Kane.*

Raquel Welch was one of the stand-outs in* A Swinging Summer *(1965).

A Swingin' Summer

Producer: Reno Carell
Writer: Leigh Chapman
Director: Robert Sparr
Music: Harry Betts
United Screen Arts; 80 minutes
Released 4/65

Cast: William Wellman, Jr., Quinn O'Hara, James Stacy, Martin West, Raquel Welch, Mary Mitchell, Robert Blair, Allan Jones

Another pretty dull flick about a summer dance pavilion, wealthy parents, romantic problems, robbery, and the happy tie-up. Highlights include appearances by the Righteous Brothers, the Rip Chords, Gary Lewis and the Playboys, and Raquel Welch singing "I'm Ready to Groove." Still, the kids kept coming: "Some of these 'smaller' pictures out-gross bigger ones in my town. This was no super, but it did okay for me." William Wellman, Jr., also graced *A Swingin' Affair, Winter à-Go Go, The Young Sinner, Born Losers,* and many others.

A return to fifties juvenile-delinquent themes sparked* Teenage Gang Debs, *filmed entirely in Brooklyn.

Teenage Gang Debs

Producer: Jerry Denby
Writer: Hy Cahl
Director: Sande Johnsen
Music: Steve Karmen
CIP Ltd.
Released 11/4/66

Cast: Diana Conti, Joey Naudic, Linda Gale, John Batis, Eileen Scott, Tom Yourk, Sandra Kane, Thomas Andrisano

Filmed in Brooklyn, this was a return to the bad-girl wild-guy motorcycle flicks of the fifties, this time updated to include more graphic sex and violence. It's a story of teen gangs, fights, stabbing, romance, rumbles, and revenge. Producer Jerry Denby also brought us such classics as *The Sexploiters, The Beautiful, the Bloody, and the Bare,* and *Pleasure Plantation,* among other wonders, in which he alternated between producer, director, and cinematographer. A true triple threat.

The Thrill Seekers *was a pretty adventurous teen film, imported from England in 1964.*

Teen-age Strangler

Producer: Clark Davis
Writer: Clark Davis
Director: Bill Posner
Ajay; 61 and 67 minutes (two versions)
Released 1964, 1967

Cast: Bill A. Bloom, Jo Canterbury, John Ensign, Jim Asp, Bill Mills, Johnny Haymer

This low-budget obscurity was filmed in West Virginia 1964, when it got limited regional release. It was reissued in 1967, and played on double bills as part of a blood-and-gore shock package. It's the story of a high school Romeo who has a disturbing tendency to kill his dates. Ajay Film Company also brought us *The Quare Fellow, Dog Eat Dog, A Taste of Blood, The Bang Bang Kid,* and others.

The Thrill Seekers

Producer: Robert Hartford-Davis
Writers: Derek and Donald Ford
Director: Robert Hartford-Davis
Music: Malcolm Mitchell
Topaz; 88 minutes
Released 7/64

Cast: Jacqueline Ellis, Annette Whitely, Georgina Patterson, Anne Kettle, Margaret Vieler, Noel Dyson, Victor Brooks, Richard Bebb

"Teenage school dolls . . . what they learned isn't on any report card!" True. What they learned was how to lose their virginity, and then they were rewarded with a yellow teddy bear pin which made them a member of the club. This British film concerned teen girls, a boarding school, a nonvirgins' club, parental neglect, pregnancy, and runaways. It was originally released in Britain in 1963 as *The Thrill Seekers* and *The Yellow Teddy Bears,* and also released in the United States as *Gutter Girls.* British pop stars Iain Gregory and Doug Sheldon carried the male roles.

Under Age

Producer: Harold Hoffman
Writer: Larry Buchanan
Director: Larry Buchanan
Music: Peter Frank Organization
American International; 90 minutes
Released 6/64

Cast: Anne MacAdams, Judy Adler, Roland Royter, George Russell, John Hicks, George Edgley, Tommie Russell, Regina Cassidy

This strange little picture was picked up by AIP after being filmed in Dallas. It's a trial melodrama about a mother who encouraged her fourteen-year-old daughter to have sex with a sixteen-year-old Mexican boy. It's a story of bad parents, ministers, a mother who denies all. The jury deliberates, then the film fades out. Either they didn't have enough money to finish it, or they wanted you to make your own decision. Larry Buchanan also brought us *Free, White and 21, Naughty Dallas, The Trial of Lee Harvey Oswald,* and later on *Goodbye Norma Jean,* and *Hughes and Harlow: Angels in Hell.* Topical guy, that Larry.

Village of the Giants

Producer: Bert I. Gordon
Writer: Alan Caillou
Director: Bert I. Gordon
Music: Jack Nitzsche
Embassy; 80 minutes
Released 10/20/65

Cast: Tommy Kirk, Johnny Crawford, Beau Bridges, Ronny Howard, Joy Harmon, Bob Random, Tisha Sterling, Charla Doherty

A wild teen picture, based loosely on H. G. Wells's *Food of the Gods.* It's the story of teen couples who eat a special food which turns them into giants. They take over and terrorize a town, consumed with greed, until an antidote is found and they're run out of town. From the *Journal of Independent Film* trade magazine: "Interesting combo in *Village of the Giants,* one with an almost certain appeal to teeners. The film unites the elements of science-fiction with teen themes to come up with a musical view of rebellion against the adult world. Youngsters will go for the idea of taking over a town for themselves and living to the rhythm of today's 'big beat,' but will also fall in line with the town's right-minded teeners that after all, right is right. Special effects soup up the fun, especially with a Watusi done by overgrown ducks, and if their variety doesn't complete the bill as the spice of life, the young lovelies shown in a variety of costumes will." Many recognizable faces here, as well as many famous Hollywood offspring: Beau Bridges was the son of Lloyd; Tim Rooney the son of Mickey; and Tisha Sterling the daughter of Robert Sterling and Ann Sothern. Also includes the Beau Brummels, Freddy Cannon, Mike Clifford, and music by Phil Spector arranger Jack Nitzsche. Toni Basil is the choreographer and also has a small acting role. Filmed in "Perceptovision." A novelty.

The Wild Angels

Producer: Roger Corman
Writer: Charles Griffith
Director: Roger Corman
Music: Mike Curb
American International; 82, 83, 85, 90 and 93 minutes (various versions)
Released 7/20/66

Cast: Peter Fonda, Nancy Sinatra, Bruce Dern, Lou Procopio, Coby Denton, Marc Cavell, Buck Taylor, Norman Alden

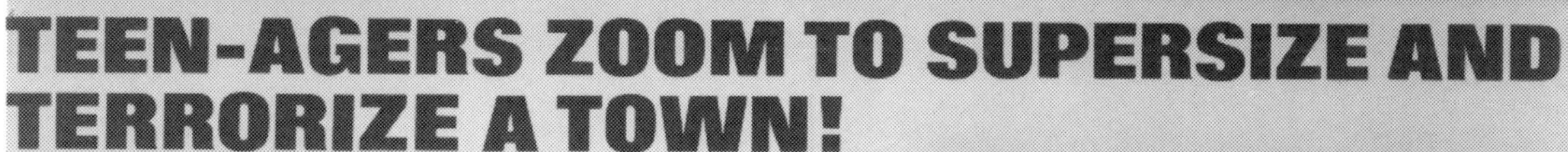

STARRING
TOMMY KIRK · JOHNNY CRAWFORD · RONNY HOWARD · GUEST STARS THE BEAU BRUMMELS · FREDDY CANNON · MIKE CLIFFORD

PRODUCED AND DIRECTED BY Bert I. Gordon · SCREENPLAY BY Alan Caillou · A BERT I. GORDON PRODUCTION IN COLOR · An Embassy Pictures Release

Is there something subliminal in this advertisement?

A landmark film, partially for its graphic violence, and partially for kicking off a wave of biker films that swamped the country. *The Wild Angels* is basically a story of the Hell's Angels, rumbles, thefts, orgies, violent attacks, rape, Nazism, and temporary retreat. The film was released in various running times, most edited to cut out the most brutal and sexy scenes. The *New York Times* called it "a brutal, embarrassing little picture, a vicious account of the boozing, fighting, pot-smoking, vandalizing, and raping done by a gang of 'sickle' riders obviously drawn to represent the swastika-wearing Hell's Angels. . . . Despite an implausible ending, and some rather amateurish acting by Peter Fonda and Nancy Sinatra, it gives a pretty good picture of what these militant motorcycle-cult gangs are." The cinema-verité style of the film added a painful sense of reality, and initially there was some support from the hippie segment of the population—they probably identified with the "outlaw" image and the pot-smoking. But soon the rampant violence and senseless activities pushed the two sides far apart. Still, the biker films that followed had their audience. Others in the cast here included Michael J. Pollard, Diane Ladd, Gayle Hunnicut, and Peter Bogdanovich. Crew members included Bogdanovich and Monte Hellman.

Wild on the Beach

Producer: Maury Dexter
Writer: Harry Spalding
Director: Maury Dexter
Music: Jimmie Haskell
20th Century–Fox; 77 minutes
Released 8/25/65

Cast: Frankie Randall, Sherry Jackson, Russ Bender, Booth Colman, Justin Smith, Jerry Grayson, Marc Seaton, Robert Golden

Beach movies were popular the world over, as can be seen by this Spanish-language poster for* Wild on the Beach. *Somehow though, I just can't picture Frankie, Annette, and all the rest conversing in Spanish.

Michael Parks was selling his imitation of James Dean in 1965's* Wild Seed. *Unfortunately, not too many people were buying.

Another beach film, this time a tale of college students, a disputed beach house, parties, romance, and a happy ending. Sherry Jackson was Danny Thomas's daughter on the original "Make Room for Daddy"; she tried to change her squeaky-clean image by wearing skimpy bathing suits, and later appearing in *Playboy*. There's also music by the Astronauts, Sonny and Cher, Cindy Malone, and Sandy Nelson. Director Dexter was a veritable superstar of B teen flicks, having helmed *The Young Swingers*, and *Surf Party*. He later moved into teen-protest films with *Maryjane, The Mini-Skirt Mob*, and *The Young Animals*.

Wild Seed

Producer: Albert S. Ruddy
Writer: Les Pine
Director: Brian G. Hutton
Music: Richard Markowitz
Universal; 99 minutes
Released 5/5/65

Cast: Michael Parks, Celia Kaye, Ross Elliott, Woodrow Chambliss, Rupert Crosse, Eva Novak, Norman Burton, Merritt Bohn

An attempt to ressurect the James Dean look, with Michael Parks as the Dean look- and soundalike. This is the story of a teen runaway, drifters, arrests, parental problems, and—surprise!—the girl sticks with Parks at the end, and doesn't return home. Parks also moped and grunted his way through *Bus Riley's Back in Town, The Idol,* and *The Happening,* before scoring mildly as the motorcycle-riding drifter in TV's "Then Came Bronson" (1969–70). Executive producer of *Wild Seed* was Marlon Brando, Sr.

Wild Wild Winter

Producer: Bart Patton
Writer: David Malcolm
Director: Lennie Weinrib
Music: Jerry Long, Frank Wilson
Universal; 80 minutes
Released 1/5/66

Cast: Gary Clarke, Chris Noel, Don Edmonds, Suzie Kaye, Les Brown, Jr., Vicky Albright, James Wellman, Steve Franken

Another student frolic, this time with college students, featuring skiing, contests, and the happy finale. For musical merriment you can catch Jay and The Americans, the Beau Brummels, Dick and DeeDee, the Astronauts, and Jackie and Gayle. Weinrib also directed *Beach Ball,* and *Out of Sight* and acted in Sonny and Cher's *Good Times.* He later wrote all episodes of "H. R. Pufnstuf" for television.

Winter à Go-Go

Producer: Reno Carell
Writer: Bob Kanter
Director: Richard Benedict
Music: Harry Betts
Columbia; 88 minutes
Released 10/28/65

Cast: James Stacy, William Wellman, Jr., Beverly Adams, Anthony Hayes, Jill Donohue, Tom Nardini, Duke Hobbie, Julie Parrish

More frolic at a ski lodge, with friends, fights, success, and the happy wrap-up. Music by Screen Gems staffers Howard Greenfield, Steve Venet, Tommy Boyce, Bobby Hart, and Toni Wine. Also features performances by Joni Lyman, the Hondells, the Astronauts, the Reflections, and the Nooney Rickett Four. William Wellman, Jr., was the son of famed Hollywood director William Wellman, and James Stacy was married to teen star Kim Darby from 1967 to 1969. Stacy also had the lead in a "Bonanza" ripoff, "Lancer," on TV from 1968 to 1970.

The Young Sinner

Producer: Tom Laughlin
Writer: Tom Laughlin
Director: Tom Laughlin
Music: Shelly Manne
United Screen Arts; 81 minutes
Released 8/65

Cast: Tom Laughlin, Stefanie Powers, William Wellman, Jr., James Stacy, Roxanne Heard, Robert Angelo, Linda March, Julia Paul

Shot in Milwaukee in 1960, and screened in 1961 as *Like Father, Like Son,* this film wasn't officially released until 1965—which helped, because not only was Laughlin a bit better known, but Stefanie Powers, William Wellman, Jr., and James Stacy were quite well-known names. This was part of an aborted trilogy, *We Are All Christ,* and concerned confessional flashbacks, high school athletes, bad parents, girlfriend problems, loose morals, expulsion from school, and the final help of a priest who will aid Laughlin. Said *Daily Variety:* "an offbeat story of teenage love . . . some frank sex angles and use of salty language are handled well." This followed Laughlin's first self-made film, *The Proper Time.*

The Young Swingers

Producer: Maury Dexter
Writer: Harry Spalding
Director: Maury Dexter
Music: Hank Levine
20th Century–Fox; 71 minutes
Released 9/19/63

Cast: Rod Lauren, Molly Bee, Gene McDaniels, Jack Larson, Jo Helton, Justin Smith, Jerry Summers, Jack Younger

An early-in-the-cycle tale of a teen nightclub, singers, romance, arson, and reconciliation. Pretty tame and pretty dull. Features Rod "I-was-supposed-to-be-a-star-but-never-was" Lauren, and Jack "Jimmy Olsen" Larson. Larson was also in *Teenage Millionaire,* while Lauren was stuck in *The Crawling Hand, Terrified!, Once before I Die,* and several other monstrosities.

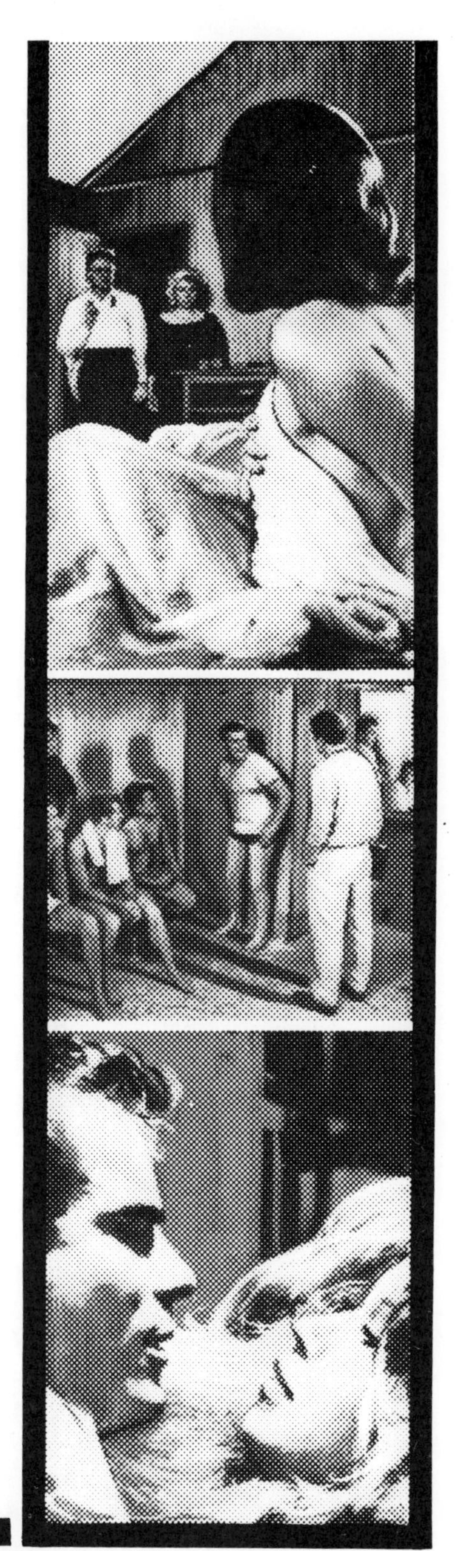

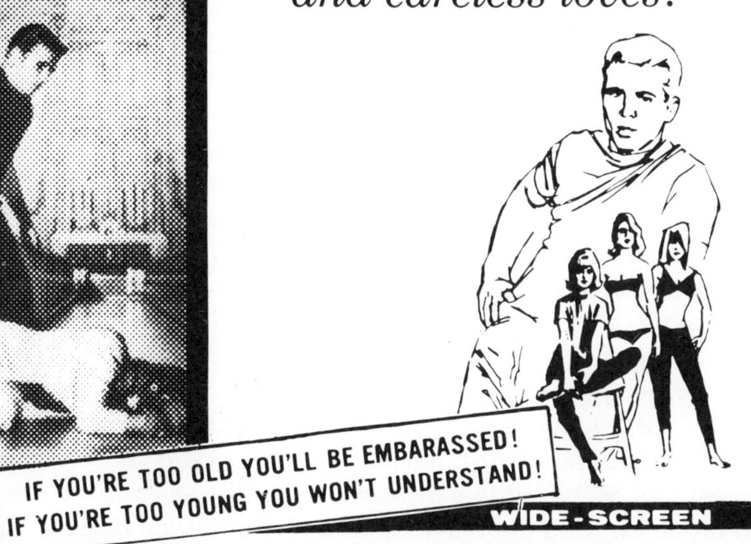

***The Young Sinner* was shot in Milwaukee in 1960, but not officially released until 1965. Writer-producer-director Tom Laughlin later struck paydirt with *Born Losers* and the *Billy Jack* films.**

1967-1969
The Protest Trip

In late 1966, Roger Corman and AIP released *The Wild Angels,* a graphic and violent look at the Hell's Angels motorcycle gang. Although (or perhaps because) the media lambasted the film for its overt brutality and cinema-verité realism, the picture went on to become a massive box-office hit, and a cult artistic triumph as well. In its initial release it grossed over $6 million, a massive amount for such a low-budget film. Over the next three years about twenty biker films would follow (with more following in the early seventies), each one trying to outdo its predecessor in sheer volume of senseless violence, sex, and, of course, theater grosses. They were usually made very cheaply, needing little in the way of interior locations or name actors, and with much of the running time spent on scenes of motorcycles roaring down the highways. Surprisingly, these pictures made a lot of money, no matter how cheaply or amateurishly they were produced. In fact, some new independent film companies like Crown and Fanfare were made almost overnight with profits earned from biker pictures. To my mind they don't really fit into the category of teen exploitation movies, because for one the actors were not portraying teenagers, and for another the films did not really examine an aspect of teenage culture. A large part of the audience, especially in drive-ins, was made up of teenagers, but so were the audiences for many other types of films. The real target audience for these films was a male in his early twenties—mostly in the South and the Midwest, where it seemed that sado-masochism on film had a rather large following.

But there was little anyone could do to stop the flood. In 1967, there was *Devil's Angels* (AIP), *Wild Rebels* (Crown), *The Glory Stompers* (AIP), and *Outlaw Motorcycles* (Hollywood Star). In 1968, the feast continued with *Hell's Chosen Few* (Thunderbird), *The Savage Seven* (AIP), *She-Devils on Wheels* (Mayflower), *The Hellcats* (Crown), *Angels from Hell* (Fanfare/AIP), and *The Angry Breed* (Commonwealth United). The decade closed out with *Cycle Savages* (AIP), *Hell's Angels '69* (AIP), *Hell's Belles* (AIP), *Naked Angels* (Crown), *Run, Angel, Run!* (Fanfare), *Satan's Sadists* (Independent-International), and *Wild Wheels* (Fanfare). Almost half of these films grossed in the $1-to-$2 million range, a few did a bit better, and the rest took in under a million dollars. But they were made so quickly and cheaply that almost all of them turned a profit. I am not a fan or connoisseur of biker films, nor do I believe they fit the criteria for pure teen exploitation films, but are worth mentioning because they were a close offshoot of teen films, patronized by a large percentage of teens, and they offered an alternative to the peace-love-and-drugs atmosphere of the true teen exploitation flicks of the era. The lines were being drawn in the real world between war and

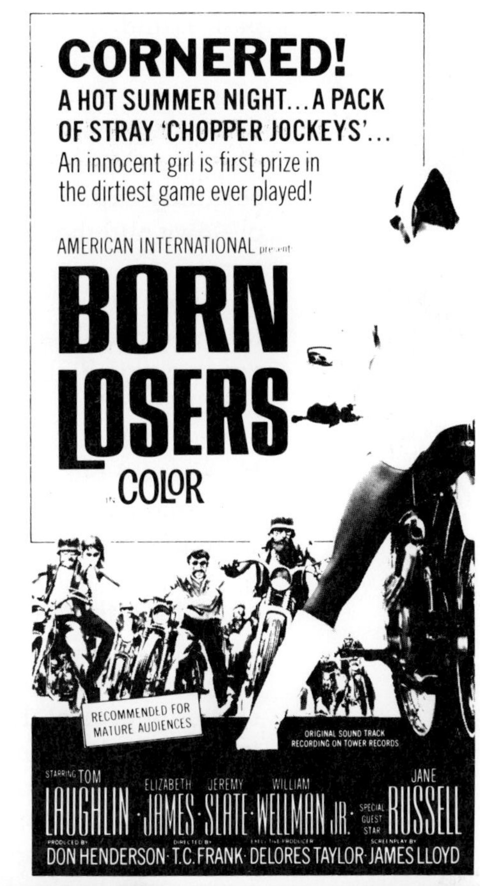

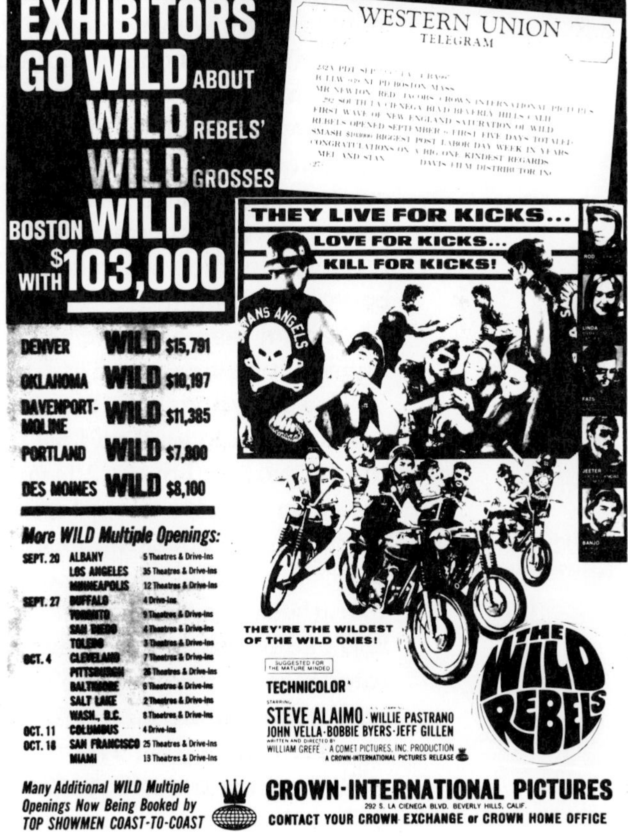

Some typical ads for biker films.

peace, and to a certain extent this dichotomy was represented by the biker-hippie film trends. But, to be sure, this wasn't a genre of teen angst, rebellion, culture, music, lingo, or even juvenile delinquency—it was a genre of brutal criminality by over twenty-ones who in these films led a life of rape, Nazism, sadism, and violence. They were certainly exploitation films, but not of the teenage genre. There are outlaws and there are outlaws. But all outlaws are not created the same.

About the best I can say for biker films is that they gave many talented people some work on their way to better things. Behind the camera was Richard Rush, Roger Corman, Jonathan Demme, and Tom Laughlin, while onscreen were such performers as Bruce Dern, Dennis Hopper, John Cassavettes, Jack Nicholson, Diane Ladd, Nancy Sinatra, Michael J. Pollard, Tyne Daley, Gary Busey, and Harry Dean Stanton. Their pictures were the best of the genre—the ultracheap imitations were pretty near horrible.

In 1967, there were still some holdovers of the beach-party fun-and-frolic variety—*C'mon Let's Live a Little, It's a Bikini World,* and a few others—but times were clearly changing. The media was filled with stories of protest, hippies, runaways, drugs, and new rock music. In fact the media was swamped, and not only from the above-ground straight media; a new breed of underground papers was now blossoming and millions of teens were being drawn to this new lifestyle. So the exploitation filmmakers jumped in to capitalize on the trend, and try to make some bucks. For the most part, these films portrayed the new movement as weird, generally distasteful, and basically degenerate. This initially may have played well in some backwoods areas, where the hippie thing was slow to penetrate, but for the most part the films were perceived of as outdated, dishonest, and laughable, and never really reached the audience being portrayed onscreen. First came the quicky cheapy documentaries—*The Hippie Revolt, Mondo Mod, Mondo Teeno, Revolution,* and the like, which were newly shot and documentary-type footage set to bad rock music. You could probably have done better watching the news and reading *Life* magazine. The two most influential teen-oriented pictures of 1967 were *The Trip* and *Riot on Sunset Strip,* and both, fittingly enough, came from AIP.

The Trip, Roger Corman's picture, was supposedly what it was actually like to take an LSD trip, with Peter Fonda as "the man on the trip." It was an honest attempt to recreate the effects of LSD, but that's pretty impossible to capture on film, especially with a low budget and 1967's limited special-effects capabilities. Although the film today seems crude and even amateurish, often stereotyped and campy, for 1967 it was a bit of a shock, and quite controversial. Was it promoting LSD use by not coming down squarely in opposition to it? Was it accurate? Was it irresponsible? Was it a ripoff? All these questions were ballyhooed in the media, and, despite its jarring visual style and lack of a traditional plot, *The Trip* became a surprise hit, grossing over $4.5 million at the box-office. *Riot on Sunset Strip* was a more traditional AIP exploitation film, and also received a lot of media attention, centering as it did on a real event. AIP and Sam Katzman (the film's producer) hoped that this too would be a major success. It was a mixture of camp Hollywood stylizations of the new lifestyle, alongside a cinema-verité–

Trade advertisements for* The Trip *stressed how much money the film was grossing.

style story of the events leading up to the real "riot on Sunset Strip." There were a few accurate moments, and some relatively true music, mixed together with some totally ridiculous scenarios, characters, and language. But the film did not draw too many fans to the box office—after all, who *really* cared about the Sunset Strip in the rest of the country? It grossed over a million dollars, but was considered a failure.

Now the flood began—*Hallucination Generation, The Love-Ins, The Hooked Generation, The Young Runaways.* For the most part these films did not do very well. The real hippies found them to be inaccurate, juvenile jokes, and the rest of the kids didn't seem all that interested. They wanted something safe and secure in the face of a fast-changing world, or something that represented a complete fantasy. They didn't want reality, and for the most part that's what these films represented.

The classics for 1968 were *Maryjane, Psych-Out,* and *Wild in the Streets. Maryjane* was a throwback to the fifties dope films, where fantasy was substituted for reality. It's a story of high schools, teachers, and pot smoking, but performed in such an unrealistic manner as to make it safe enough to draw fans to the box office. And, after all, it was only pot—something that by this time was infiltrating every high school in the country. *Psych-Out* was a Dick Clark production, directed by Richard Rush, which was one of the better looks at the Haight-Ashbury scene. Perhaps it was the fact that they had a hip and experienced cast—Susan Strasberg, Dean Stockwell, Jack Nicholson, Bruce Dern, and Henry Jaglom—that kept it from becoming a horribly out-of-date and ridiculous look at the drug culture. It does have its campy moments and funny Hollywood hippie clothes, but there is still much worth seeing here. Many of the participants in *The Trip* and *Psych-Out* would later unite to make *Easy Rider,* a solid and inventive look at the alternative culture, which would go on to become one of the largest grossing and best-respected films of its time. *Wild in the Streets* was another AIP film, this one quite expensive to produce, which offered a satirical fantasy vision of what life might be like in the future with LSD and youth-culture power taken to their extremes. It was well done, with good characters and situations, but perhaps the fact that it reflected fantasy rather than reality was really the reason it became so popular. It was a significant box-office success, grossing over $4 million in its first six months of release. Today it's a classic of sorts, and, for its time, it's not totally off-base in its predictions. Sure there's a lot of laughs, but a strong dose of social commentary weaves in throughout the story as well.

By 1969, the hippie-protest-LSD cycle had just about died out. The violent biker pictures were still going strong, but Hollywood just could never find the right balance in the teen exploitation genre to guarantee success. Things were moving so fast that, by the time a picture came out, it seemed hopelessly outdated. Moreover, by this point drugs, youth, and looser sex were becoming staples of almost every Hollywood picture, so the exploitation pix were just squeezed out on both ends. Teens were also being lured to more thoughtful and intelligent pictures like *The Graduate,* which with its teen *and* adult audience grossed over $40 million in 1968 and 1969. This was an absolutely staggering amount, and, along with the success of *Easy Rider* and other more realistic youth-oriented pictures, left the exploitation film-

Two "hippies," wearing sandwich signs, parade Baltimore streets as a stunt for AIP's "The Trip" at the JF circuit's New Theatre. The pair also distributed brightly colored neck cards, which read: "Turn in, turn on, trip out."

'Angels From Hell' Bows in Wichita

During the "Angels From Hell" world premiere festivities at Commonwealth's Meadowlark-Twin Drive-In at Wichita, Joe Solomon, upper left, producer of the American International Pictures release, introduces Jack Starrett, who has a role in the film. Upper right, the marquee of the Joe Borders-managed drive-in points to the premiere and the appearance of the recording group, which did the background music for the picture. Lower left, Manager Borders has members of a motorcycle group to display their vehicles to add atmosphere to the film about a motorcycle gang. Lower right, an autograph party is being held by members of the cast of "Angels From Hell"—Tom Stern, Ted Markland, James Murphy, Starrett and Luana Talltree.

Car in Psychedelic Colors For 'Psych-Out' in Omaha

A. H. Cohn, manager of Ralph Blank's Chief Theatre in Omaha, stirred up a lot of interest when he painted a car in psychedelic water colors and paraded it through town to promote "Psych-Out" and "The Trip" at the Admiral, Chief and Sky View.

Cohen even drew the attention of police, who agreed that the paint job was a knockout as an attention-getter, but thought it was a bit too much. After a bit of the decoration was removed from the windshield he passed with screaming colors. Cohn promoted the car in return for a small display in the lobby.

"I paint my own signs, so it wasn't any effort to decorate the car and make a small banner announcing the playdate for the Admiral, Chief and Sky View," Cohn said.

Detroit Newspaper Refuses Ad With LSD Mentioned

DETROIT—The psychedelic drug LSD apparently has become "unmentionable" in theatre advertising here in the Free Press, according to William Brown, president of the 5,000-seat Fox Theatre, concerning ads for "The Weird World of LSD."

"They will use LSD in news stories, but not in ads," Brown says. "They wanted me to change the title, but I couldn't." He says he was told the picture was not a factual story, and did not deserve to be advertised.

The Detroit News accepted the ads without question, Brown says.

makers confused and in disarray. Their fortes were not realism, accuracy, sincerity, emotional depth, or true situations, yet it was these elements that now seemed to be drawing kids into the theaters in droves. The high school kids were put on a back burner, while the college generation took hold. The exploitation filmmakers appeared to have lost their core audience, and they turned to other, more specialized films to reach their audience—sex, blaxploitation, prison films, martial arts, gore, and so on. But now, instead of shooting for one big mass audience, they were splitting up their market into different subgenres, so their overall impact and trendsetting nature was diminished. It wouldn't be until the nostalgia boom *(American Graffitti, Grease)* and the disco boom *(Saturday Night Fever),* that they would once again turn their sights on the pure teenage market, followed by graphic horror films, college and high school hijinx movies, slasher films, and so on. Once again, each cycle would last for only three years at best, and then they had to search for something new to entice their core audience back into the theaters.

But despite the ups and downs of the teen exploitation market, it always seems to stage a comeback, just when pundits have pronounced it dead. Perhaps this is because kids want to see things only they understand or relate to, and perhaps, ultimately, it is because teens are teens and trends are trends. Adults may look down with disdain at teen exploitation trends—and despite much change in the world, the target is still the teenage male—but the trends go on. It seems that there is room for everybody, and there's always a lot of junk and some good stuff in there too. Today it's the Brat Pack, tomorrow it's somebody else and something new. But the power of peer pressure and mass media advertising campaigns cannot be discounted. The whole idea of exploitation films is to get the kids into the theaters. After that, it's a problem for the sociologists. The films are cheap. They're lurid. They're stereotyped. They're stupid. They're ridiculous. They're rip-offs. They're immature. They're scary. They're campy. They're sexy. They're violent. They go for the jugular and cost five bucks to get in. Perhaps that's why they're called exploitation films.

The Battle of the Mods

Producer: Luggi Waldleitner
Writers: Ennio de Concini, Adriano Bolzoni, Michael A. Scheiber
Director: Franco Montemurro
Music: Robby Poitevin
GG; 97 minutes
Released 9/68

Cast: Ricky Shayne, Joachim Fuchsberger, Elga Andersen, Eleonora Brown, Orchidea De Santis, Enzo Cerusico, Solveig D'Assunta, Cristina Gajoni

This Italian–West German co-production, starring German teen idol Ricky Shayne, was a story of a mods 'n' rockers battle, death, police chase, flight to the Continent, bad parents, decadence, and final escape. It was originally released in Rome in August 1966 as *Crazy Baby,* so by the time it received its limited U.S. release, it was pretty far out of date. The ads promised that it was filmed "in all the colors of a psychedelic seizure, and not recommended for those over thirty." Gee, if it might cause a seizure, I don't know if those under thirty should have gone either—and not many did.

Born Wild

Producer: Maury Dexter
Writer: James Gordon White
Director: Maury Dexter
Music: Les Baxter
American International; 100 minutes
Released 10/68

Cast: Tom Nardini, Patty McCormack, David Macklin, Joanna Frank, Zooey Hall, Sammy Vaughn, Michael Wood, Keith Taylor

Filmed in Tucson, this teen epic concerned Mexican-American students, bigotry, rape, violence, revenge, chases, a student strike, and in the end a fair hearing for their grievances. Said *Boxoffice:* "This might well be described as an Andy Hardy movie for student radicals. Naive in concept, and peopled by what must be the oldest high school students in the world, *Born Wild* is nonetheless a sincere and surprisingly effective vehicle with a timeliness that might well make it very popular with the teen crowd. Maury Dexter has directed with great style, and there's also the standard quota of violence and enough sex to inspire the more unimaginative drive-in patrons. . . . This is just different enough in theme and execution to be a big hit with the youngsters." The film's title was originally *The Young Animals* and at the last minute a new title was edited onto the film, and all press material was replastered with *Born Wild* stickers. Said the *Times:* "Another bargain priced, glib commentary. This was originally more appropriately titled *The Young Animals.* It was filmed in color, but it is colorless." Child star Patty McCormack later became a teen exploitation star in *Maryjane, The Mini-Skirt Mob,* and *The Young Runaways.*

A Boy. . . a Girl

Producer: Jack Hanson
Writer: John Derek
Director: John Derek
Music: Joe Greene
Four Star Excelsior/Cannon; 69 minutes
Released 4/25/69

Cast: Dino Martin, Jr., Airion Fromer, Karen Steele, Kerwin Mathews, Peggy Lipton, Trace Vernell, Gene Walker, Michael-Maxim Nadar

This is a kind of drama-fable concerning a fifteen-year-old couple in love, loss of virginity, LSD, and an older man; in the finale, the girl leaves the boy behind. This low-budget film was originally shot in sixteen-millimeter and blown up to thirty-five. In 1970, it was re-edited and rereleased at seventy-six and eighty-five minutes as *The Sun Is Up.* Special music was written and recorded by the duo Jamme, a group whose LP was produced by John Phillips of the Mamas and Papas. John Derek, a matinee idol in the 1950s who appeared in over two dozen films, later directed *Tarzan* and *Bolero,* starring his third wife, Bo Derek. His first two marriages were to Ursula Andress and Linda Evans.

Chastity

Producer: Sono Bono
Writer: Sonny Bono
Director: Alessio De Paola
Music: Sonny Bono, Dan Peake
American International; 85 minutes
Released 6/69

Cast: Cher, Barbara London, Stephen Whittaker, Tom Nolan, Danny Zapien, Elmer Valentine, Burke Rhind, Richard Armstrong

Born Wild ***starred Patty*** **Bad Seed** ***McCormack, and was also released as*** **The Young Animals** ***— I guess that sounded too much like a wilderness film.***

This is a showcase for the dramatic acting talents of Cher, after Sonny and Cher's musical romp in *Good Times.* This concerns a female teenage hitchhiker and her exploits on the road—robbery, a trip to Mexico, brothels, lesbianism, and general worldly problems. In the end Chastity (Cher) is seen going back on that long lonely road. Said the *Times:* "Purposeful, rather pretty and completely banal. The film seems to have been directed simply by keeping Cher in focus. Mostly, however, *Chastity* is like a small child's frown, solemn and innocent."

C'mon, Let's Live a Little

Producers: June Starr, John Hertelandy
Writer: June Starr
Director: David Butler
Music: Don Ralke
Paramount; 85 minutes
Released 5/3/67

Cast: Bobby Vee, Jackie DeShannon, Eddie Hodges, Suzie Kaye, Patsy Kelly, Ethel Smith, Bo Belinsky, John Ireland, Jr.

An out-of-date teen romp, this film concerned folk singers, college, campus politics, romance, and a happy ending. This was so conservative, it was almost radical. Said the *Times:* "Idiotic? Perhaps. But it aims to please, and for the life of us we can't see how it will harm teenagers. For one thing, the picture is clean—much cleaner in fact than a lot of rock 'n' roll rhythmic beach frolics that cloak on-the-brink sexuality in sunshine and surf. For another, some of the youngsters are generally appealing, especially Mr. Vee and Jackie DeShannon. Finally, the tunes the youngsters warble and occasionally bellow are several cuts above average." Also look for Kim "Bette Davis Eyes" Carnes, and Ken "Eddie Haskell" Osmond in small roles.

The Cool Ones

Producer: William Conrad
Writer: Joyce Geller
Director: Gene Nelson
Music: Lee Hazelwood, Ernie Freeman, Billy Strange
Warner Bros.; 94 minutes
Released 4/12/67

Cast: Roddy McDowall, Debbie Watson, Gil Peterson, Phil Harris, Elvira Miller, Robert Coote, Nita Talbot, George Furth

This satirical look at the music business, although quite exaggerated, has its moments of truth and entertainment. It concerns rock 'n' roll singers, an egotistical manager-tycoon (Phil Spector?), media manipulation, romance, and a happy ending. There's some good character acting, especially from Nita Talbot, as well as musical spots by the Bantams, Glen Campbell, and the Leaves. The choreographer was Toni Basil. This is good, campy fun. Director Gene Nelson also helmed *Hootenanny Hoot, Your Cheatin' Heart,* and two Elvis films, *Kissin' Cousins* and *Harum Scarum.* In addition, he also directed over 175 episodes of television series including "I Dream of Jeannie," "Mod Squad," and "Dan August."

Free Grass

Producer: John Lawrence
Writers: John Lawrence, James Gordon White, Gerald Wilson, Paul Stevenson
Director: Bill Brame
Music: Sidewalk Productions
Hollywood Star; 83 minutes
Released 10/15/69

Cast: Richard Beymer, Russ Tamblyn, Lana Wood, Elizabeth Thompson, Warren Finnerty, Casey Kasem, Joel (Jody) McCrea, Lindsay Crosby

This low-budget quicky was a little late in the cycle, as it concerned hippies, pot smuggling, murder, LSD, gang fights and death, and finally free pot for hippies. This film had lots of Hollywood offspring in it, but the biggest character change was for former Disney star Russ Tamblyn—his next film was *The Blood Seekers.* Most of the rest just faded away, except for Casey Kasem, who became one of America's most successful DJs.

Hallucination Generation

Producer: Nigel Cox
Writer: Edward Andrew Mann
Director: Edward Andrew Mann
Music: Bernardo Segall
Trans American; 90 minutes
Released 12/66

Cast: George Montgomery, Danny Stone, Renate Kasche, Tom Baker, Marianne Kanter, Steve Rowland, Claude Gersene

Filmed in Spain, this was an early-in-the-cycle LSD picture. It told the story of expatriate Americans in Spain, LSD, sex, romance, gambling, robbery, murder, arrest, and retreat to a monastery. This was the first film released by Trans American Pictures, a subsidiary of American International—these were the films that were even too low-budget or sleazy to bear the AIP tag. Other Trans-American releases included *Mondo Teeno, Sadismo, The Cycle Savages,* and *It's a Bikini World.*

TONIGHT

YOU ARE INVITED TO A 'PILL PARTY'

You will experience every jolt... every jar of a Psychedelic Circus...The Beatniks...Sickniks... and Acid-Heads...and you will witness their ecstasies, their agonies and their bizarre sensualities... You will be hurled into their debauched dreams and frenzied fantasies!

The revealing story of today's...

HALLUCINATION GENERATION

STARRING GEORGE MONTGOMERY · DANNY STONE ·

Herbert R. Steinmann Presents
An Edward Mann · Robert D. Weinbach Production
Produced by NIGEL COX · Written and Directed by EDWARD MANN
A TRANS AMERICAN RELEASE

Here We Go 'round the Mulberry Bush

Producer: Clive Donner
Writer: Hunter Davies
Director: Clive Donner
Music: Simon Napier-Bell
Lopert; 96, 114 minutes (two versions)
Released 3/4/68

Cast: Barry Evans, Judy Geeson, Angela Scoular, Sheila White, Adrienne Posta, Vanessa Howard, Diane Keen, Moyra Fraser

This is a British mod movie about a teenage boy who seeks to lose his virginity, and has a series of wild encounters. The screenplay was written by Hunter *(The Beatles)* Davies, and taken from his 1965 novel of the same name. This film captures the feel of swinging London quite well, and features music by the Spencer Davis Group, Stevie Winwood, Traffic, and Andy Ellison. Musical director Simon Napier-Bell was an important manager and producer in Britain in the mid-sixties (the Yardbirds was one of his groups), and he spent the early eighties as manager of the megagroup Wham!

The Hippie Revolt

Producer: Art Lieberman
Director: Edgar Beatty
Music: Tom and John Bahler
Headliner; 85 minutes
Released 12/19/67

This is a documentary filmed in the spring and summer of 1967 in Haight-Ashbury and other California locales. There are scenes of love-ins, discotheques, crash pads, body painting, pot and LSD use, communes, and interviews with hippies. This was also released as *Something's Happening,* and featured music by the Love Generation. Edgar Beatty also directed several hundred television commercials.

The Hooked Generation

Producer: William Grefe
Writers: Quinn Morrison, Ray Preston, William Grefe
Director: William Grefe
Music: Chris Martell
Allied Artists; 92 minutes
Released 11/13/68

Cast: Jeremy Slate, Steve Alaimo, John David Chandler, Willie Pastrano, Cece Stone, Socrates Ballis, Walter Philbin, Milton Smith

This low-budget picture was filmed in Florida, and was a story of drug dealers, murder, robbery, kidnapping, rape, and death. The final scene of death by hypodermic needle in the neck was quite original. Director Grefe also helmed *Racing Fever, Want a Ride, Little Girl, The Wild Rebels,* and *The Devil's Sisters,* among others. Jeremy Slate also graced *Born Losers, The Mini-Skirt Mob, Hell's Angels,* and *The Girl in the Leather Skirt,* while would-be teen star Steve Alaimo emoted in *The Wild Rebels* and *The Naked Zoo.* Said one exhibitor: "*The Hooked Generation* is a timely film that my audience loved. We did terrific business all week. This one can make money for you." Ah yes, but is it art?

Hot Rods to Hell

Producer: Sam Katzman
Writer: Robert E. Kent
Director: John Brahm
Music: Fred Karger
MGM; 92 minutes
Released 2/67

Cast: Dana Andrews, Jeanne Crain, Mimsy Farmer, Laurie Mock, Paul Bertoya, Gene Kirkwood, Tim Stafford, George Ives

This is a rather dull and silly story of a middle-class family terrorized by wild teenagers. The acting is overdone, and the story is full of holes, especially the ending where Dad teaches the kids a lesson they won't forget. This was taken from the story "Fifty-two Miles to Terror," which appeared in the *Saturday Evening Post* of January 14, 1956. Songs are performed by Mickey Rooney, Jr., and

Hot Rods to Hell was originally supposed to be a TV movie, but the powers at the network found it too violent and distasteful.

his group. Teen wild girl Mimsy Farmer also appeared in *Riot on Sunset Strip, Devil's Angels, The Wild Racers,* and the 1969 drugs-and-sex classic *More.*

It's a Bikini World

Producer: Charles S. Swartz
Writers: Charles S. Swartz, Stephanie Rothman
Director: Stephanie Rothman
Music: Mike Curb, Bob Summers
Trans American; 86 minutes
Released 4/67

Cast: Deborah Walley, Tommy Kirk, Robert Pickett, Suzie Kaye, Jack Bernardi, William O'Connell, Sid Haig, Jim Begg

This is a very late-in-the-cycle beach movie, perhaps saved a bit by the slightly feminist plot line. It's a story of teen athletic competitions, dual character roles, beaches, and the happy ending. It also features screen appearances by the Animals, the Toys, the Gentrys, and seminal punk group the Castaways. Said one exhibitor: "I used this second run as part of a double bill. It seemed to be only fair. Some walkouts on it. Not as good as an AIP produced beach picture." Stephanie Rothman later became a cult director for her low-budget films, including *The Student Nurses, The Velvet Vampire, Group Marriage,* and *The Working Girls.*

Just for the Hell of It

Producer: Herschell Gordon Lewis
Writer: Herschell Gordon Lewis
Director: Herschell Gordon Lewis
Music: Larry Wellington
Unusual Films International; 85 minutes
Released 11/6/68

Cast: Rodney Bedell, Ray Sager, Nancy Lee Noble, Agi Gyenes, Steve White, Ralph Mullin, Larry Williams, A.V. Dreeson, Sr.

Blood 'n' guts director Lewis took a slight departure with this film, a tale of a delinquent teen gang on a rampage. There's lots of violence, dope, police chases, and death. Lewis also directed *Blood Feast, The Gruesome Twosome, She-Devils on Wheels,* and *The Wizard of Gore,* among other cult classics. For afficionados only.

The Love-Ins

Producer: Sam Katzman
Writers: Hal Collins, Arthur Dreifuss
Director: Arthur Dreifuss
Music: Fred Karger
Columbia; 91 minutes
Released 7/26/67

Cast: Richard Todd, James MacArthur, Susan Oliver, Mark Goddard, Carol Booth, Marc Cavell, Janee Michelle, Ronnie Eckstine

This timely bit of film history comes from the ever-current Sam Katzman. It's a story of an underground newspaper, expulsion from college, LSD, happenings, false gurus, pregnancy, attempted suicide, murder, and martyrdom. Said the ads: "The hippies and diggers are here—with the way out excitement that's turning on America today!" Besides the leading cast, also look for controversial talk-show host Joe Pyne, the Chocolate Watch Band, U.F.O.s, New Age, and Donnie Brooks. Said the *Times:* "The hippie couple who submitted to matrimony in the Victoria Theatre yesterday morning before the opening of *The Love-Ins* (it was, as you may guess, a publicity stunt), were more fortunate than the gaggle of customers who sat through this shrill and predictable Hollywood cop-out on the whole current hippie happening. It's a gaudy, gleeful glorification of the fun that hippies have at their jolly outdoor love-ins and on their phantasmagorical trips. . . . Evidently Mr. Katzman wanted his picture to be both psychedelic and socially indignant. It is neither. It's a very weak trip." Campy fun.

A trade magazine advertisement for Maryjane promised that AIP was "always timely with the NOW scene" — and they were.

'THE LOVE-INS' *IS FOR HIP EXPLOITATION!*

'The Love-Ins' Language

Listed below are definitions of several words used by hippies in everyday conversation. Print these definitions on throwaway cards, with credits and a scene from the film.

'HIP' TALK

THE HASHBURY — That section of San Francisco where Hippies live.
HIP - Wise or tuned-in. A Hippie "knows" what's really happening.
HEAD — A user of LSD, marijuana and other psychedelic drugs.
JOINT — A helping or dose of a psychedelic drug.
GURU — A leader of Hippies.
DIGGERS — Hippies who provide food and shelter for "heads."
MILL-IN — A sitdown or protest in the streets.
NARK — A narcotics agent.
PAD — Apartment, living quarters.
HASH — Hashish.
GRASS or POT — Marijuana.
MELLOW YELLOW — Scrapings of banana peel, smoked to induce a "high."
HIGH — Under the influence of a psychedelic drug.
BUST - Under arrest. If a Hippie is "busted," he's been arrested.
COMMUNE — An apartment where anyone can live without charge.
ACID — LSD, a psychedelic drug.
TEENY-BOPPER — Under-age boy or girl who looks-in on the Hippie scene.

Know the Language of the Hippies When You See
'THE LOVE-INS'
starring
RICHARD TODD JAMES MacARTHUR SUSAN OLIVER
A Columbia Pictures Release in Eastman Color
Wednesday, State Theatre

- Stage "The Love-Ins" Art Show, with paintings by art students to be exhibited in the theatre lobby. In addition to guest tickets to all entrants, promote art items for the best and most unusual paintings.
- Psychedelic facial make-up is popular with girl hippies, who paint tear drops, small hearts and other symbols on their cheeks. In a tie-up with a local beauty shop, offer girls a psychedelic cheek decoration and a guest ticket to "The Love-Ins" if they wear the make-up throughout the day.
- For a street bally, send a girl dressed in hippie fashion-barefooted, mini-mini-skirted, sweater, long straight hair and dark glasses—through town with a sign on her back: "The Hippies Are Here! See 'The Love-Ins!' State Theatre."
- Work with a local dance studio on a "Dance-In," in your theatre lobby or out-front. Or, perhaps with dancing in the aisles of your theatre. Youngsters participating wear "in" costumes, of course. Offer prizes for best costumes, best dancers.
- Sandals or bare feet, weird clothing styles, beards and long hair are some of the ways hippies show their independence of modern customs. Offer guest admissions to the first ten or more residents who attend "The Love-Ins" at your theatre in similar fashion. Arrange for newspaper and television coverage.
- Hippies have been known to express themselves by painting each other. Relate this to "The Love-Ins" via a painting party in the lobby, with a girl in a bikini being painted while radio announcer describes the action. Furnish water color paints and cosmetic colors for the stunt, which might also be worked in a downtown store window.
- Hippies have been known to paint automobiles, with bright "psychedelic" colors in weird designs. Promote a car from a used car dealer, park it in front of the theatre a week in advance of playdate and let local hippies paint it. Drive the car through town with credit banners.
- Brighten up the scene by having hippies, or volunteer artists, paint the sidewalk with a psychedelic painting! They can demonstrate their art in front of the theatre or other sections of town where it would be permissible, such as empty lots. Local merchants might give permission to have their windows painted with water colors.
- Set a competition among local go-go girl dancers to perform in a downtown store window, or on a platform in the theatre lobby, giving their impressions of a hippie at a "love-in." The girls should wear home-made and way-out costumes or they might model the "Psychedelic Fashions" provided by a neighborhood store.

Some typical marketing strategies for hippie films, in this case* The Love-Ins. *Note hippie dictionary.

Maryjane

Producer: Maury Dexter
Writer: Richard Gautier, Peter L. Marshall
Director: Maury Dexter
Music: Mike Curb, Lawrence Brown
American International; 95 minutes
Released 1/24/68

Cast: Fabian, Diane McBain, Kevin Coughlin, Michael Margotta, Patty McCormack, Russ Bender, Booth Colman, Baynes Barron

Said the ads geared to theater owners: "American International—Always timely with the 'wow' scene. The shocking FACTS behind the marijuana controversy!" Well, not exactly the facts—more like a fable—in this story of a high school, pot smoking, teachers, violence, and rescue. Said *Motion Picture Herald:* "In the wake of mountainous publicity on LSD, STP, and the hard narcotic drug forms, producer Maury Dexter has chosen to go back to what is probably the oldest and most widespread narcotic—'pot,' 'tea,' more conventionally, marijuana, and in this particular case, *Maryjane*. . . . For the most, however, stereotyped punks and stiff officials abound and little is provided to illuminate the unfortunate situation. Rating—Fair." *Boxoffice:* "Action is typical of films made on delinquency problems, featuring orgies of youngsters high on pot. . . . The police chief and town mayor are not given a very good image and there are sadistic angles to the juveniles' conduct that have the shock impact intended. . . . A popcorn-crowd thriller that asks topical questions." From the *Times:* "The idea is packed with good, unstereotyped dramatic potential. Considering how AIP has previously gone hog-wild in sadism and sex, notably in those motorcycle frolics, the tone here is surprisingly restrained. Unfortunately, the dialogue is generally wooden, the pace is static, the acting is generally second-level, and the cynicism of the arrogant youngsters is rampant." Said one exhibitor: "I don't like dope as a subject for teens, but this rallies about midway and winds up on the right side of the ledger morally." Written by TV comedian Dick Gautier and game show host Peter Marshall, also look for Terry (Teri) Garr and future director *(American Hot Wax)* Floyd Mutrux.

Just don't ask these gals for help in changing a flat tire.

The Mini-Skirt Mob

Producer: Maury Dexter
Writer: James Gordon White
Director: Maury Dexter
Music: Les Baxter
American International; 82 minutes
Released 5/68

Cast: Jeremy Slate, Diane McBain, Sherry Jackson, Patty McCormack, Ross Hagen, Harry Dean Stanton, Ronnie Rondell

"They're hog-straddling female animals on the prowl!" Well, actually they straddle motorcycles in this tale of miniskirted female cyclists, featuring violence, revenge, assorted mayhem, murder, and police chases. *Motion Picture Herald:* "This time, AIP's big bikes are manned by a flourish of strumpets in a state of semi-undress. . . . Maury Dexter's handling of the material is straightforward to the point of being heavy-handed. . . . The film should enjoy some success among fans of miniskirts and mobs. Rating—Fair." *Boxoffice:* "Creamy thighs straddling motorcycles figure prominently in AIP's *Mini-Skirt Mob*, and they should offer the big draw for the summer drive-in trade. The screenplay will draw laughs, but the young set doesn't take this kind of film seriously to begin with. There is some exciting motorcycle footage and a hair-curling cat fight between the two female leads. There's really not much to the story of a pack of post-puberty Amazons who travel with their somewhat adolescent boyfriends, except a surprisingly cynical conclusion in which Miss Jackson calmly allows McBain to fall off a cliff." The *Times: "Mini-Skirt Mob* is simply a monotonous exercise in sadism, as a bunch of girl cyclists and their male partners torment a honeymooning couple. It is sickening." Maury Dexter began directing in 1960, hooked into beach movies in the middle sixties, and spent the late sixties helming *Maryjane, Born Wild,* and *Hell's Belles.*

Mondo Daytona

Producers: Bill Packham, Gordon Craddock
Director: Frank Willard
Music: Bill Lowry
Craddock; 80 minutes
Released 5/68

Documentaries abounded in the late sixties—many inspired by the successful *Mondo Cane* and promising a behind-the-scenes look at one subject or another—and often not making it clear that the film they were selling was indeed a documentary. They were quick, cheap, (no actors, sets, or screenwriters), and easy to market. This one was rather tame—a look at vacationing students at Daytona Beach during spring holiday, along with the requisite rock 'n' roll parties, beach frolic, and motorcycle gangs—and filmed "with a hidden camera." This was narrated by pop star Billy Joe Royal, who also contributed songs along with the Swinging Medallions and the Tams. This film was subtitled *How to Swing on Your Spring Vacation,* and the low-budget Craddock Films also brought us *Forty Acre Feud, From Nashville with Music,* and *Passion in Hot Hollows,* among others.

Mondo Mod

Producer: Peter Perry
Writer: Sherman Greene
Director: Peter Perry
Music: The Gretschmen
Timely Motion Pictures (later distributed by AIP); 89 minutes
Released 6/21/67

A look at the world of youth, aged thirteen to twenty-five, in this documentary narrated by Harve Humble. There are surfers, mod clothes, Sunset Strip, LSD and pot, rock clubs, and music by Sam the Soul and the Inspirations, the Group, and the Gretschmen. "Parents: If you don't understand your children, see this motion picture!"

***Bragging about theater grosses in this ad from* Boxoffice *for the low-budget documentary* Mondo Mod.**

***Another teen documentary* Mondo Teeno *was also released as* Teenage Rebellion.**

Producer Peter Perry also worked on *Blood of Dracula's Castle, Five Bloody Graves, Horror of the Blood Monster,* and other filmic tranfusions.

Mondo Teeno

Producer: Norman Herman
Writer: Norman Herman
Director: Norman Herman
Music: Mike Curb, Al Simms, Mike Summers
Trans American; 81 minutes
Released 4/67

Another youthquake documentary, this one narrated by the producer-director Burt Topper, who first began making teen exploitation flicks in the fifties, *(Diary of a High School Bride)*. These films show teenagers around the world in revolt against society—sex, drugs, fashion, music, and unwed mothers—from the United States, Britain, Sweden, France, Italy, and Japan. The British sequences were directed by Richard Lester, and this was also released as *Teenage Rebellion.*

Privilege

Producer: John Heyman
Writer: Norman Bogner
Director: Peter Watkins
Music: Mike Leander
Universal; 103 minutes
Released 7/24/67

Cast: Paul Jones, Jean Shrimpton, Mark London, Max Bacon, Jeremy Child, William Job, James Cossins, Frederick Danner

A searing look into the near future by director Peter *(The War Game)* Watkins, where pop music has become a matter of social control. It takes place in 1970, and tells the story of a wild singer who is tamed by the government (British) and used to dictate to the kids. In the end, thanks to Jean Shrimpton, he rebels, but is rejected by the Establishment and his brainwashed followers. Said the *Times:* "In general this vigorous protest picture generates reason and power, with excellent performances conveying a taut belief in the characters. . . . The director's apprehensions are pictured with brilliance and startling satiric bite in his new quasi-documentary, *Privilege.*" The movie has excellent music and is worth catching; it now seems more like realism than fantasy.

Psych-Out, *featuring Jack Nicholson and Bruce Dern had its hip moments mixed inbetween the Hollywood hippie hype.*

Psych-Out

Producer: Dick Clark
Writers: E. Hunter Willet, Betty Ulius, Betty Tusher
Director: Richard Rush
Music: Ronald Stein
American International; 101 minutes
Released 3/6/68

Cast: Susan Strasberg, Dean Stockwell, Jack Nicholson, Bruce Dern, Adam Roarke, Max Julien, Henry Jaglom, Linda Gaye Scott

Good, fun Haight-Ashbury drug movie, with an excellent cast and appearance of the Strawberry Alarm Clock, the Seeds, and lesser-knowns. It's a story of runaways, rock groups, LSD and STP, death, and reconciliation. *Boxoffice:* "Dick Clark, former TV star and author of many articles on teenage problems, debuts as a full producer with this exploitation film which reunites two stars from *The Trip,* Susan Strasberg and Bruce Dern. *Psych-Out* presents the hallucinating world of the flower children of San Francisco's Haight-Ashbury district, who disavow the ills of society by isolating themselves in a unique culture of their own. The film delves only superficially into the hippie problem and tends to be more exploitational than insightful. Will appeal to mature young people." And the *Times:* "Nonetheless the film, directed by Richard Rush, has considerable élan. There is music. There are a lot of beads and spangles and prisms and fabric and pads. The onturnage and the outfreaking leave room for a lot of surreal and science-fiction effects . . . although Miss Strasberg's STP delusions are not very imaginative." Richard Rush also directed *Hell's Angels on Wheels, The Savage Seven, The Stunt Man,* and an early Jack Nicholson film (1960), *Too Soon to Love.*

Revolution

Producer: Jack O'Connell
Writer: Jack O'Connell
Director: Jack O'Connell
Music: Ben Shapiro
Lopert; 87 minutes
Released 8/7/68

Cast (Documentary): Today Malone, Herb Caen, Ronnie Davis, Louis Gottlieb, Jurt Hirschhorn

Another hippie documentary. This one intercuts scenes of Haight-Ashbury, LSD use, acid rock, gurus, and be-ins with interviews with hippies, doctors, psychiatrists, and policemen about the dangers of the hippie lifestyle. Your guide: a fresh-faced flower child, dubbed Today Malone. Said the *Times: Revolution* is a documentary about the drug scene last summer in the Haight, and already its hippie star, Today Malone, might as well be last year, or the Day before the Day before Yesterday. The community is over—scattered by hepatitis, mental illness, crime, the horrors, social pressure—and *Revolution,* although it is for the most part very dull and on one note, may be the best documentary record we shall have of it." Good music by Mother Earth, Quicksilver Messenger Service, the Steve Miller Band, and Country Joe and the Fish. "The sex is free. The pot is cheap. Everyone can afford the acid." Yeah, but it cost two bucks to get into the theater.

Riot on Sunset Strip

Producer: Sam Katzman
Writer: Orville H. Hampton
Director: Arthur Dreifuss
Music: Fred Karger
American International; 85 minutes
Released 3/67

Cast: Aldo Ray, Mimsy Farmer, Michael Evans, Laurie Mock, Tim Rooney, Gene Kirkwood, Hortense Petra, Anna Mizrahi

Wild exploitation film about the Sunset Strip protests, hippies, rebellious daughter, pot and LSD, and a violent confrontation which ultimately leads to "the riot on Sunset Strip." Good music by the Standells, the Enemies, and the Chocolate Watch Band. Ninth-billed is Schuyler *(Rat Fink)* Hayden. Said one exhibitor: "Oh boy, it will do business. There was one bad scene in it, but you can pass it, by changing reels just before it gets to it. It's doing business in small towns." Arthur Dreifuss began directing in 1940, and, as he neared the age of sixty, directed such late-1960s teen items as *The Love Ins, The Young Runaways,* and *Riot on Sunset Strip.* This one is campy fun.

Ski Fever

Producers: Wolfgang Schmidt, Mark Cooper
Writers: Curt Siodmak, Richard L. Joseph
Director: Curt Siodmak
Music: Guy Hemric, Jerry Styner
Allied Artists; 98 minutes
Released 3/5/69

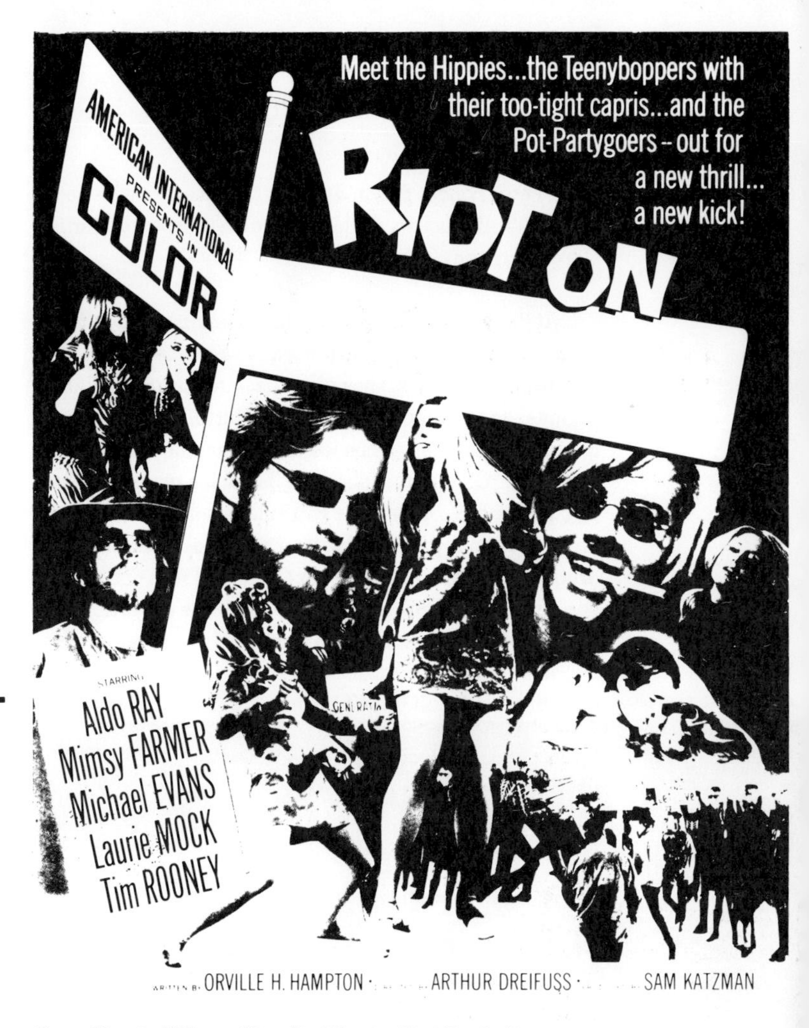

Cast: Martin Milner, Claudia Martin, Vivi Bach, Dietmar Schonherr, Toni Sailor, Dorith Dom, Kurt Grosskurth, Curt Bock

This dated college-kids flick was an American-Austrian-Czechoslovakian co-production, and was originally released in Europe in 1967, when it made more timely sense. It's a story of American students in a European college, ski teachers, sex games, romance, competition, and a happy ending. Said *Boxoffice: Ski Fever* is faintly reminiscent of all those go-go stuffed-bikini-beach pictures that flooded the AIP release schedule a few years back, except this one substitutes snow for surf, skis for bare feet, and the Alps for Malibu. The other ingredients are the same, including an almost perverse preoccupation with virginity, and a cast of aging Lotharios who have the kind of sexual responses expected from mental defectives. Adults will find little of interest, but the impressionable pre-teen set may respond." Dean's little girl Claudia also graced *For Those Who Think Young* and *The Ghost in the Invisible Bikini.*

The Trip

Producer: Roger Corman
Writer: Jack Nicholson

Director: Roger Corman
Music: The Electric Flag, Al Simms
American International; 85 minutes
Released 8/23/67

Cast: Peter Fonda, Susan Strasberg, Bruce Dern, Dennis Hopper, Salli Sachse, Katherine Walsh, Barboura Morris, Caren Bernsen

At the time a controversial film, because it didn't preach against drugs, it just tried to show the effects of an LSD trip. There are scenes of gurus, visions and hallucinations, good and bad vibes, sex, rebirth, and the like—not to mention the famous washing-machine scene. From *Boxoffice:* "Given great shocking boxoffice material, *The Trip* pulls no punches. This is a smash commercial picture on the national youth problem of taking psychedelic drugs. Producer-director Roger Corman doesn't miss the sex, 'freakouts,' and 'trips,' showing all the distortions of reality, with their fearful and terrifying reactions. Peter Fonda's smash performance shows constant resourcefulness in his difficult role of the man on 'The Trip.' Because this is almost entirely a rapid-fire visual story, backed with strong sound, great credit goes to the writer, Jack Nicholson, and to the very fine technical crew. . . ." But the *Times* didn't agree: "Familiar cinematic images are accompanied by weird music and sounds. Is this a psychedelic experience? Is this what it's like to take a trip? If it is then it's all a big put-on. Or is this simply making a show with adroitly staged fantasy episodes and good color photography effects? In my estimation, it is the latter. And I warn you that all you are likely to take away from the theater is a painful case of eyestrain and perhaps a detached retina." The theater owners didn't seem to get it either. Said one: "Good boxoffice on a very sorry picture. A lot of walkouts with very sad comments." And another: "I have been seeing pictures for twenty years and this is the worst movie I have ever seen—simply disgusting. Don't be fooled by Susan Strasberg's name—she's in it for two minutes." Filmed in "psychedelic color" and also featuring Dick Miller, Luana Anders, Peter Bogdanovich, and an unbilled Brandon de Wilde. Nicholson, Fonda, and Hopper next went to create the supersuccessful *Easy Rider.*

Roger Corman's* The Trip *was one of the surprise box-office success stories to come out of the hippie-protest-drug cycle of exploitation films.

Wild in the Streets

Producers: James H. Nicholson, Samuel Z. Arkoff
Writer: Robert Thom
Director: Barry Shear
Music: Les Baxter, Al Simms
American International; 97 minutes
Released 5/29/68

Cast: Shelley Winters, Christopher Jones, Diane Varsi, Ed Begley, Hal Holbrook, Millie Perkins, Richard Pryor, Bert Freed

A fun, satiric fantasy film, telling a story of rock-star idolatry, a fourteen-year-old voting age, LSD, power politics, and more. Christopher Jones is elected president, a wild government bordering on anarchy takes charge, everyone over thirty-five is sent to camps where they must take LSD, and in the end the question looms whether even younger kids will take over. There are many good performances, especially by Winters, Jones, and Varsi, and also Kevin Coughlin and Salli Sachse. There are also some good pop songs by Mann and Weil that capture the mood excellently. This was based on a story in *Esquire* (December 1966), "The Day It All Happened Baby," and is definitely worth catching. One exhibitor said: "This is a real weird one. The kids seem to like it and it's worth a playdate. The adults probably will not like the subject matter, but the end might strike their fancy." This was a very big moneymaker for AIP.

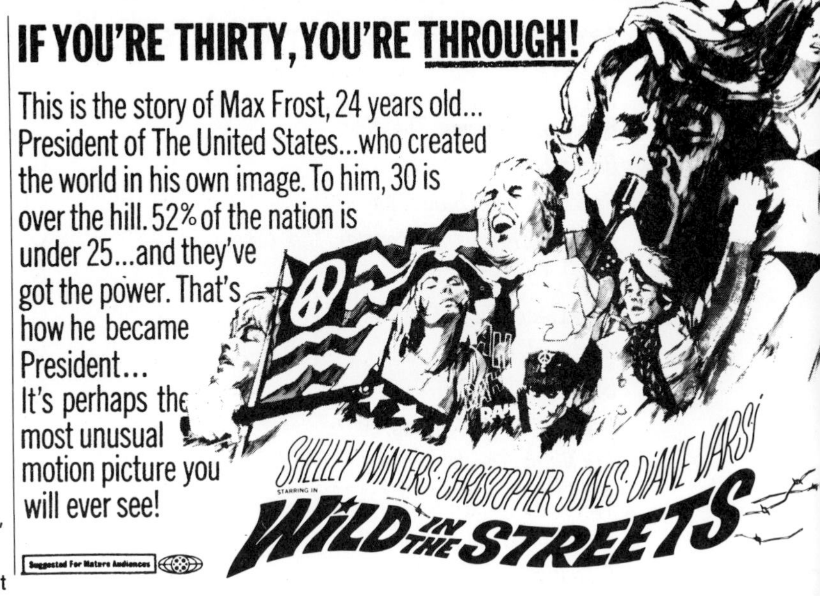

Wild in the Streets: ***A campy teen classic featuring Christopher Jones, Diane Varsi, and Richard Pryor.***

The Young Runaways

Producer: Sam Katzman
Writer: Orville H. Hampton
Director: Arthur Dreifuss
Music: Fred Karger
MGM; 91 minutes
Released 9/11/68

Cast: Brooke Bundy, Kevin Coughlin, Lloyd Bochner, Patty McCormack, Lynn Bari, Norman Fell, Quentin Dean, Richard Dreyfuss

Katzman continues onward in this story of runaways, hippies, prostitutes, violence, death, and partial reconciliation. From *Boxoffice:* "While its approach is superficial, and its execution cliché ridden, its message to youth is loud and clear: don't run away, as things are often worse away from home and a violent end could be met. These messages and portrayals are presented through some rather lurid sequences. . . . It is suggested for mature audiences, and its exhibition will be limited to saturation bookings and drive-ins." Featuring teen exploitation star Patty McCormack, and Kevin Coughlin, who also appeared in *Wild in the Streets* and *Maryjane* after first appearing onscreen in 1958 at the age of thirteen.

On a highway...in a crash-pad...
AT YOUR BOX-OFFICE...
THERE'S NO STOPPING THE YOUNG RUNAWAYS!

And in the end, still standing tall, was producer Sam Katzman who was there when it all started in the mid-fifties with **Rock Around the Clock.** ***In the late sixties, he was still churning out teen exploitation films like*** **The Love-Ins** ***and*** **The Young Runaways.**

Index to Filmographies